T0367507

NIGERIA

Contemporary Commentaries
&
Essays

Alfred Obiora Uzokwe

Nigeria:
Contemporary Commentaries and Essays

iUniverse books may be ordered through booksellers or by contacting:

iUniverse
1663 Liberty Drive
Bloomington, IN 47403
www.iuniverse.com
1-800-Authors (1-800-288-4677)

ISBN: 978-1-4917-7407-6 (sc)
ISBN: 978-1-4917-7408-3 (e)

Library of Congress Control Number: 2015912456

Print information available on the last page.

iUniverse rev. date: 08/13/2015

DEDICATION

This book is dedicated to the memory of my beloved mother, Mrs. Lilian Uzoma Uzokwe. She lived all her life in service to humanity.

TABLE OF CONTENTS

ACKNOWLEDGMENTS

A load of gratitude to my brother, Nnamdi, for always
pushing me to reach beyond my comfort zone.
Thanks to my family for continuing to support
me in my writing endeavors.
Special thanks to my readers that have, through their
feedback over the years, made me a better writer.
Thanks to the publisher of Nigeriaworld for being
the first to introduce my writing titled, "I want
Nigeria back", to the world in July of 2001.
Thanks to my father, Mr Sylvanus Chukwukadibia
Uzokwe, the man that drummed the essence of excellence
in the spoken and written English into my ears.
To my wife, Anthonia and my children: Alfred Jr, Lilian,
Sylvanus, Jennifer and Chris, thanks for putting up with
my many hours on the computer away from you.

INTRODUCTION

This book is a collection of published and unpublished commentaries I have written, over the years, about Nigeria. The subjects are diverse, ranging from health, welfare, politics, aviation, infrastructure, to accounts of some of my visits to Nigeria.

Since July of 2001, I have written more than 2,000 pages of commentaries about the sociopolitical and economic situation in Nigeria. These commentaries, many critical of the leadership of Nigeria and their modus operandi, and published biweekly on the internet news magazine website called Nigeriaworld.com, often attracted volumes of emails to me from readers across the globe. In the commentaries, I proffer solutions to many of the problems I highlight and these trigger robust and constructive debates with my readers, through emails.

Some of my readers who are government functionaries or public officials, sometimes engage me in debates about returning to Nigeria and offering my services if I thought I had worthwhile ideas on the way forward for the country. I always countered that writers who unearth problems and proffer solutions do not necessarily have to be in government or serve as public officials to be effective. I lightheartedly add that it is my chosen responsibility to unearth and highlight issues and proffer solutions and it was theirs, as public officials, to take and implement. Hopefully, my writings over the years have not only made a difference by shining the spotlight on the failed policies of our leaders and public officials, but have also provided ideas to some of the leaders on the way forward.

Before now, my writings were scattered all over the internet. Hence, some policy makers in Nigeria as well as scholarly researchers and students often inquired if there is a central location where they can easily get to all my writings in one swoop. This book effectively answers their question. It is a collection of some of my most "celebrated" writings as evidenced from the volume of email feedback received from my readers when the commentaries were published. Also, the frequency with which some of these writings have been quoted, excerpted or re-published in policy and scholarly articles and books globally, were considered in selecting them for this book.

Nigerians are resilient, ingenious and resourceful. Add that to the fact that the nation has one of the most sought-after natural resources in the form of oil and the image of an Eldorado or land of milk and honey begins to develop in one's mind. Unfortunately, the country has not made appreciable progress since independence. The country continues to flounder, plagued by corruption, unemployment, runaway inflation, insecurity and poor standard of education. Many of the major roads are pothole-ridden and the currency continues to slide downwards vis a vis other currencies.

Nigeria's problems can be traced to the fact that 54 years after independence, she is yet to be blessed with truly selfless leaders. Her leaders lord themselves over the masses and treat the nation's treasury as their personal purse. In the end, they leave the nation more impoverished than they met it. Oil has sustained the economy for very many years but instead of using proceeds from oil to diversify the economy, Nigerian leaders continue to preside over a one-dimensional economy. Now that oil price is plummeting and the United States has curtailed procurement of Nigeria's crude oil to nothingness, the nation's economy has gone from bad to worse. Her foreign reserve which is supposed to be for the rainy day, is being depleted at a rate so drastic that it may be gone before Nigeria even experiences a truly catastrophic economic event!

When Nigeria began her current democratic experiment, there was hope that being extricated from military dictatorship would throw a major life line to the masses. Sixteen years later, the expected lifeline has been a mirage at best. Until May 29, 2015, the Peoples' Democratic Party(PDP) bestrode the land like a colossus, fostering corruption and creating a nation where citizens go hungry in the midst of plenty. This national malaise created an unbridled yearning for change of leadership and direction. When, therefore, a couple of political parties pulled together and developed a formidable opposition party called All Progressive Congress(APC), with General Muhammadu Buhari as their flag bearer, Nigerians flocked towards the party and eventually dethroned the ruling party. Buhari is now the new president of Nigeria and the world is keenly watching to see if the soldier-turned politician would make a positive difference.

It has not been all doom and gloom for Nigeria though. The advent of democracy meant the banishment of military rule, hopefully to oblivion. Today, Nigerians, like this writer, can at least freely express their opinions verbally or in print, a far cry from what happened during the military rule. The just-concluded presidential election, which was adjudged successful by many, as well as the peaceful acceptance of defeat by former President Goodluck Jonathan, is a huge progress when compared with the uncertainty and subsequent carnage that seemed to follow most elections in the country. In spite of this partial progress, the nation is not yet where she needs to be. Nigerians must continue to strengthen democracy and its institutions by unashamedly demanding that her leaders operate the ship of state in line with the dictates of the constitution and tenets of democracy. There is no better way to ensure accountability than by calling the leaders to the carpet, on the pages of newspapers, the internet and other available forum, whenever they head down the wrong path.

In spite of the difficulties of the present time, I foresee a great future for Nigeria and I intend to, along with many other writers, help shape same through the power of the pen. My goal is public enlightenment, influencing opinions, setting discussion agenda and shinning the searchlight on often-neglected issues in Africa's most populous nation.

This compendium of some of my commentaries about Nigeria is my own modest contribution towards the national discourse and nation-building.

PART 1
Health and Welfare

Citizens of other Nations Now Live Longer, Why Can't Nigerians? - August 2010

Archbishop Benson Idahosa, founder of the Church of God Mission International, one of the pioneers of TV and evangelical ministries in Nigeria, passed away in 1998 at the young age of 60. He died suddenly in the midst of colleagues that had come to visit him from Oral Roberts Ministry in the United States. His wife recalled that on the fateful day, after having lunch with his guests, he started muttering, "Glory to Jesus" or something like that. The rest of the people around him thought he was praying and so closed their own eyes and started chorusing the same line in unison. After a while, an awkward silence ensued, prompting some of his guests to open their eyes. That was when they discovered that he was on the floor! That was it.

I do not know the exact cause of death but it is almost safe to assume that since he was not sick before then, his passing may have had something to do with his heart – some form of cardiac anomaly. This untimely death syndrome has become a malady on its own, plowing through the landscape like a hurricane, uprooting and laying to waste unsuspecting Nigerians, leaving heart-break and anguish in its wake. The more this pandemic continues, the more average life expectancy depresses. As I write, average life expectancy at birth for Nigeria, according to CIA World Fact book, is 47 years for the general population. For the female population, it is 48 years and male population is 46 years! The surprising part is that in 2003, average life expectancy for Nigeria was 50 years. It has declined to 47 years in just 7 years!

One does not even need the CIA Fact book to conclude that life expectancy is at its lowest point in Nigeria. All one needs to do is attend a village or family meeting there. It is comical when people refer to such meetings as "meeting of elders" because it is filled with men and women in their 50s and early 60s. In a typical Nigerian village today, one can count off the fingers the number of people above the age of 70. Even the leadership echelons in churches are now the exclusive preserve of men and women in their 40s, 50s and early 60s.

By comparison, the average life expectancy for the United States is 78.2 years for the general population and 81 years for the female population. Life expectancy for the Japanese has moved to a new high of 86.5 years for women and almost 80 years for men. In Germany, it is 79 years for the general population. Canada is 81 years and United Kingdom is 79 years.

The other day, John Boehner, the minority leader in the United States House of Representatives suggested that the retirement age should be raised. His contention was that in the United States, people are living longer and if someone retires at age 62, the person could still live another 38 years, collecting social security. This, to him, will bankrupt the social security system. John Boehner is right about one thing and that is that people in the United States are living longer. I however refuse to accept the assertion from some quarters that citizens of advanced nations are genetically predisposed to live longer and so there is nothing Africans can do to catch up. I just believe that there is something that advanced nations are doing right that makes them live an average of 30 years more than African nations and Nigeria needs to adopt those things. As they say in sports, if you want to be the best you can be, then you must learn to use the best athletes as your measurement yardstick and work towards that goal.

One major reason why people live longer in advanced countries is that at a very early age, their doctors help them identify diseases that they may be genetically predisposed to. If a doctor knows that a patient is genetically predisposed to a certain disease, maintenance medications and lifestyle changes, as the case may be, tailored to that person are prescribed. This type of early intervention, plus health education awareness, goes a long way in prolonging life.

In case the reader is wondering what I mean by a doctor helping to identify the diseases someone may be genetically pre-disposed to, I will answer by telling a story. The first time I went to a hospital here in the United States, I was asked to complete a health questionnaire. It started with questions about my susceptibility to certain ailments, surgeries I may have had, and then progressed to ailments any member of my family, both living and dead, may have had. The doctor explained that because members of immediate and extended families have genetic

4

linkage, they not only pass on physical traits but also medical traits, including predisposition to diseases. Someone could actually inherit a disease that the grandparent or a great uncle or auntie or nephew suffered from. That explains why a woman who died of breast cancer may have grandchildren with the disease even though her direct offspring did not suffer from the same disease. If a doctor knows some of the ailments that family members had or have, the doctor will be in a position to design yearly medical exams that specifically look for any sign of such ailments in their patients. That is a pre-emptive strike.

The idea of a doctor using medical information about a patient and family members to design medical checkups sound so simple but that remains elusive in Nigeria for many reasons. Nigerians do not always know, for sure, what ailments their family members died of because of incorrect diagnoses and the absence of autopsies at death. Moreover, people still feel embarrassed to discuss their ailments even with family members because ailments are either seen as personal weakness, a curse or disadvantage. I have heard people insinuate, when someone gets sick, that it was a punishment from God for an atrocious sin that person or family members may have committed. People therefore hide ailments they or family members have and choose to die with it rather than divulge it. All this is compounded by the unwillingness of some doctors to insist on getting such information from new patients.

I was lifting weights beside a black American the other day at the gym and after a while, he turned around and introduced himself because he wanted me to spot for him. As I was doing that, he said he was 40 years old and that his father passed away at an early age of 45 from heart disease. Later in life, his mother developed heart problems too. He said he was afraid that he might inherit heart disease so with the help of his doctor, he has made lifestyle changes that include diet and exercise, and that was why he joined the gym.

If Nigeria must join advanced countries in enjoying longer life span, then it is important for two things to happen: Doctors must imbibe, as good practice, the idea of using family medical history to design medical checkups and treatment for their patients. There must also be a massive health awareness campaign to sensitize our people to the need for seeking out and providing their doctors with family medical history to use for designing their health checklists for yearly physicals. Yearly physical is important in the prevention of diseases and proactive identification of diseases at very early stages, enabling successful treatment. Advanced nations like the United States understand this and so most citizens, even very healthy ones, religiously observe that yearly trip to their doctors like a pilgrimage. Every ailment goes through different stages before manifesting itself via symptoms. If caught at the very beginning stages, treatment is easier, less costly and usually the patient has better chances of survival. During yearly visits for physicals, doctors subject the patient to a battery of medical tests and physical examinations. Anomalies are noted, isolated and treated promptly. Through research, they have identified medical and physical tests that should be administered on a patient at certain age range. They know the age range when women are most vulnerable to diseases like breast cancer and hence breast examinations and mammograms are religiously done at those stages in a woman's life. They know when to order pap smears to screen for the onset of ovarian cancers. All these prophylactic actions are saving a lot of lives in the United States and positively affecting longevity.

Talking about yearly physicals for Nigerians may be a tall order for several reasons: Most Nigerians do not believe in going to the hospital if they are not sick. Even when they are sick, some would not visit the hospital but would rather go to one of the roadside pharmacies, buy the drug of their choice and self-medicate. The general result of this attitude is that ailments are mainly detected only when they must have advanced and become symptomatic. The first step in stemming this is again an awareness campaign that discusses how yearly physicals lead to early detection and hence cure. Plaster the message on billboards all over the nation, put them on radio and television jingles, organize health education seminars in local government headquarters and schools and talk about it. Enlist pastors to talk about it in churches and imams in mosques.

It is true that many may not be able to afford yearly physicals because of poverty and joblessness. That is true but that is where Nigeria's stupendous oil wealth comes in. Part of the dividends of democracy is a robust health care delivery system. The United States just passed the healthcare bill that essentially says that everyone is entitled to good healthcare. The bill places premium on preventive health care which is yearly physicals. Nigeria should follow suit and put our oil money to good use. Universal healthcare should be the goal. Physicals uncover asymptomatic ailments or those at the early stages that could be treated and taken care of with minimal cost. It is these types of early medical interventions that will improve the quality of life for Nigerians and invariably beef up life expectancy.

Availability of world-class medical facilities in advanced nations is probably the most important factor that continues to assure higher life expectancy. In the United States, there are so many hospitals that continue to push the envelope of science. They are curing diseases that would normally kill people just a few years ago. They are complemented by state- of- the-art medical labs that invest heavily in research. New discoveries are made each day regarding the medical and anatomical composition of the human body, leading to disease containment or outright cures.

Compare the above with what we have in Nigeria. The country cannot boast of a medical facility in the same league as the ones found in advanced nations. This fact was proven when the nation's number one man, President Yar'Adua, slowly dying from kidney problems and associated complications, had to be flown out of the country, in search of a good medical facility to give him the proper care. He eventually died. It is no secret that all of Nigeria's elite delight in flying out of the country for medical treatment and checkup. The absence of well-equipped hospitals in Nigeria results in continual wrong medical diagnoses and wrong treatment that culminate in the senseless deaths of citizens from ailments that should normally not kill. Nigeria has the money to invest in state-of-the-art hospitals. The government can also go into private-public partnerships with private individuals to build state-of-the-art hospitals and equip them with the best in medical technology. Also, Nigeria has a lot of qualified medical doctors outside the country that can pull resources together to build and operate state-of-the-art hospitals in the nation.

Another factor that has helped in advanced nations is the presence of disciplined medical boards that regulate the activities of doctors. These medical boards realize that no matter how well-intentioned a doctor is, as humans, sometimes they become complacent and make mistakes that cost lives. They therefore dole out stiff penalties that include precluding an errant doctor from ever practicing medicine to requiring retraining. Citizens understand their rights and when they smell malpractice by doctors, they speak up and the medical boards and the justice system take over. All complaints against doctors are thoroughly investigated and punishment meted out where warranted. For doctors in the United States, the fear of the medical board and the justice system is the beginning of wisdom. Doctors are forced to do due diligence in their practice and the nation is better off for it.

The above is not the case in Nigeria where some doctors do as they please without consequences. During a visit to Nigeria, a few years ago, I listened in horror as one of our relatives told the story of how he was operated on. He had appendicitis. He was wide awake in a filthy room that was used by the doctor as his operating theater as the unscrupulous doctor cut open his stomach, literally brought out his intestines and dumped them on an adjoining filthy table while he fished for his appendix. Of course a few days after the procedure, he became violently ill, obviously from infection. He was lucky to have survived that but if he had died, the family would have accepted that as his destiny and the doctor would say he did his best and that would close the chapter. I once narrated how another relative lost his sight because during eye surgery, in one of the northern states, National Electric Power Authority(NEPA) struck and the hospital building lost power. Before they could get gas into the standby generator to resume operation, something had gone very wrong with the procedure. Nothing came out of this negligence except that he lost his sight permanently. This happens every day in the nation.

Sordid stories abound about cases of medical malpractice all over Nigeria. One story that beats the imagination is where patients in the throes of death, rushed to hospitals by relatives, are told to pay admission fee first otherwise the patient will not be attended to. Accident victims suffer that all the time and many die just because the doctor refused to intervene to close the source of profuse loss of blood. In advanced nations, such doctors will be disbarred for refusing to offer medical services to people in emergency cases. The solution is for the medical boards in the nation to add more teeth to what it does. Sensitize the public to the fact that they can report suspected cases of malpractice to the board and get justice. Also, through public awareness, people should be made to understand that when they suspect malpractice, they can go to court to seek redress.

Some of the good practices that account for increased longevity of people in advanced nations are as follows:

Presence of functioning emergency medical call system:
Anyone who lives in an advanced nation must be conversant with the emergency call system. Here, every resident that has access to a telephone has the right to dial an emergency medical number during a medical or fire emergency. In a medical emergency, as soon as that number is dialed, a team of emergency medical personnel quickly hop into their emergency vehicles, blaring the siren that alerts motorists and pedestrians of their presence on the highway. Regardless of the urgency of their trips, motorists clear the roads as the vehicles approach them, averting hold-ups that could lead to delays.

At the scene of a medical emergency, emergency personnel quickly use first aid procedures to stabilize the patient before evacuation to the closest hospital for full medical attention, if warranted. They carry out their work with utmost dispatch, mindful of the fact that time, sometimes mere minutes, makes the difference between life and death. For emergencies like cardiac anomaly, if real help does not arrive within minutes, the patient may die or become permanently incapacitated due to restricted flow of blood and oxygen to vital parts of the body. Timely arrival and intervention of medical personnel, to scenes of medical emergencies, continue to save lives of countless citizens and account for the high average life expectancy in the country.

When the above system is compared with what obtains in Nigeria today, the difference is as clear as day and night. On a daily basis, people die from medical emergencies in their homes; in their places of business or work; in the market places; along the streets under the baking sun; in schools and other places too numerous to mention here. Cases abound where people suddenly collapse in their homes from heart problems, diabetic complications, food poisoning, excessive heat, gastrointestinal ailments and more. They die needlessly because of the absence of emergency call system. If Nigeria must join other nations in improving the average life expectancy of her citizens, it is imperative that a nation-wide medical emergency call and response system is quickly put in place.

A robust emergency response system is not the mere procurement of one or two ambulance vehicles and the hiring of a few uniformed drivers. There is much more to it. The effort must start with the establishment of a dedicated phone system, procurement of vehicles well equipped and appropriate for the purpose, proper training of the right personnel for emergency medical work. I say "right" personnel because emergency medical work is not just for anybody. It is not a job that someone should take just to put food on the table. It requires selflessness, sacrifice and absolute dedication. As straight forward as all this may sound, establishment of an emergency call system is still a tall order in the country. For one, infrastructure, especially bridge and road decay and dilapidation, militate against this. Furthermore, the way the country is structured, the attitude of the populace and the corrupt nature of the ruling class, make things even harder.

When I visited Nigeria recently, I drove from my home to the closest teaching hospital in my home town. From the condition of the road, which was riddled with potholes, if an emergency vehicle tries to evacuate a heart patient from a location such as my home to that teaching hospital, by the time the vehicle would get to the hospital, the patient would have died from gallops. Furthermore, hospitals are so scantily equipped that successfully evacuating a patient, in emergency to the hospital, does not guarantee adequate medical care. As a result of years of neglect, some of the hospitals are so filthy that infection of patients is always a clear and present danger. I paid a visit to a friend in the hospital during one of our Christmas visits. He had been involved in an accident. I was shocked by the filthy ward and bed where he was kept. Soon, with stethoscope around his neck and white coat, the doctor walked in. The dirt ring around the collar of the doctor's overcoat was enough to show that hygiene was not a priority in the hospital. I kept wondering how patients beat infection in such an environment. Add all the above to the fact that in that hot afternoon, there was no power. The hospital windows were wide open to let in air but they were letting in more dust instead. All these inadequacies are obstacles to the establishment of an adequate and fully functioning emergency medical system but can it be done? Of course. Nigeria has the money to do it. What we need is the will. Citizens must demand it and hold the feet of politicians to the fire for it.

Health Education and Awareness:

Another issue that accounts for high average life expectancy in the United States is that in almost every family, there is at least one person trained on how to administer CPR (Cardio-Pulmonary Resuscitation) or chest compression on a patient in emergency. You hear of and watch on TV, emergency calls that people make from home about a patient having a heart attack. You observe that the first step that the families take, as they call the emergency hotline, is to start administering CPR (Cardio Pulmonary Resuscitation) or just chest compression. That intervention helps the patient buy time before the medical emergency team arrives. Statistic shows that because of that, many lives have been saved. This is a far cry from what happens in Nigeria where many have not even heard of the word CPR talk less of knowing how to administer it. In many cases, when someone is going through a medical emergency, especially those associated with the heart, family members hurriedly haul the patient into a vehicle and dash off to a hospital. Without any actions that would help the patient buy time, the result is almost always catastrophic! You hear of people dying on the way to the hospital or shortly after arrival in the hospital. Even if the patient gets to the hospital on time, there is no guarantee that a doctor will be on duty and sometimes nurses insist on admission fees before the patient will even be touched, losing valuable time that could be used to save the patient.

I recall a CNN story by Dr Sanjay Gupta how a boy who basically "died" for seven minutes, was brought back to life. The miracle was credited to his family (mother and father) because while they were calling 911, after the young man became unresponsive, they were applying rigorous chest compressions on him. This guaranteed the continual distribution of blood and remnant oxygen throughout his body, especially the brain. The circulation of remnant oxygen kept his body tissues alive until emergency personnel came and did their thing. If the parents had merely tried to haul the young man off to the hospital, by the time they would get there, because of oxygen deficiency in vital tissues, he would have passed on. They did what they did because of health awareness education. They understood the process of CPR and chest compression and most importantly applied same when it was needed most. Because of health awareness education in this country, people are being helped to live longer.

Health awareness education is a must in Nigeria if things must improve in the health sector. One does not need a formal education to learn how to apply CPR or chest compression. The Heimlich maneuver, which is used to dislodge food that cause choking, a frequent cause of medical distress and sometimes death, can also be learned without any formal education. Local government centers should start holding short classes on how to help people in medical emergencies. Elementary, secondary and tertiary schools should make compulsory a course in emergency procedures. In public places like places of work, businesses, market places, life-saving equipment like defibrillators, for chest compression, should be placed at strategic locations for use in emergencies

Regimented and monitored drug prescription process:
The strictly regimented nature of the process of drug prescription, in the United States, also helps to save lives. To get prescription drugs in the United States, one first has to see the doctor for examination. After examination, the doctor makes a diagnosis and then writes a prescription for drugs for the patient. The patient then takes the prescription paper to a registered pharmacist and submits. After contacting the doctor, to assure the authenticity of the prescription, the pharmacist dispenses the drug to the patient. All medications dispensed must be genuine, authentic, FDA-approved and the patient must be schooled on how to use the medication. Possible side effects and what to do in the case of a serious side effect are disclosed to the patient. This process makes it difficult if not impossible for someone to just walk into the pharmacy and purchase a drug without prescription. Also, it is easy for the doctor

to monitor the drugs a patient takes to prevent drug interactions and overdose that could lead to death.

The opposite is true in Nigeria where self-medication is the norm. Many go to the hospital only when the symptoms of an ailment has reached alarming levels. In the interim, they merely walk into unregulated "pharmacies", ask for any medication they want, sometimes the quack pharmacists even prescribe drugs. The symptoms of many ailments like chills, loss of appetite and general weakness, mimic those of malaria. As a result, when most Nigerians experience such symptoms, they rush to the pharmacy, purchase malarial pills and start ingesting. Meanwhile, the real ailment will gradually be worsening and sometimes lead to death. Also, people often ingest multiple drugs, ignorant of the drug interactions. We read about sudden deaths that occur after the ingestion of certain drugs. The other often overlooked issue is that when patients self-medicate, they often take more than the recommended dose because some feel that if a certain dose makes you feel better, doubling it will even stop the ailment dead on its tracks. They do not understand that certain medications, taken at certain doses, actually become poison!

These days, people with certain diseases have to take powerful medications. Some of these medications that treat diseases like high cholesterol, diabetes and heart disease, also have side effects that include kidney and liver damage. The drugs, therefore, need to be taken under the close supervision of a doctor. Continual blood tests are run to ensure that the kidneys and liver are not being adversely affected. Here in the United States, I have heard people say that through blood tests, their doctors found out that a drug they were taking was affecting their kidneys or liver and so had to change the drug or lower the dose. Nigerians take the same powerful drugs too. The difference is that sometimes it is through self-diagnosis and self- medication. They are unaware of the side effects and have no doctor to monitor side effects on vital organs. The result is almost always lethal. Most people love life and if they know the side effect of the medication they are toying with, they will change course.

Absence of or reduced presence of fake and adulterated drugs:

Ingestion of fake and adulterated drugs continues to lead to untimely deaths in developing countries like Nigeria. Advanced nations realized, through many decades of trial and sometimes costly errors, that fake and adulterated drugs have no place in the society because of their lethal effect on the citizenry when ingested. They know that drugs made up of unadulterated ingredients, mixed in the right proportions, administered at the right dose and right time to a patient, makes a great and positive difference in the life of the patient. As a result of this awareness, before any drug is released to the public for consumption, rigorous clinical testing and trials take place. During this period, the drug is administered on human volunteers. This testing is done over a long period of time that sometimes frustrates people who want life-saving drugs in the market immediately. As the testing takes place, results are noted, including any adverse reactions on the volunteers or even death. In the United States, only after a new drug has been tested exhaustively, its efficacy certified and assurance obtained that it does not contain dangerous, fake or adulterated ingredients or chemicals, is it released to the public for use by the FDA (Food and Drug Administration).

Even after the release of a drug to the public for consumption, FDA continues to monitor complaints from users. If at any time adverse effects, including death, are reported, the drug is pulled from the market on grounds of public safety. This and other safeguards, in place, reduce adverse reactions and deaths from new drugs.

It has always been the norm in Nigeria, before the advent of NAFDAC, for any Tom Dick and Harry to introduce a new drug into the Nigerian market without proper testing. I recall the days, back in the early 70s, when someone released a medication called "Ikampower" to the market. In the bus, in the market place, along the streets, you would hear promotional jingles extolling the virtues of Ikampower. It was touted as a 'cure all' medication. People bought and ingested it in droves. One of the promotional jingles, touting the "cure all" capability of the drug went thus:

Isi n'awa gi, Ikampa - If you have headache, take Ikampower
Afo n'alu gi, Ikampa - If you have stomach ache, take Ikampower
Anya n'egbu gi, Ikampa - If you have eye problems, take Ikampower, etc

The question then was: how was it possible that this one drug took care of all types of ailments? It later went away but not before some people started complaining about serious adverse effects after ingesting it. Nigeria later became a dumping ground for untested drugs from places like India, Poland, Belgrade and you name it. Some heartless people even imported expired drugs and people were buying and taking them. With NAFDAC, hopefully, this problem will be tamed.

Declare War Against Diabetes - It is Blinding, Maiming and Killing Nigerians - July 6, 2009

Many years ago, as a construction engineering inspector in the United States, I worked with a project engineer, Mr. Buchanan (not his real name) on two bridge projects. Mr. Buchanan had a personal regimen that caught my attention as soon as I joined the project team. During lunch time, when the rest of the engineering inspectors would settle to scrumptious meals with assorted cans of soda to wash the food down, Mr. Buchanan would head into the woods and would not reappear until thirty five to forty minutes later. It took a while before I found out what he did while in the woods. He used the entire time to get his daily exercise by briskly walking two or three miles.

On return to the office, he would settle into his chair, gingerly retrieve his lunch from a small Ziploc bag and slowly start eating. His lunch pack always contained fruits and a few other items that looked measured and could pass for the lunch pack of a kindergarten pupil. Because I did not understand what was going on at the time, I saw him as a very strange and miserly man that did not want to spend the money he was making to "live well". Considering that he was very well paid, I did not understand why he could not "eat big" like every other person on the project team. Mr. Buchanan always wore sunshades and did not smoke. He told me that he quit alcohol several years back.

As time went on, I began to understand that there was a method to Mr. Buchanan's "madness." The man I saw as a miser was actually a very wise man. He was doing everything possible to live long enough to see his grandchildren. The mild mannered man was working hard to surmount an uphill but winnable internal health battle that nature had dealt him. It was during a routine conversation with him that it all began to make sense to me. In a somewhat subdued tone, he said to me that he had lived with diabetes for a while. He explained that an attempt to control and even defeat the ailment necessitated several changes in his life style that included quitting smoking, watching what he ate, exercising regularly and wearing shades to protect his eyes.

Mr. Buchanan also stated that he was always in control of his temperament to avoid spiking his blood pressure. To him, all the precautions he had been taking had proved fruitful so far because in spite of the number of years he had lived with the disease, he was still free from any of the opportunistic ailments like retinopathy and neuropathy. "Alfred", he had said to me, "the greatest gift any man can ask for in life is to live a life free from diseases. When this is not possible because of heredity or other factors, the quality of a man's life depends on the effort invested in the upkeep and maintenance of life. I realize I did not ask to be struck by diabetes but since it can be controlled through what I eat and do, I am going to do my best to control it."

From that day on and as the years passed by, Mr. Buchanan's words of wisdom have continued to make sense to me. The relevance of the above story will become apparent as this commentary unfolds.

I must admit that while I was still in Nigeria, in the early eighties, diabetes was an ailment I knew very little about. I thought it was one of those very rare ailments that struck one in a million in Africa and Nigeria. The reason for this is obvious, I rarely heard people say they had diabetes or that family members had it. Something must have happened between then and now. It is either there was stack ignorance about its presence in Nigeria before or something in the environment, lifestyle or diet has drastically changed in the country to cause a geometric proliferation of the disease. Since I started visiting Nigeria more often, I have been alarmed at the ubiquity of the ailment in the country. It has come to the point where one believes that as much as sixty five percent of the adult population is grappling with pre-diabetes or have the full blown disease! My conclusion is of course not based on any tested scientific analysis but a small population sampling of the people I come in contact with during the Christmas season.

The Yuletide season is always a time to visit friends and families or be visited. It seemed that every single compound one visited, there was always at least one person that had been diagnosed with diabetes or is already suffering one or more of the opportunistic ailments that result from the disease. Not quite three years ago, a distant relative suddenly passed away. He died sometime in April or June of that year but I had seen him the previous Christmas season where he was the

17

chairman of a family meeting. I saw him many more times during that period and we even sat down several times to have conversations about general issues. This man looked hale and hearty and the reader can imagine how shocked one was, a few months later, to hear that he had passed away because of diabetes. Since then, I have talked to many Nigerians that concur that diabetes had proliferated geometrically in the last ten or fifteen years, maiming, blinding and killing Nigerians in droves.

Now, what do you make of this heartbreaking story? A few nights ago, I was woken from sleep by a phone call. As soon as I saw the time, I could tell that the call was not an ordinary one. No one would be calling at that ungodly hour if there was no emergency. I was right. It was a relative calling to inform me that diabetes had caused the amputation of a young woman we all know. It was the result of diabetic neuropathy. I last saw this woman this past December and we all attended one of the festive occasions we had in the village. She was very active. On several occasions during that period, I sat down with her for conversations on several issues of interest and saw no outward sign of the ailment. It was after the news of the amputation that I became aware of the fact that she had been diagnosed with the disease sometime back. Typical of the progression of the ailment, she soon started having a tingling sensation on one of her feet. The tingling sensation quickly progressed to loss of feeling on that foot.

She dutifully went to the doctors in one of the respected University Teaching hospitals and got treatment. When the loss of feeling did not improve, one of the doctors referred her to what they call "icha oku"-heat or thermal treatment. This is where the patient's leg is placed inside an enclosed heat source for a period of time each day. The rationale is that since the loss of feeling is the result of blockage of the blood vessels going to the foot, the heat treatment would help "dissolve" the congealed blood and allow flow again. While this woman was undergoing this unconventional treatment, she was losing valuable time that could have been used to save her leg. After several of the heat treatments, when it became clear that the condition was not improving, the young woman was airlifted overseas. There, her case was declared critical. The so-called heat treatment had damaged more nerves and any remaining living tissues and quickly progressed to gangrene. The doctors had no choice than to amputate the leg.

This story exposes the fact that while there are great doctors in the country that know what they are doing, there are those fly-by-night doctors and therapists who have no idea what they are doing. A doctor that sent a diabetic patient to a therapist that roasts people's limbs alive, all in the name of therapy for diabetes, is not fit to be called a doctor and families should never send their loved ones to such people.

It is not clear to me whether the medical board in Nigeria is able to regulate the activities of its members like defrocking incompetent ones that send unsuspecting patients to untimely deaths or cause them to lose body parts that could be saved if the right treatment was applied. If there is no provision for serious sanctions for toying with people's lives and body parts, one should quickly be put in place by the medical board. Just as the woman unexpectedly lost her leg because of following the wrong course of treatment, so do many diabetic patients lose their sight, sustain kidney damage, become heart patients or even die because they trusted the management of their ailment in the hands of fly-by-night doctors. Treatment and control of diabetes, from what I can tell as a lay person, depends largely on whether the doctor in charge prescribes the right course of action regarding drugs to take, life style and eating habits changes to make.

Mr. Buchanan, the project engineer I talked about in the opening paragraphs of this commentary, had a good doctor. The doctor prescribed the right medications; advised on needed lifestyle and dietary changes. The doctor also followed up with periodic blood tests to ensure that the drugs Mr. Buchanan was taking were not having toxic effects on his kidneys and liver as is often the case with medications that are metabolized in the liver or kidney. The doctor knew when to change Mr. Buchanan's prescription drugs or reduce the dose to avert liver or kidney damage. Nigeria needs doctors that are knowledgeable, dedicated and not just profit-driven. I am sure we have many of such doctors but we need to have a way to fish out the scam artists and weed them out so that diabetic patients will not go through what the woman above is going through now. Clearly, if it were to be in the United States that a doctor prescribed a treatment course that resulted in loss of limb, that doctor better be ready to be sued and decertified by the medical board for malpractice. We must begin to move in that direction.

Some of the doctors in Nigeria do not even keep abreast with developments in the pharmaceutical industry. They carelessly prescribe healthful but dangerous drugs without monitoring their patients to avoid liver or kidney toxicity. They do not even know when the drugs they prescribe have been recalled so as to warn their patients to stop taking them. For example, one of the drugs that had been used to control high cholesterol, in this country and elsewhere, was recently recalled and doctors quickly sent out information to their patients warning them to discontinue the use of the drug. I am almost certain that there are doctors in Nigeria that still use the proscribed drug to treat their patients.

It is time for the Nigerian government to declare an all-out war against diabetes. This means earmarking substantial amount of money to make available necessary drugs for treatment. The drugs should be subsidized so Nigerians on the lower rung of the income ladder can have access to them. Also, a substantial amount of the earmarked money should be used for mass education about diabetes. The mass education component of the campaign should include TV, Radio, newspaper and billboard advertisements that address the signs and symptoms of the disease, when to see a doctor, what to expect from a good doctor, lifestyle changes to make once a diagnosis is made, dietary changes and more.

Furthermore, the medical board in Nigeria must do its part. It must come down hard on the doctors that give the generality of the brilliant doctors a bad name by their fraudulent practices. Doctors should be compelled to get some sort of recertification before they can treat patients living with the disease. Recertification should include relearning signs and symptoms of the disease and treatment options that advancement in technology has unearthed. It must include relearning the necessary lifestyle and dietary changes needed by patients. Most importantly, recertification should include keeping abreast of new and emerging drugs for the disease and knowing when a drug is recalled so as to warn patients. Also, the importance of constantly running kidney and liver tests on patients placed on diabetes drugs to know when toxicity has set in cannot be overemphasized.

The war against diabetes requires concerted effort from all and sundry. It requires action from the government of President Shehu Musa Yaradua. It requires effort from Nigerian doctors and the certification board. It requires effort from the patients and their families.

Heed Professor Wole Soyinka's Admonition and Fight Prostate Cancer Now! - Dec 16, 2014

In December of 2010, I visited Nigeria and on Christmas day attended morning service at my hometown church. Service had already started when we arrived at the church grounds. As I hurriedly made my way towards the building entrance, my eyes momentarily settled on a man that was standing on the far end of the steps that led up to the foyer under the bell tower. My eyes were about to wander away from him when it dawned on me that something about him seemed familiar. It took casting a steady gaze on him for a few more seconds for me to realize that he was an elementary school classmate of mine that I saw last more than 30 years earlier. For the sake of privacy, I will call him Chuma. I walked up to him and as soon as he recognized me, he smiled and stuck out his hand in greeting. I shook his hand. "Unu anatalu?", - "did you guys return?" he asked smiling. Yes I said sizing him up. I was surprised that he grew taller and bigger than I would have imagined when we were all playing soccer and climbing trees in my neighborhood many years earlier. After exchange of pleasantries, I left him and went into the church.

The thought of meeting him after so many years did not leave my mind but there was something unusual about the meeting. His smile seemed forced and even somewhat pained. I had expected a more boisterous greeting but when I sensed that he seemed reserved, I pulled back and settled with the hand shake he seemed to prefer. I eventually concluded that his reserved disposition was the result of the fact that after many years of not seeing each other, we had in so many ways become strangers to one another. Our interests had diverged so much that we did not have much to discuss except to ask about our families.

A few weeks later, I was back in the States after the Christmas vacation. The reader can imagine my shock when I later heard, I am not exactly sure how long later, that he had passed away! "What happened?," I had asked in bewilderment when I was told of his passing. "I just saw this guy the Christmas of 2010", I had said to the guy breaking the bad news to me. "He started having constant pain around his waist", the man had told me, "and when he visited the doctor, he was told that the waist pain was attributable to constant sitting during long vehicle rides. He was a transporter. Of course he had other symptoms but the waist pain was said to be more pronounced and lingered. Later he fell sicker and sicker and that was when they discovered that he had advanced prostate cancer. I could not believe what I was hearing. Apparently, he was already experiencing the many symptoms of the disease when I saw him at church and it could have been the reason for his seeming "pained" smile and reserved disposition. I was very sad that a young man had been taken away at the prime of his existence.

It was with this in mind that I read the interview where Professor Wole Soyinka revealed that he had become a prostate cancer survivor. He followed his revelation with an admonition to the federal government to establish cancer-screening clinics in Nigeria. In line with Soyinka's classy way of doing things, instead of hiding his diagnosis as many Nigerians would do, he spoke up about it and used his clout to ask the government to do something about it. I was hoping that many more prominent Nigerians will join his call but of course since it does not involve sharing of money, they will not speak up in support of Soyinka's prescription.

Chuma's case is not the first time I have had to contend with the news of someone I know suffering from the ailment or even dying. In fact, the number of people I know that are living with the disease is so staggering that one is tempted to believe that it has become one of the most common but deadly diseases in Nigeria for men. When I visited Nigeria in 2007, a friend told me the story of his contemporary that had undergone prostate cancer surgery in the country. The surgery had gone wrong and all manners of complications had developed. I was almost moved to tears as the story was narrated of what a once boisterous and ebullient man was going through including loss of appetite for existence. I began to wonder if the doctor that performed the operation was even trained to do so or whether he even fully understood how the disease worked before embarking on the operation. Up to this date, I have not mastered the gumption to ask how things eventually turned out for the man. I am always hoping and praying silently that the day I ever toughen up to ask, I will be told that he beat the disease. Now, just a few weeks ago, I got the sad news that a relative had passed away as a result of the disease. I am still trying to process the news of my relative's passing.

In all, prostate cancer is real. It is said to be the number four killer of men worldwide. It can be deadly if not detected early but the good news is that early detection has proven to be the key to survival. If detected early, it can be cured fully through a combination of surgery and therapy and the patient will live a full and productive life. Just here in the United States, high profile personalities like John Kerry and Colin Powel are good examples of survivors that are living normal lives because their cases were detected early and treated.

I will never forget what happened in my doctor's office when I turned 50 and visited my doctor for routine yearly physical. After conducting the rest of the physicals, my doctor said, "now that you have turned 50, there are two screening tests that you will now be subjected to every year you show up for your physical. The goal of the test is to ensure that your prostate is working well" "It is recommended for every male 50 years and over", he continued, "but could start earlier for those with genetic disposition for prostate cancer". I knew what the test was from stories of older contemporaries and had long dreaded being subjected to it but at this moment, I had to do what my doctor said, I had no choice. "It is a two part test", he continued, "one of the tests will be done here in the office and the other will be done using your blood in the lab". "Ok", I answered, already feeling embarrassed but trying to hide my emotions. "I will caution you", he said further while scribbling some notes on a pad in front of him, "that the one that will be done here can be uncomfortable". With that, he asked that I turn around! The bottom line is that I did not like having someone probe my rear yet it was a life-saving necessary evil. The screening is a procedure that would tell the doctor whether the prostate has started enlarging beyond normal levels or if lumps of any sort had developed that would warrant attention. Any reader that wants more information on how the office screening is done could google it.

This test was followed up in the lab with a blood test called PSA or prostate specific antigen. The presence of the antigen in the blood in certain amounts provide indication of whether the prostate had become diseased especially with cancer. Most survivors of prostate cancer are men that their doctors became alerted of the disease through a combination of this test and the rear "body cavity" probing. Of course some had already developed symptoms like constant and burning urination and the sorts but the bottom line is that early detection made the difference between survival and death.

My classmate Chuma may not have died had his disease been detected early. He only went to a doctor when the symptoms had started manifesting. Yet, most probably, the disease developed and progressed years before he became symptomatic with waist pain, constant urination and the rest. It is possible that yearly physicals capped with PSA blood tests would have detected the disease early and his life saved but that is water under the bridge now for Chuma. A young man with children that depended on him not just for subsistence but for guidance, has passed away, leaving broken hopes and shattered dreams. He also left a young widow to fend for the children. The living must now learn from that experience and begin to take control of their health through proactive yearly physicals that must include these tests.

Nigeria must heed Wole Soyinka's admonition and begin to establish, as a priority, more cancer screening clinics and testing labs all over. Also, there has to be a regulatory body that oversees what these testing labs do as it is my considered opinion that some are not fit to be in business. I have seen situations where lab test results seem to vary depending on where they were done. Sometimes, false positives or false negatives result, confusing doctors into making the wrong diagnoses. Furthermore, there has to be a way to bring down the costs of these tests to a level that the common Nigerian can afford. Everything costs in the thousands in the country and such situations may be contributing to the aversion of some people to going to the labs or seeing doctors regularly.

When I saw Wole Soyinka's interview, I decided to write about this with the hope that the average Nigerian reading this will become more sensitized to take action now. As the Igbo would say, "tata bu gboo" "today is early".

Urgent Open Letter To President Umar Yaradua:
Save Nigerians from senseless deaths occasioned by poorly equipped hospitals - November 29, 2009

For quite some time now, every time I open the pages of Nigerian dailies, I read about the state of your health. Some tell us that the situation is so hopeless that it is just a matter of time. Then you suddenly traveled to Germany and the word was that your situation had deteriorated. They said it started with swelling that mimicked allergic reaction but then deteriorated into something more serious.

The talk in the press is that your ailment was misdiagnosed by your doctors in Nigeria. Your doctors, according to media reports, had diagnosed your condition as respiratory in nature and were therefore treating you accordingly with the medications they thought were right for you. It was only later, the reports added, that your German doctors found out that your condition had to do with your kidneys. According to the reports we read, your German doctors concluded that your treatment was not started early so your situation was no longer curable and could only be managed. Alas, the doctors in Nigeria had misdiagnosed your condition!

Sir, be aware that I am not in a position to tell if what we are reading is the true picture of your medical condition but that is irrelevant. The fact is that what we are reading about you completely describes what average Nigerians are going through day in day out. Their medical conditions are being misdiagnosed daily in Nigeria.

As I read, on a daily basis in the Nigerian dailies, what amounts to the anticipation of the passing of a fellow Nigerian and an important one at that, it pains my heart. It would have been different if you had attained at least the ripe age of three score and ten. It becomes even more painful to think that, as media reports speculate, your situation worsened because of incorrect diagnoses. If the story about incorrect diagnosis of your ailment is true, Mr. President, have you taken time to pledge to yourself for the sake of posterity, that what happened to you will not and should not happen to any other Nigerian? As one of the most powerful men in Africa today, have you pledged to yourself to take bold steps to save other Nigerians that face, on a daily basis, the same predicament of medical misdiagnosis that you went through?

Mr. President, it is worth emphasizing, in fairness to Nigerian doctors, that most of the time they misdiagnose ailments not because they are incompetent but because the hospitals, clinics or health centers where they work, do not have the requisite equipment for pathological analysis and differential diagnoses. I was once a student at the University of Nigeria Nsukka and so know the caliber of doctors produced then. I shared hostels with medical students who were taught by the likes of famed Dr. Udekwu. Along with students from other Nigerian universities like Ibadan, Lagos and Ife, these were Nigeria's best brains and it showed in everything they did. Upon graduation, each batch of graduates continued in the tradition of excellent delivery in the medical sector. They did not always have the best medical equipment or labs to work with but the situation at the time had not become as grave as now. Mr. President, it was about this time that one of your predecessors, General Babangida, instituted austerity measures. It began to take its toll on every aspect of life in Nigeria. Medical doctors could no longer be rewarded in consonance with the critical nature of the service they delivered. Some could no longer find good jobs. Not long after that, Nigeria's best brains began to leave the country, one after the other, in search of greener pastures. Many have continued the tradition of excellence in their adopted western countries and continue to win awards in places like Britain, United States and Australia. But the gains of other nations have become Nigeria's loss as you can attest from the experience you have had so far where you have to jet out to Germany for medical care.

Mr. President, in case you have not truly noticed, the medical sector in Nigeria has deteriorated. For starters, the many schools of medicine in Nigeria are no longer what they used to be. This is not the fault of the students. They are still bright and eager to learn but what they find in the schools are mere class rooms that lack medical equipment and labs for instruction. They lack books and lack access to the internet to keep up with other medical institutions in the world. Even after graduation, because of the complete neglect of the medical sector by successive governments, including yours, sir, they have not found their footing in practice. Without the proper equipment for medical instruction in schools, without the proper equipment and diagnostics labs in hospitals, clinics and health centers, Nigeria is now a country where ailments are routinely misdiagnosed. If your own ailment could be misdiagnosed, can you imagine how many Nigerians whose lives are being cut short on a daily basis because of the same malady? Could you imagine how many doctors take their best guesses in an attempt to satisfy the obvious curiosity of a patient because they have no equipment or truly equipped lab to make informed analysis?

Sir, MRI equipment that are used to differentially diagnose many ailments are lacking in many so called hospitals and Nigerians are dying in the hundreds as a result. Kidney dialysis machines that have the capability of giving a new lease in life for thousands are nowhere to be found in many so called hospitals in the country and many are dying. Mr. President, even common equipment like X-ray machines, ultra sound machines, and equipment for the early detection of colon polyps that later become cancer are lacking. How could you, in all honesty and sincerity, think you are moving Nigeria forward when your administration has done nothing in the medical sector to help improve the quality of life for average Nigerians? If it is true that your doctors did indeed misdiagnose your own ailment, then you do understand the point I am making here. I am sure your doctors are smart, intelligent and well experienced otherwise you would not be going to them. That is why I am convinced that their error must be the result of lack of the requisite equipment or inability to keep abreast with new development in the medical field. This is the result of the total neglect of the medical sector.

Now you have to shuttle between Nigeria and Germany just to get treatment. It is my fervent hope that you will get well soon. But the question is how long are you going to be shuttling between both countries? Furthermore, have you wondered how many Nigerians find themselves in your type of medical predicament where their best hope of survival is getting help abroad but cannot travel because they do not have the money or the connection? Have you wondered how many Nigerians have died simply because they were unable to get the type of treatment you are currently getting in Germany? Have you wondered how many Nigerians, breadwinners for their families, fathers, mothers, uncles, aunties that have died or are about to die because the Nigerian hospitals they depend on do not have the requisite equipment to diagnose their ailments and treat them properly?

Mr. President, I need to tell you a story. Not long ago, a hitherto happily married woman poured out her heart to me in an email. She talked about the death of her husband after a long illness. When the symptoms of the illness initially began to manifest, the man dutifully went to the hospital but because of poor equipment, the doctors were never able to tell what was wrong. It was only in the end, when the ailment had eaten deep into him and ravaged every part of his body, that the right diagnosis came. The cancer diagnosis was given when he was finally airlifted to Britain but by then it was too late for the doctors to help him. He died leaving a grieving widow and innocent children. I want to reiterate that many more Nigerians are daily taking their last breath, leaving loved ones who depended on them just because Nigerian hospitals are underfunded, under-equipped and understaffed.

One of the reasons why I am writing to you, Mr. President, is that the issue of wrong diagnose of ailments has hit home for me! A family friend in Nigeria is going through what amounts to a serious medical issue. He has been to hospitals, including the one at Abuja and it has been difficult for the doctors to give a concrete differential diagnosis. One of the doctors has advised him, in confidence, to seek medical treatment outside Nigeria. As a young graduate in Nigeria, this very humble young man is not affluent or well-connected as you are. The idea of quickly sending him to Germany, like you do, is almost out of the question. My heart bleeds to think that in a nation as affluent as Nigeria, there are no hospitals properly equipped to handle the diverse medical issues that people face. It is equally embarrassing that in this day and age, Nigerians have to be jetting out of the country to places like Ghana, South Africa and the like to get proper medical treatment. It is hurtful that as advanced as Nigeria, which is under your responsibility now, claims to be, we still have empty hospitals with doctors that are not keeping pace with medical and technological advancement through no fault of theirs.

Mr. President, during your inauguration, you stated that you would be a servant leader. A true servant leader is one that is able to gauge the true situation in the country you lead and take urgent measures to come down on the side of the masses. If you are a true servant leader, if you have learned any lesson from your own experience, you must declare a medical emergency in the country. With that, you should use your office to mandate the design, construction, staffing and equipment of four major hospitals in each of the four regions of the country - North, South, East and West. This should not be one of those projects that have to needlessly get bogged down by bureaucratic red-tape. It should be a presidential mandate supervised and shepherded as such. We have been getting oil windfall for many months now and we have enough money in Nigeria's coffers for the design, construction, staffing and equipment of the hospitals. Even if this is the only thing you succeed in doing for Nigerians, at the end of your tenure, they will always remember you. Do not let people deceive you into thinking that this is an impossible task or that the design and construction of ultra-modern hospitals cannot be completed during your tenure. It could be done in 30 months as long as there is no restriction in cash flow.

I am almost certain that this issue will not be of utmost priority for the people that surround you; even your own commitment is still questionable. This is because you have all found solace in hospitals outside the country and easily fly out on the drop of a hat for medical attention. There was yet another rumor, a few days ago, that Maryam Babangida was flown to Los Angeles on medical emergency. At least, she could afford it. But remember, if we go by what we have been reading about you, your own medical situation is not good either. While we pray that you will recover soon, you must now become pragmatic about things. The time you use in shuttling between Nigeria and Germany for medical treatment could make the difference between life and death. Have you considered the fact that in a medical emergency that requires prompt action, the 6-hours or so you use in jetting out to Germany could make the difference between living and dying? What do you see wrong in duplicating the type of hospital you visit in Germany in the four corners of Nigeria and if need be, staff them initially with foreign doctors, including Nigerian doctors from abroad?

Mr. President, be aware that as I write, many prominent and well-meaning Nigerians are out of the country to seek medical treatment for life threatening ailments. They have discovered that most Nigerian hospitals are not equipped with the right tools, the right buildings, the right doctors and the right labs to treat certain ailments. My favorite democracy crusader, Chief Gani Fawehinmi, is out of the country for medical treatment. One of my favorite artists, Sunny Okosun of the Ozzidi fame, is out of the country because of the same problem. You, the president of Africa's most populous nation, continue to shuttle between Nigeria and Germany when you can build, in Nigeria, the best hospitals that Africa could ever have. That is actually a disappointment.

Think seriously about this, Mr. President. Since you have experienced the issue at stake first hand, you would understand it much more than those that ruled Nigeria before you. I mean those that used Nigeria's billions to enrich themselves rather than make it possible for Nigerians to have a second chance at life via well-equipped and staffed hospitals.

I await your response and most importantly urgent action. The clock is ticking Mr. President.

Some Nigerians Use Skin-Bleaching Creams That May Be Harmful to the Skin - September 2003.

Remember the song by the late Afro-beat musician of Nigeria - Fela Anikulapo- Kuti - christened "Yellow Fever?" The song satirized the use of bleaching creams to lighten the complexion of the skin in the quest for beauty. The song is a classic example of how Fela used his songs to focus awareness on some of the problems that he saw in the Nigerian society. He describes, in the song, the transmogrifying effects the bleaching creams had on the skin: "your face go yellow, your eyes go yellow, your skin go yellow…" he sang.

Right after the release of the song, the practice of skin-bleaching, which had almost gained acceptance in the Nigerian society, started on a downward trend. The song had raised awareness about the deleterious effects that the creams could have on the skin of the user. In fact, at the sight of any one perceived to have bleached, children would be heard shouting invectives at the person, including: "iru Fanta, ukwu Coke," meaning: Fanta-colored face but Coke-colored legs. This was in reference to the way the creams bleached the face, giving it a yellowish, Fanta-colored hue while the rest of the body remained as dark as the Coca Cola.

The use of the creams, at the time, was so widespread that it almost became difficult to tell the actual complexion of our young girls and some women! Suddenly it seemed like every young girl and young woman all became fair complexioned. The aftereffects of the use of the creams began to lend credence to the Latin phrase, "culculus non facit monarchum"- the hood does not make the monk. Essentially, just because someone looked fair in complexion does not mean that the person is actually fair in complexion. I failed to see the rational in the bleaching of the skin because even women with beautiful dark-complexioned skin also took to the practice.

I must confess that even though I disagreed with the practice of skin-bleaching, I never really thought seriously about the probability that these creams could be causing harm to long-term users until I read an article on CNN.com/World of August 14, 2001. It stated: "Uganda is set to follow Kenya's example and outlaw dozens of popular creams and soaps used by African women to lighten their skin as awareness grows of their harmful side effects"

Apparently, sometime in the past, the Kenyan government banned these creams for reasons related to their damaging effects on the skins of long- term users. My assumption here is that the Kenyan government did not take this type of drastic step based just on mere hear-say, but must have undertaken some type of research which led them to the conclusion that these creams and soaps were really damaging to the skin. They did what any government interested in the welfare of her people would do - ban the use.

The CNN article further stated: "Millions of women throughout Africa use creams and soaps containing hydroquinone and mercury to lighten the color of their skin, believing that it makes them more beautiful. Dermatologists say prolonged use of hydroquinone and mercury-based products destroy the skin's protective layer. Ultimately, it can damage the nerves or even lead to kidney failure or skin cancer."

After reading the CNN article, I did a quick search to get a better idea of what the ingredient hydroquinone was and how it accomplished its bleaching action. Hydroquinone and products containing it are used as de-pigmenting agents to lighten the skin. It works as a skin-lightener by killing the cells that produce melanin (melanocytes) Because of safety concerns, hydroquinone is banned in a number of European countries and limited to a maximum concentration of 2% in North America.

Obviously, I am not a clinical scientist and so the real ramifications of the use of these creams may remain fuzzy to me. I do know, though, that prolonged use of the creams result in an unevenly toned, dry-looking, blotchy skin.

The awareness raised by the CNN article, in my mind, has elevated my level of consciousness about skin-bleaching. On a recent trip to the Northeast, to an event that attracted a large gathering of Nigerian and indeed African folks, I noticed that the "iru Fanta, ukwu coke" syndrome is very much alive and well within our African women folk. Africans living in the Diaspora still use bleaching cream heavily. The telltale signs of the effects of the creams on the body are unmistakable - "the face go yello, the fingers go brown, the knuckles, the ankles and the knees go black! Some go look very fair for face but when them stretch them hand to shake you, you go notice say them fingers black". I am trying to use some humor to soften the seriousness of this matter, but the fact remains that it is far from being a laughing matter.

The aim of the article is to draw attention to the fact that bleaching creams actually cause lasting damages to the skin and our womenfolk may be putting their lives in danger unknowingly. The banning of these creams in Kenya, Tanzania and with Uganda readying to follow suit is sufficient reason for Nigeria's health Ministry or Food and Drug Administration to act. They should take a closer look at the creams to ascertain their efficacy and any probable damage as alleged in the CNN article.

In fairness to our women folk, however, it is incorrect to assume that anyone who uses bleaching cream is doing so in the quest for beauty. Just as Michael Jackson stated that he started bleaching his skin to cover up vitiligo, some of our people actually use the creams to ward off skin ailments like acne, pimples and other skin rashes. I know this for a fact because during my early years in secondary school in Nigeria, as puberty was setting in, I could not escape the onslaught of facial pimples. I naturally sought reprieve from pimples by using the most popular medicated soap at the time (which contained mercury. After three days of continuous use, it "burnt" my face as we used to say. Even though this happened over two and half decades ago, I still have the scars to show for it. Needless to say that the experience caused me to refrain completely from the use of these "medicated" soaps.

I have no problems per se with people using these creams since most are of adult age anyway and make decisions for themselves, but as a public service, the government should institute a research into these creams and soaps and make the results known to the public. Government research could be as simple as just conducting a literature search of existing and factual documentation and delving into the reasons for which the other African countries banned the creams. Most would agree with me that if these creams and soaps are proven to be harmful to the body, most people would stop using them of their own volition.

I believe we have a highly qualified pool of Nigerian experts (both in Nigeria and the Diaspora) who would willingly join forces with the Nigerian government to get to the bottom of this issue. They could help by providing research information, commentary and any germane information to prove or disprove the assertion that the creams are harmful. Valuable commentary and evidence could also be obtained from the countries that have already banned these creams as to why they took that course of action.

At the end of the exercise, all findings must be made public. At that time, the government should become satisfied that it has fully discharged a public service obligation.

Fake Medications in Nigeria - August 13, 2001

Self-medicating is a phenomenon that is rife in Nigeria and in other African countries, especially amongst the people in the lower echelon of the economic spectrum. Most of us grew up under that type of environment where you always assumed that you understood the symptoms of your ailments. You could therefore go to the chemist, procure and ingest any medication without consultation with a physician. But the danger in self-medicating is that very serious diseases are sometimes misdiagnosed and the wrong medication administered. By the time the real ailment manifests itself, it would have become too late.

Since in Nigeria people could easily buy and ingest any medication, would it not make sense that for the safety of the citizens, drugs sold by the chemists are at least authentic? Self-medicating is bad enough, but if the medication you are taking is fake, expired or adulterated, the problem becomes compounded manifold.

A very disturbing trend has been on the rise in Nigeria for the past several years. The importation of fake and expired medication has been the vogue and some "chemists" make a career out of this illicit trade. These people collude with foreign nationals, import fake or expired drugs and distribute them throughout the nation for consumption. The public buys these medications and takes them hoping for the symptoms of their ailments to subside to no avail.

Lamenting the influx of fake drugs into the country and the wickedness inherent in this unpatriotic act, the director-general of the National Agency for Foods and Drugs Administration in Nigeria, Dr. Dora Akunyili asked, "Have we ever asked ourselves if the countries that produce fake drugs for some of us to import, distribute those drugs to their people? The answer is no. The fake drugs are for export only" She further stated that "when people take fake or substandard anti-hypertensive drugs, their blood pressure will continue rising until they go down with stroke or even die"

A few weeks ago, a relative of mine told me a story of how she bought some antibiotics to relieve a child of cold infection. After some days of administering the medication, the ailment would not subside but took a turn for the worse. At this time, it occurred to her that the medication did not have the characteristic odor of the said anti-biotic. To confirm her suspicions, she obtained a urinary sample of the patient and discovered that the characteristic odor of the antibiotic in urine was also absent. When she opened the remaining capsules, she realized that they were mere chalk-like powders! Imagine how many people this happens to on a daily basis? Imagine how many lives may be gradually drifting away just because of this?

We must take a closer look at the incidence of untimely deaths in Nigeria especially deaths from ailments that are usually non-life threatening. These days it is not uncommon to hear that people easily die of malaria, headache, diabetes and stomachache. These are diseases that could be successfully treated or at least managed. Who knows if the medications they took were expired or fake? An international workshop which evaluated the state of drug distribution in Nigeria in 1988 revealed that 33 percent of drugs emanating from open markets were fake. That survey also confirmed that seven percent was actually dangerous to the health of the consumers. This was in 1988, who knows what the statistics are today?

The question that needs to be answered: why has this gone on for so long without real action to stamp it out? Fresh investigations must be instituted to unearth how much damage this may have done to our citizenry while seeking permanent solutions.

A couple of weeks ago, the National Agency for Food and Drug administration(NAFDAC) destroyed millions of naira worth of fake and adulterated drugs at Onitsha Anambra State. According to them, that signaled an all-out war on the menace of importation of such drugs into the country. After the destruction of the drugs, one of the men allegedly responsible for the illicit trade, asked for forgiveness of Nigerians. The story took a bizarre twist when, according to a story reported on Guardian Online of August 3, 2001, "hired assassins, believed to be agents of fake drug barons, went after Dr. Dora Akunyili" It was reported that Mrs. Akunyili escaped unhurt but is this the beginning of a ding dong warfare between fake drug importers and the Nigerian Government?

Whatever the case may be, this is a fight the government must fight and win. Since 1989, several laws have been enacted to deter importation, manufacturing, distribution and selling of fake drugs but the situation has continued unabated. Desperate situations must be met with desperate actions. Destroying the drugs while a welcome action step, is just not enough as it is akin to treating the symptoms of an ailment without taking care of the root cause. Measures adequate to the current exigencies must be devised.

There must be strict enforcement of the laws in the books and culprits summarily brought to book. Penalties must not be a mere slap on the hand but must be commensurate with the gravity of the offense. People are certainly dying from taking expired drugs as stated by Dr. Akunyili when she asked, "Do you know that the growing number of people dying of hypertension, heart failure and stroke in this country today is because of fake and adulterated drugs?" If fake drugs cause deaths in Nigeria, then the perpetrators of these nefarious acts cannot absolve themselves of murder. When apprehended, they must bear full responsibility for taking lives.

Those countries from which these drugs emanate must formally be made aware of the situation by the government of Nigeria (if we haven't already done so). Officials of the NAFDAC should develop bilateral agreements with these countries to help track down the foreign counterparts of the Nigerian culprits to stop the problem at the sources rather than wait for the drugs to get to Nigerian shores.

Before now, I was opposed to the policy of 100 percent inspection of imported goods at our ports. My reason was that it would cause untold hardship to legitimate importers and give the custom officials the opportunity for more corruption. Even though some of the problems I anticipated are taking place, I now support the inspection because it would afford the government the chance to combat importation of fake and expired drugs into the country.

Finally I would end this piece by once again quoting the director-general of NAFDAC: "When we import and distribute poisons, substandard, non-efficacious, expired and or about to expire drugs, are we not making blood money? Is there no other way of making money without killing people through fake and counterfeit drugs? Let us remember that our God is a God of justice. Those who become rich by killing other people with fake and counterfeit drugs will neither live to enjoy the money, nor will their children" I could not have said it any better. We should all support the effort put forth so far by Dr. Akunyili and her agency.

Alfred Obiora Uzokwe

Health Concerns Trigger Clampdown on Bakeries that Use Potassium Bromate- November 3, 2003

Believing that potassium bromate, an additive that Nigerian bread-makers frequently add to make bread rise causes cancer, The National Agency For Food and Drug Administration and Control(NAFDAC) issued a blanket ban to save lives.

The National Agency for Food and Drug Administration and Control (NAFDAC) has continued to live up to its name and mandate in Nigeria. Employees of the agency have set an unprecedented legacy of probity, action and positive results in a country where personal enrichment at all costs seems to be the guiding principle of many. Under the leadership of the Director-General of the agency, Dr. Dora Akunyili, NAFDAC has been uprooting, with surgical precision, dubious and unscrupulous businesses that have once operated freely in the country.

Not too long ago, NAFDAC boldly took on businesses and individuals that imported and manufactured fake and adulterated medications. In the face of threats from some of the businesses, the agency fought back fearlessly, steadily and relentlessly. Today, that line of business has been whittled down appreciably. Fake and adulterated medications are now harder to come by. Unregistered pharmacies and pharmacists that once littered Nigeria's landscape have either been closed down or are running scared. The era when "pharmacists" sold glorified chalk instead of antibiotic to unsuspecting victims is fast coming to an end. Genuine drug manufacturers in the country, who were beginning to think of moving their businesses elsewhere, because fake drugs had become more popular than the real ones they manufactured, have started doing well again and are vowing to stay put.

West African countries like Ghana and Sierra Leone which banned importation of medications from Nigeria, because of the bad name fake drug importers gave the industry, have started lifting their sanctions. The good work of the agency has not gone unnoticed in international circles. The agency has continued to receive all types of equipment from international bodies to help fight the scourge of fake medications.

NAFDAC employees sometimes utilize unconventional methods in the discharge of their duties. For example, anytime it determines that a shipment into Nigeria is of fake medication, the entire shipment is confiscated and burnt in open arenas with members of the public watching. The exercise is designed as a deterrent to would-be importers or manufacturers of fake drugs. At the time of this writing, it was estimated that NAFDAC has burnt goods worth more than 5 billion naira!

The agency has now set its sights on perpetrators of another type of crime: it has begun a massive clampdown on bakeries that still use banned potassium bromate in making bread. The chemical is an additive that bakers add to bread dough, during the mixing process, to make it stronger and moldable. In trying to defend the use of the additive in making bread, Theresa Cogswell of the American Society of Bakery Engineers said it is used to help bread rise in the oven and to create a good texture in the finished product. The catch, though, is that even with the benefit bakers seem to derive from the use of potassium bromate, there are concerns that it has deleterious effects on humans when consumed in certain quantities. The average person eats bread about five times a week and hence may just be consuming unsafe levels of potassium bromate. In light of this and cognizant of the fact that the additive "is termed a cancer threat"[1,] concern about its use is right. The Director-General of NAFDAC stated that toxicology studies show that potassium bromate degrades the essential vitamins in bread. She added that research shows that bread treated with bromate proved carcinogenic in oral administration in rats but that in humans, it reportedly brought about cough and sore throat on inhalation, abdominal pain, diarrhea, nausea, vomiting, kidney failure, hearing loss and redness in the eyes on ingestion[2]

Researchers became concerned about the additive when in a 1982 study, they discovered that potassium bromate brought about the development of various types of tumors on lab animals like tumors of the thyroid and kidneys. This development caught the attention of the American Food and Drug Administration. As a result, in 1992 and again in 1998, the agency conducted rounds of tests on baked goods. The tests revealed that many baked goods in the country contained potassium bromate at levels considered unsafe for humans.

In 1990, the United Kingdom banned the use of the additive in baking because of health concerns. Four years later, Canada followed suit. Surprisingly, it turned out that Nigeria was also following the findings that point to the health risks inherent in the consumption of goods baked with the additive, because in 1994, NAFDAC banned its use for making bread in the country. However, as is the case with everything else in Nigeria, bakers ignored the ban and continued to use it to the detriment of unsuspecting consumers.

On assumption of office, Dr. Dora Akunyili took interest in the baking industry just as she did in the drug importation and manufacturing industry. Her agency began to work towards enforcement of the ban on the use of potassium bromate. On March 4, 2003, bakers in Nigeria were ordered to end the use of the banned additive by June 4 or face the music. That deadline has now come and gone and enforcement has begun in earnest. Recently, NAFDAC officials arrested six Master Bakers in Bauchi State for continued use of the banned substance They have since been handed over to the police for prosecution.

It should be noted that the nature of the job of NAFDAC employees makes temptation inevitable. Just as an importer of fake drugs could try to bribe the employees to look away, users of potassium bromate could also attempt to offer bribe money to be left alone. However, the example set by the no-nonsense director of NAFDAC, where no business is a sacred cow, is being emulated by employees. They are demonstrating their willingness to shun bribery and corruption and do their jobs the right way. The few employees that have succumbed to bribery temptation have been shown the way out.

The exemplary behavior and leadership model that the agency's director has displayed and continues to espouse is the type of model that all of Nigeria needs. It is a leadership model that says: do as I do not just do as I say. Dr. Akunyili uses an effective system of reward and punishment to run her agency. Forthright and hardworking employees frequently go to free seminars organized outside the country. It not only makes them feel important and appreciated, but it also motivates them. During the seminars, they get to meet people from other countries and continue to see the need for love of country. They also learn how to combat the scourge of fake medications and adulterated food.

As far as potassium bromate is concerned, Nigeria cannot afford to wait for clear and convincing evidence that it causes cancer in humans before strictly enforcing the ban on its use. Canada and the United Kingdom have banned its use based on exhaustive investigations. Furthermore, tests by the FDA in the United States point to the fact that it is unsafe. In Nigeria where many die daily from ailments that could at best be described as mysterious, continued use of the banned additive should not be an option. We can never be sure what role the ingestion of the additive plays and rather than wait to find out the hard way, it is better to err on the side of caution. This, in my mind, should be the wisdom and impetus behind the strict enforcement of the ban.

Ban All Overseas Medical Trips For Public Officials:
They will be forced to build modern health facilities
or equip existing ones in Nigeria- January 15, 2007

There is a dialogue currently going on between the lawyers for the former governor of Bayelsa State, Diepreye Alamieyesiegha and the Economic and Financial Crimes Commission(EFCC). The former governor, who is currently being tried for corruption, slumped in court for unexplained medical reasons. Since then, reports have been filtering into the public domain that he has a medical condition that is fast deteriorating. His lawyers decided that he should be sent abroad for treatment, probably at the expense of Nigeria! Surprisingly, the judge presiding over the case agreed with Alamieyesiegha's lawyers and has since been hounding the EFCC to procure visa for the corruption suspect to proceed abroad.

Alamieyesiegha's lawyers and the undiscerning judge conveniently forgot that in the governor's heyday, he could have used the millions he is being accused of embezzling to build an ultra-modern hospital, equipped with all the necessary gadgets for medical diagnoses and treatment in Bayelsa state. He did not do that because, just like most Nigerian public officials, he reveled in traveling abroad for his physicals. Now that he needs medical intervention, he wants Nigerians to finance a trip to a choice hospital abroad and the judge is siding with him. This is a travesty that must be resisted. He should be sent to the same hospitals he neglected in Bayelsa state when he was the governor. It would serve as a radical but instructive lesson to other politicians in Africa's most populous nation.

Nigeria must ban, as a matter of urgency, all overseas medical trips for all elected public officials and their appointees. It should be a blanket ban cutting across the executive, judiciary and the legislative arms of government. It should not be restricted to just the trips financed with public money but should include all medical trips whether paid for by the official or the government. This may sound draconian and undemocratic but as this article unfolds, it will become clear to the reader why this writer has gone this radical.

There are two forms of overseas medical trips that public officials embark on in Nigeria. The first type is the routine trip where they fly to choice hospitals outside the country. During the visits, they undergo elaborate physicals, blood work and prophylactic treatments. In the absence of any "remarkable" findings that require medical intervention, doctors certify them as healthy. Subsequently, they head back home to Nigeria, satisfied that they will yet live another year to continue their unbridled assault on Nigeria's treasury.

The second type is where they travel overseas for treatment of a budding or fully developed ailment. During such visits, doctors conduct diagnostic tests and carry out medical procedures that could include surgery. The patients stay a while for recuperation before heading back home to Nigeria.

In both cases described above, the price tag is staggering! It is not just the cost of medical treatment that is involved, air fare and cost of hotel accommodation for the officials, personal physicians and the retinue of staff members that accompany them on such trips, are included. The costs are directly or indirectly being borne by the tax-paying public!

During a recent visit to Nigeria, I had the opportunity to visit a few government-owned and private medical facilities in places like Lagos, Awka and of course Nnewi. I was appalled and horrified at the condition of the facilities. These are dilapidated and poorly equipped hospitals staffed with poorly paid and hence "laid-back" physicians. When patients go to the hospitals, they meet filthy buildings with little or no modern equipment for testing and diagnosis. The pharmacies stock few or no drugs for treatment. The patients come face to face with doctors who have become disillusioned because of poor pay and hence have abandoned their Hippocratic Oath of "do no harm". They provide substandard and questionable diagnosis and treatment. In one of the hospitals, because of the stench that greeted my nose, I had to step outside for a while before a re-entry. It even had an operating theater where patients undergo surgery! No wonder we hear of patients dying after minor medical procedures.

As I toured these facilities, the question that continually came to my mind was: "what have our elected officials been doing?" Why

45

have they not found it attractive policy-making to embark on serious cleaning, rehabilitation and equipment of our hospitals? I wondered if they ever hear the horror stories of patients dying in our hospitals due to the absence of equipment for diagnosis and treatment as well as the absence of drugs in our pharmacies. That was when it hit me: Why would they be interested in rehabilitating our hospitals when they could easily travel abroad for medical checkup and treatment? Why would they be interested in building ultramodern hospitals when they are easily airlifted overseas for medical treatment. Why would former governor Alamieyesiegha or members of the National Assembly want to improve the medical sector when they and their relatives have direct access to choice hospitals abroad? It dawned on me that if the medical sector must be improved and all Nigerians given equal access to good health care, overseas medical trips must be banned for public officials whether financed with tax-payer's money or not.

In a democracy, people have the right to do whatever they want with their money including going abroad for medical treatment. This is true but the intent of the suggested blanket ban is to force our officials to use the same hospitals that the rest of Nigerians use and so witness, first-hand, the sorry state of our medical sector. If a Nigerian public official goes to one of the hospitals for treatment and is confronted by poorly equipped facilities, disenchanted doctors or empty pharmacies, they will be forced to rethink their policy of inaction towards the healthcare sector.

To make my point a little more forcefully, I suggest that whenever President Obasanjo's routine physical is due, he should be sent to Nnamdi Azikiwe Teaching Hospital in Nnewi, Anambra State. He should not be flown in by helicopter either. By the time the vehicle conveying him to the hospital has navigated the pothole-laden Teaching Hospital road, his rear end would be so sore that he would quickly initiate action to rebuild the road. I am even more convinced that by the time he is done in the hospital, he would quickly earmark a more reasonable sum of money to improve the condition of things in that hospital and others like it around the nation.

The need for modern diagnostic and treatment equipment in Nigerian hospitals cannot be overemphasized. Stomach and colorectal cancers continue to take the lives of Nigerians in great numbers. Yet, in advanced countries, procedures like colonoscopy are helping doctors detect and treat early cases of these deadly ailments. Colonoscopy is where the doctor gets a full picture of the intestinal tracts via endoscope cameras and a probe inserted into the patient. They use it to detect colon polyps and excise them before they become deadly. They also use it to detect colon cancers in early stages where they could still be removed and the patient's life saved.

A medical facility that has the requisite equipment for detection and where doctors are paid well for their services will serve not only the average and poor Nigerian, but would be a good alternative to overseas trips for public officials. Ensuring the presence of such equipment in as many hospitals as possible will reduce concentrated demand and keep costs down so that the average Nigerian would also benefit.

Sometime ago, a woman sent me an email and said that her husband suddenly started having certain medical symptoms. Every time she went with him to the hospital, the doctor would conduct a physical and tell them that he did not find anything. The ordeal continued for a long time and the answer continued to be the same but she could tell that something was very wrong. He was losing weight and stamina. The best the doctor ever did was to send the man for blood work and when the results came back, he asserted that nothing was wrong.

At long last, the woman mustered some money and her husband was airlifted to London. There, he was subjected to more advanced tests and a diagnosis of advanced prostate cancer was. The man later died leaving a heartbroken widow and little children that are now growing up without a father. While this may be a case of medical malpractice by an incompetent doctor, if Nigeria paid doctors well and properly equipped the hospitals, they would attract the best minds to our hospitals and cases like the above would be few and far between. What we see is that the best minds in medicine in Nigeria are leaving in droves. The remaining ones float private clinics and charge exorbitantly for their services, thereby driving away the common person. Even at that, they still fall short in diagnoses because of the absence of the right equipment.

Prostate cancer does not have to automatically lead to a man's death. If detected early and excised, men lead normal lives thereafter. Simple finger tests from a man's rear and PSA (Prostate Specific Antigen) tests reveal the presence of the disease early enough. Here in the United States, notable figures like Collin Powel and John Kerry have both had the operation and are both cancer-free. Why can't Nigerians have the same benefit? If our leaders are determined, the same benefits can be replicated in the "Giant of Africa"

There was also the case of my former classmate's sister. Again, she was having certain medical symptoms a few years ago. Her hospital of choice was the Lagos University Teaching Hospital. Why not? After all, it is supposed to be one of the best since it is a Teaching Hospital. As she complained to her attending physician about her symptoms, he dismissed them as nothing serious. By the time the diagnosis was made, the cancer had metastasized and was in its final stages.

When my friend narrated his story to me, he said something that saddened me immensely. "As my sister lay dying in our hometown, after the case was branded hopeless", he said, "I placed a call to my family home in Nigeria from the United States. After talking to my father, I asked to speak to my dying sister. She was too weak but cheered up when she was told that I was the one on the phone". My friend told me that as they talked, the last thing from her mouth to him was: "brother, please make sure that they do not bury my corpse until you return from the USA"

All the above sounds like mere stories until it affects one personally. There are many more stories like the above where people died senselessly because of misdiagnosis occasioned by the absence of adequate equipment or the incompetence of mediocre or disillusioned doctors.

Sometime in the mid-1980s, during Babangida reign, he was flown out to France for treatment of a foot ailment called radiculopathy or so! One would think that the experience would have spurred the man to invest money into the medical sector to build ultra-modern hospitals. He did not do that.

Nigeria has enough money to build two modern hospitals in each state. Nigeria has the money to recruit and pay the best physicians to man these hospitals. Nigeria has the money to ensure that our pharmacies are stacked with requisite drugs. Nigeria has the funds to clean up filthy medical facilities that pass for hospitals and prevent deaths occasioned by post-surgery infections. Nigeria has the money to advance low-cost loans to private doctors to acquire advanced diagnostic and treatment equipment to take the load off of public hospitals. Why is this not being done? Because our public officials can run overseas and get well. If that alternative is completely taken away, they will look inwards and we will all be better for it.

I am longing for a Nigeria where my 47-year old childhood friend will tell me that he can go to the Teaching Hospital in my hometown and get all prophylactic medical tests recommended for people in his age bracket at very affordable cost. I look forward to the day when my former school-mates at the University of Nigeria who studied medicine and are now in private practice in Nigeria, will tell me that with the help of low-cost government loans, they have acquired requisite diagnostic and treatment medical equipment for their practices. I look forward to a Nigeria where senseless deaths occasioned by the neglect of the health sector will peter out considerably. This may never be realized unless our leaders are forced to face what the average Nigerian faces in hospitals at home. They will not face that unless overseas medical trip is taken away from them.

PART 2

Politics

President Jonathan is Handing the Presidency to General Buhari on a Platter of Gold - January 18, 2015

These days, President Jonathan seems to have come to terms with the fact that presidential campaigns are not for the soft-at-heart or the fainthearted. He is no longer timid but has been delivering his own attacks at Buhari. When the campaigns first started, he seemed excessively deferential to Buhari, to the chagrin of his supporters

The problem, though, is that the statements that Jonathan makes on the campaign trail tend to deepen the belief by some that he is clueless about what really matters. It is one thing to respond to a campaign attack or to make an attack of your own but it is important to ensure that the things you say make sense, are effective and are capable of creating doubt about your opponent. Nigerians are looking for Jonathan to specifically tell them why, after 6 years in power, they still have to reelect him. They want to hear the specifics of what he did to move the nation forward and what he plans to do if reelected. They want to hear tangible reasons why he feels he is better than his challenger and why his challenger is bad for the country. Nigerians want to know why he should be given 4 more years to fight corruption when he has had 6 full years without tangible results. Unfortunately, so far, he has not been able to make the case. He says things that are rather peripheral or even tangential to the issues at hand and does not display mature grasp of the issues Nigerians are grappling with and care deeply about.

For example, most Nigerians believe that the bane of the nation has been endemic corruption and so want that cankerworm excised. That was why Nigerians hailed when the EFCC was first born under Obasanjo. They relished watching on TV as Obasanjo paraded some of the corrupt officials although he later turned that into a witch-hunt. But one would not know how badly Nigerians want corruption rooted out of the system by listening to President Jonathan. Jonathan was once quoted as saying that "stealing is not corruption". Then he said he is averse to building prisons to house never-do-wells. He is also skewering Buhari for jailing people who defrauded the nation and was quoted as saying that Governor Jim Nwobodo was jailed for stealing funds akin to what you use to buy a car. The impression this writer and many have developed, based on the utterances of Jonathan, is that he has no appetite to fight corruption. By continually castigating a former head of state for daring to fight corruption, he seems to be signaling that he will not pursue that and EFCC will remain docile under his watch. If I were him, I would actually be saying that Buhari and I agree that corruption should be fought and that I will keep fighting it. Unfortunately, he has lost credibility on that issue.

Most Nigerians still remember that General Babangida was and is still despised for what he did when he was in office. It was under his watch that Dele Giwa was killed and many media houses silenced in one way or the other. Corruption basically became institutionalized during Babangida's administration and inflation ran amok. He annulled the freest and fairest election in Nigeria that was won by Moshood Abiola. IBB has tried to come back a few times as a president but Nigerians roundly rejected him. One would think that with this type of resume, any politician would keep far away from Babangida. No, that is not Jonathan. He has, by his statements, started portraying Babangida as a saint to the chagrin of many Nigerians, including this writer. During one of Jonathan's campaign rallies, he took time to recite the reasons that IBB adduced for overthrowing Buhari and said it was for the same reasons that Nigerians should reject Buhari. So Jonathan is now using a former corrupt dictator's reasons for staging a coup to back himself up. If he says that Buhari was draconian in his time and used IBB's utterances to justify that, he seems to be implying that he is in bed with IBB in spite of the things that took place during his regime including corruption, annulment of the election, the killing of Dele Giwa and heavy-handedness. Jonathan is trying to legitimize IBB. This does not make sense.

During a speech recently, Jonathan said Buhari cannot even remember his phone number and yet wants to rule Nigeria. If he makes that statement in the United States, senior citizens would come after him because it smirks of age discrimination. As if that was enough, Jonathan made a statement that was so hyperbolic that even a kid would wonder what he was thinking. He said that part of the reason why the army was failing in the anti-terrorism fight was that Buhari did not buy a single rifle for them when he was in power. It not only sounds unbelievable but childish especially when he says that it is the reason why he, Jonathan, cannot fight insecurity. First of all, by that, he is admitting that his administration has failed in the fight against terrorism. Also, laying the blame on the doors of a head of state that ruled 20 years ago for just 20 months before being booted out of office, is a wild stretch. What Jonathan does not realize is that by saying that, he actually indicts his own party, PDP, which has, since Buhari's ouster, had the presidency for 15 years. He is inadvertently making the case of why PDP should not be reelected, including him as part of them. He could simply have made a case that he has been doing his best to fight insurgency, cite examples of some of the successes that the army has made and say he has been equipping them and the battle will continue to be ramped up until insurgency is rooted out. Frankly, the president and PDP seem to have the foot-in-mouth disease.

These days, attention has been shifted to Buhari's school certificate and Jonathan's camp are expending a lot of energy talking about school certificate for a man that has been the head of state for 20 months and has had training in army War College and other places. This issue will eventually amount to nothing. Let's face it, the poor Nigerian does not care about his certificate and so expending time that Jonathan should be using to frontally attack this guy's deficiencies on inanities makes him look silly.

The other week, PDP again expended a lot of energy and political capital asking for Buhari to show his wife, something this writer thought was trivial and had no bearing with governing Nigeria. For some reason, PDP thought they would get political mileage out of it and spent the time they should spend on hammering Buhari on economic issues on it. Eventually, Buhari brought out his wife. Someone sent me a cartoon that showed a picture of Buhari's wife side by side with Jonathan's wife. Jonathan's wife seemed to be looking at Buhari's wife in awe and the writing was, "chei, there is god o". Inotherwords, Jonathan's wife was awestricken at the beauty of Buhari's wife. I recall that the person that tweeted the Buhari wife picture to me simply said, "this woman is beautiful-o; this Buhari get taste–o". So that ended a silliness that raged for weeks.

On the converse, Buhari seems to be landing very effective blows. He simply talks about the economy that has gotten worse under Jonathan and says he will fix it. He has not truly said how he will fix it but says he will. He says he has fought corruption before and will fight it again. He says there is insecurity in the nation and he will fight it. He has not said how but says he will in simple sentences. He says the roads are bad and he will fix them. He says the office of first lady will be abolished because it is costing too much to Nigerians. These are populist statements that resonate with Nigerians and that is why this guy is making inroads. No complexity in his statements, In fact, one could argue that he over-simplifies things but that is the language the generality of masses speak and understand.

With the way Jonathan and PDP are going, if he loses the election, and it seems he is poised to, it will not be because Buhari is a superior candidate; it will be because of poor messaging by Jonathan. It will also be because of an incumbency that has little to show for the six years he was in the saddle. After all, Buhari has no clue how to fix the economy. Buhari's utterances show that he does not seem to fully understand the mechanics of macro and micro economics. For example, Buhari was quoted as saying that he "will stabilize oil price". How would he stabilize oil prices that market forces are dictating? This is the type of issue that Jonathan and his handlers should be nailing Buhari on but they are not doing it. Instead they want to see Buhari's wife and his certificates. What a shame. They are poised to hand the presidency to Buhari on a platter.

If I were Jonathan, I will go back to the drawing board, re-craft my message so that while responding forcefully to APC and Buhari on all counts, he will tell Nigerians specifically why they should reelect him in spite of the poor state of the economy and why specifically Buhari is bad for Nigeria.

Merits and Demerits of Postponing the Scheduled 2015 Presidential Elections - Feb 9, 2015

As Nigeria's presidential elections approach, the nation is at crossroads. The ineptitude of the Independent National Electoral Commission has made it difficult for all registered voters to get their voter registration cards. This means that if the elections were actually held on the 14 of February, millions will be disenfranchised. If millions are disenfranchised, then the outcome of the election will not of course be the wish of the people. Attahiru Jega maintains that INEC is ready but how can he continue to say that when millions still do not have their PVC's? All said, rather than gamble with the right of Nigerians to vote, it was right to postpone the election to give INEC more time to fulfill their constitutional mandate of providing PVC's to all registered voters assuming they are capable.

Many abhor the idea of postponing the election and this writer certainly abhors it. Some posit that it is a gambit by the ruling party to catch up. It may well be true but if voting proceeds and we later find out that many were not able to vote, the losing party will have reason to reject the outcome of the election on the grounds that their supporters did not participate. This is what Nigeria, a very volatile nation in terms of sentiments, must always seek to avoid. From this perspective, Jega's call was in order. Postpone the election so that all Nigerians that want to vote but have not received their PVCs will do so.

More specifically, security was cited as the reason why the election is being postponed. Security agencies asked for postponement because they currently cannot guarantee the safety of INEC officials at the hot insurgency zones. They need time to clear out the area. Every Nigerian knows that the north east is the strong hold of APC. If the election goes forward and parts of the north east do not participate because of the threat of Boko Haram, and APC loses, the party will cite the inability of their supporters to cast their votes as a veritable reason to reject the election results. They may be pushing for the election to go ahead as scheduled now but if the party loses without the full participation of voters in the north east, the tune of the current music will definitely change. In this respect, Jega's postponement call is right.

However, weighty questions remain to be answered. The INEC boss has known for years that the election was scheduled to take place February 14. Why are we still talking about PVCs not reaching all registered voters at this time? The simple answer is ineptitude and mammoth planlessness. This is a good reason for this to be Jega's last dance as the INEC boss. This singular fact makes it impossible for him to say that he acquitted himself creditably on the job. Nigerians need a doer and he has shown that he is not one.

Furthermore, the security guys have known for years that the elections were coming. They have known about insurgency in the area. Why did they not make the effort to flush out Boko Haram before now so that the elections will go on? One is not sure what to attribute the inability of the security agencies to do their job but someone needs to answer to Nigerians why we have to wait until a week before general elections to begin an operation that should have taken place earlier.

Now, the biggest question is that there is no guarantee that on March 28, all Nigerians would have received their PVCs. There is also no guarantee that on March 28, all the areas in the north east that are currently under the threat of insurgents will be cleared. We know there are no guarantees because security agencies have been in ding dong affair with Boko Haram for a while there. If it were that easy to set a date and wipe Boko Haram out, they would have done it. If by the 28th we are still status quo antebellum, what will INEC do? Will they postpone the elections even further? Will this not become a slippery slope that knows no end? May 29 is sacrosanct as they say but if postponements do not change things and May 29 comes nigh, what happens?

Jega has to search his soul deeply to ascertain whether this extension will be an exercise in futility. Because Nigerians will really cry foul and rightly so if after six weeks we are still talking about people without voter cards. Also the president must search his soul. If after six weeks, Boko Haram is still marauding in vast areas of the north east, and hence make voting impossible, Nigerians will believe he fooled them and only wanted to extend the date of the election just to catch up on electioneering.

People's Democratic Party Should Merge with Smaller Parties and Go Into Robust But Constructive Opposition Now That Elections Are Over – April 4, 2015

APC party will now be in the saddle at the presidential and senatorial levels for the next four years. There are very high expectations of Buhari, especially from those that voted for him. Most of his supporters believe he will tame corruption, tackle and even defeat terrorism, unravel and solve the nation's economic and electricity woes and more. He has unveiled his covenant with Nigerians and it looks promising.

I was talking to a friend of mine in Nigeria. She is a staunch supporter of Jonathan. Just after Buhari was declared winner, I called her. "How about the PDP guys", I asked. "They are all in mourning", she said. "Many believe that PDP is now dead", she opined. I hasten to say that Nigerians believe in instant gratification. If they are not in the ruling party, if they are not provided with the platform to vie for and win elections immediately, if they are not in a position to get juicy contracts and oil blocks, then everything else is failing as far as they are concerned. For them, there is no such thing as taking time to build or rebuild a solid foundation over a period of time and reaping dividends later. PDP was alive, to them, when it was the ruling party, but as soon as it lost, they are declaring it dead forgetting that there are other patriotic things a party can be doing even if it is not in power.

As soon as the election results were called, I predicted on Facebook that Nigerians will soon witness an avalanche of defections from PDP to APC. I prognosticated that political harlots and perambulators in PDP will soon commence an exodus from the party. After repudiating APC during the elections, some will now start groveling for platforms to run for elective offices. Others will be seeking new oil blocks or opportunity to keep the ones they already have. Many will be looking for ministerial appointments and the like. Then there is Fani Kayode, the tactless PDP henchman who spewed hate and lies as far afoot as his duplicitous influence could reach. He will be one of the first to slowly start eating his erstwhile caustic words, preparatory to begging to be taken back by

APC. Recently, he said he was just doing his job and all he said during the campaign were not personal. For the avoidance of doubt, this writer likes robust and constructive political arguments but lies that overheat the polity and stoke ethnic sentiments should be anathema.

The unfortunate danger in political defections that we will soon witness from PDP to APC, is that it will force Nigeria back to square one. For sixteen years, the ruling party turned Nigeria into a one-party state. The party was too big, too well financed and too dug-in to lose presidential elections or be defeated. Hence, they became complacent. Knowing that the party would always win elections no matter how they governed, members paid little or no attention to the needs of the people. Under the party, Nigeria's economy tanked, insecurity grew, standard of education fell, the value of the naira continued on the downward trend. This dominance and attendant complacency would have continued had APC not merged with smaller parties, becoming a viable opposition that eventually dislodged PDP. Nigerians just needed to change the one-party system that is akin to the military administrations we had in the past.

Now that APC has won, the advice to PDPians is this: lick your wounds, dust up your behind and spend the next three months in retreat. Use that moment to take stock of what caused the defeat of the party. This frank analysis should include: what PDP did wrong, what Jonathan did wrong. Should Jonathan have unleashed his wife on Nigeria as he did or should she have taken up just a measured and dignified role? Mrs. Jonathan helped alienate President Jonathan from many Nigerians. The way she carried herself and spoke to Nigerians, shutting down traffic whenever she visited a place, attempting to deny Chibok tragedy, fighting a sitting governor as if she was an elected official, was strange and uncalled for. I must say that every time I listened to her speak, I was embarrassed that the office of the first lady had been debased. Sages like Wole Soyinka cautioned the president many times, to no avail, to ask her to pull back a little bit.

PDP must also look at issues like the unnecessary time they expended on inanities. For example, while the issue of Buhari's certificate may have made some dent on the man's popularity, it is now clear from the election results that it had little impact on actual voting especially in the north and hence was not worth the time and effort.

One of the issues that split Jonathan's camp and began to portray him as "King Nebuchadnezzar", is the fact that he unnecessarily denied Gov Amaechi the opportunity to head the governor's forum when the man clearly won. Once Amaechi became alienated from Jonathan, he played a major role in opposition that helped APC. Should Jonathan have gone down the part he did? The after action review will help PDP decide.

PDP should also review Jonathan's response to Boko Haram threat. Initially, he seemed to be doubting the authenticity of the abduction of Chibok girls. It was only a few weeks to election that he sat up and visited the war front. Should he have done differently? Yes and these are some of the things the PDP should review. One other issue that bears mentioning is that Jonathan surrounded himself with people who were not really passionate for his reelection. They paid lip service but did little because of what they gained from him but were not enthusiastic about his reelection. Some were ethnic jingoists that simply wanted their kinsman to win. It is even evident in the fact that Jonathan could not win Aso Rock polling precinct!

Also, the after action review should include looking closely at what APC did right and even what they did wrong. For example, there are videos circulating of underage kids thumb-printing ballot papers in the north in favor of APC. I cannot authenticate this but if it is true, PDP should strategize on how to ensure that it does not happen again. It may be to send election watchers to strategic places in the north during every election. Lastly, PDP should fully articulate how to tackle the myriad of problems that Nigeria is grappling with: economy, naira devaluation, insecurity, joblessness, power sector, health, agriculture and the likes.

The result of this analysis and after action review will help PDP restructure the party in readiness for the next round of elections and then go into robust but constructive opposition. I say constructive because if they go into opposition of unwarranted obstructionism, Nigerians will further repudiate the party.

Healthy opposition means watching closely what the ruling party is doing with respect to governing. When they get it wrong, PDP should criticize them and offer to Nigerians what they would have done if they were in the saddle. PDP should also consider coopting other small parties into their fold. The nation needs just two parties or three at best. That way, they can match the ruling party in size and money. To cap off the process, PDP should elect a good leader that will shepherd their journey for the next four years. A leader that is patriotic, pragmatic, magnanimous and who puts the nation first.

General Buhari Refuses to Participate in Presidential Debate– He Just May Not Be Ready To Lead Nigeria - January 18, 2015

In politics, debates do matter. President Jonathan and General Buhari both owe Nigerians at least two presidential debates before the February elections and Nigerians must demand it. Nigerians already know the capabilities of President Jonathan because he has been on the saddle for almost six years and, during this period, Nigerians have come to know how he thinks, how he acts and what he does in response to crisis. Nigerians also know the results of his policies based on where Nigeria is today socially and economically. Based on Jonathan's record, there are some, his supporters, who believe that he has done well and deserves to be reelected. There are others, his non-supporters, who believe that he has further damaged Nigeria after six years and does not deserve to be reelected. The latter group is supporting General Buhari but they do not have much to judge him by. Just 20 months in the saddle as a military head of state does not provide enough information for them to accurately judge the man or tell what he will do under certain circumstances. This group of Nigerians started supporting Buhari because they simply want change but they are itching to hear him in unscripted moments answer to various questions. They want to hear him assure them that they are not backing the wrong horse. They want to see him stand toe to toe with President Jonathan to prove that he is not a fluke. They simply want him to give them true reasons to continue to support him.

It was therefore a disappointment to many when they heard that Buhari would not participate in the presidential debates. Some say it is because the questions may have been leaked to Jonathan and his handlers. Before I proceed with this treatise, let me state in unequivocal and unflinching terms that if this is true, Nigerians must stand on roof tops and condemn it. Debates may seem inconsequential but transparent debates are one of the building blocks of a strong democracy. In strong democracies, debates have made and unmade candidates. Debates have changed the tide of elections. If the process is bastardized because people want to perpetually hang on to power, then our fledgling democracy will continue to be fledgling for many years to come. For the sake of our nascent democracy, a neutral body must be set up immediately to take up this and ensure that a transparent debate is conducted before February 14.

Having said the above, the fact remains that, as someone opined on Facebook, a candidate that knows his onions will face and answer any and every question that comes to him. If Buhari is conversant with Nigeria's socio-politico and economic issues and has viable solutions to the myriad of problems bedeviling the nation now, he should actually be itching to showcase them in any debate, whether questions are leaked or not. Totally refusing to debate, instead of calling for a neutral body to ensure that a debate is held, only means one thing and that is that he in either unsure of himself, does not fully understand Nigeria's challenges or does not have any real answers. He should remember that as an incumbent president whose records are there for all to see, while people will listen to Jonathan during the debate, they will judge him more by what he has done in office than by what he says. So seeing the debate questions ahead of time may not necessarily give him a great advantage. If Jonathan has the questions, he can give flowery answers during the debate but people will in their mind be judging him by the mantra: "are we better off for the past six years he has been in office". If Buhari has what it takes, it is during the debate that he should poke holes into any and all answers that Jonathan has no matter how flowery. For example, Nigeria has been bedeviled by corruption. If Jonathan says he has plans to fix it as he has said, Buhari can counter that he has had 6 years to fix it and did not. But Buhari cannot just say that Jonathan has failed, he should then tell Nigerians how he plans to fight corruption in a democracy where he cannot just impulsively jail everybody.

People look forward to political debates. They use it to gauge the ability of a candidate; they use debates to determine how quick a candidate can think on their feet. Debates reveal a candidate's understanding of the issues and hence ability to proffer viable solutions because one can only solve problems one fully understands. Debates are used to gauge the countenance of a candidate and hence how temperate the candidate is under pressure. For example, a candidate that is quick to anger will not give people a level of comfort that will enable them support the candidate.

I once wrote that Buhari has everything to lose by not debating and everything to gain by debating. As it stands, PDP has successfully hung certain issues like an albatross around his neck. Some of the issues are frivolous but others are weighty. Nonetheless, the issues have stuck in the national psyche. For example, they question the authenticity of Buhari's WASCE certificate insinuating that he only passed primary six and hence unfit to be the leader of a nation like Nigeria. They have planted doubts in the minds of Nigerians about his understanding of the huge economic issues facing the nation and his ability to proffer and implement viable solutions. They have even questioned his mental acuity, saying that he forgets things and a forgetful president would lead Nigeria into social and economic catastrophe because the "vultures" around him will be running the affairs of government. He has been cast as a religious zealot that would attempt to Islamize Nigeria. Some even opined that he has some hand in Boko Haram. On my own part, I have listened to him on many occasions and sometimes find it hard to fully understand what he says, may be because of his heavy accent. With all these issues hanging around his neck, a debate would have been the right time for him to rebut them one by one and with clarity. Some say he has been answering these charges during his campaign stops. That may be true but campaign talks are scripted and prove nothing. Nigerians want to see him perform in unscripted moments. They want to hear from him in an unscripted setting and see how he thinks, what his demeanor is when annoyed or irritated and whether he thinks quick on his feet. They want to see him respond to difficult economic questions and say what he would do.

Unfortunately, some of Buhari's supporters just want Nigerians to take him at his words that he will make a great president and not ask for a debate. They point to his military background and say that military men are born leaders. Some military men are born leaders but not all. General Buhari may be a soldier but being a soldier is not necessarily coterminous with the ability to think quick on his feet. It does not necessarily translate into knowledge about national affairs and how to deal with them. If he cannot debate simple Jonathan, how would he stand at the world economic forum in Davos Switzerland and articulate Nigeria's stance on economic issues? How can he stand in front of the world at the United Nations and represent Nigeria? If he is not confident enough to debate Jonathan and talk confidently about Nigeria's economic situation and how he would change it, how would he know when his economic team is leading him astray?

Buhari and his handlers may think the debate gate is a non-issue but they will later find out that by saying that Buhari will not participate, they have truly stirred the hornet's nest and people are now curious. People are now wondering if he is shying away because he knows he is not up to the challenge. They are wondering if he is afraid of forgetting his answers when he mounts the podium. They are now wondering if he is afraid of demonstrating his ignorance of national issues in front of millions of Nigerians. Heck, they are wondering if the allegation that he just passed primary six is true and he is trying to avoid showing it on national TV. People are simply beginning to feel that following a guy they do not know his record and who does not want them to know him may just be a bad idea. Unless he changes his mind, this writer has now started to wonder if Buhari has what it takes to lead a secular and democratic Nigeria. This writer is wondering if he is truly ready for prime time. He should start seriously pushing for a neutral body and demonstrate that he is not just trying to dodge the debate because "the dog ate his homework"

Viable and Formidable Opposition From APC Forcing Jonathan and PDP to Do a Rethink - January 5, 2015

President Jonathan will square off with General Buhari in a few weeks for the presidency of Nigeria. Unfortunately, Nigerians have been presented with a choice between the devil and the deep sea. The two men are deeply flawed and if the goal here is to select a messiah for an ailing nation, it's not happening!

After six years in office, the current president cannot be said to have done anything remarkable enough to warrant another term that will push his tenure into a total of 10 years. He basically turned his back on the war against corruption because every time one looks, his administration seems to be clearing and setting free people who had hitherto been indicted for corruption and even elevating them to greater positions of authority in the PDP. Infrastructure development has not fared much better: Projects like the second Niger Bridge continue to stall. The power sector that Jonathan himself once said he was obligated to fix is still groaning under the yoke of underperformance. Huge amounts of money that should go into improving Nigeria is being used by the presidency to acquire unneeded airplanes and engage in profligacy. A large chunk of the budget is being used for food and entertainment in Aso Rock and estacode for the retinue of staff that travel abroad with the president. Most of all, security situation continues to worsen and there seems to be no discernible way out of the mess. With all these deficiencies, reelecting Jonathan to office will make no sense.

On the other hand, General Buhari is not better. His biggest claim to fame is that he ruled Nigeria with iron hand, so much so that Nigerians were temporarily frightened into behaving the way they should as human beings. He does not have enough macro and micro economic experience that Nigerians need at this time of tumbling oil prices to sustain her economy and move her in the direction of diversification. Of course some see him as a religious fundamentalist that may make the security situation worse in the country if elected. So voting Buhari into office is not a great alternative either.

The reader can already tell that this commentator is not enamored by the prospects of either Buhari or Jonathan as Nigerian president. However, a prediction I made after APC merger is slowly beginning to take hold. In an article published on Nigeriaworld, November 30, 2013 entitled, "PDP-APC Merger Will Be Good for Democracy If It Endures", I posited that the merger will present a viable opposition to and force PDP to truly start competing for the people's votes and hence do what they hitherto promised to do if voted for. Before now, PDP has arrogantly been telling Nigerians that the party will remain in power for 50 years to come. They predicated their prognostication on the fact that the party was the only viable one with structures in all regions of the federation. It was a well-financed political machine that most prominent Nigerians pitched their tent with. Their sense of invincibility made members of the party to take Nigerians for granted knowing that their sheer size and reach will make it hard for Nigerians to get an alternative or for any other party to dislodge them in federal elections. The result was that no matter how bad a PDP presidential candidate was, no matter how much the candidate was despised, no matter how ineffective, just the mere fact of being in the PDP guaranteed that the person will get into or stay in power. General Obasanjo enjoyed two terms in spite of his tyrannical tendencies and the fact that he achieved very little. At the end of his tenure and again because there was no viable opposition, Obasanjo handpicked a sickly successor! Even though Nigerians knew that he was imposing a sick man on them, the overpowering influence of the party drowned out the voices of reason and hence a sick man was thrust upon the nation by an overbearing party and president. The rest is history but here we are again stuck with an ineffective president. But when PDP thought that they were about to coast home again in the presidential elections, a seeming monkey wrench was tossed into their plan by APC merger. There is now a viable opposition party ready to give PDP a run for its money. The days of presidential election walk-overs for PDP are over.

When APC merger was concluded, I noted that it was the greatest thing that would happen to Nigeria. I was not saying that as an endorsement of APC because they may even be worse than PDP, but from the perspective that for once, the votes of Nigerians would be competed for. The parties would be forced to actually campaign and tell the people what they would do. There would be no anointments because the masses would make the final choice.

This writer recalls that PDP seemed unperturbed when the merger initially took place but the merger has produced a party strong enough and well-financed to challenge PDP. Analysts predict that APC would pull a lot of votes from the north, get a lot of votes from the south west because of Tinubu and Fashola and make sizable inroads into the South east and even the south south. This scenario has stoked a lot of panic in the PDP. The places and people that PDP once took for granted, the zones they once failed to campaign in because they felt they were theirs are now very competitive. This is politics at its finest! When you have such situations in any democracy, politicians suddenly remember that the final arbiters are the voters and they start taking them serious, start going to them to canvass for votes and start doing what they originally said they would do if elected. Now, it may be that in the final analysis, PDP will eke out a win but even if they do, PDP will never be the same in governance. They will now be forced to work to establish a trail of achievements. They will want to truly build roads, seriously tackle youth unemployment, diversify the economy, bring insecurity to tolerable levels and improve education so that they would have worthy legacies to brandish before Nigerians when they go before them next time for votes. That is good for Nigeria.

Jonathan seems to have now gotten the message that he will no longer be handed the presidency on a platter of gold as before. He now responds to criticisms he would have dismissed before as idle talk. He tells Nigerians who feel he is not doing much to secure the country that his administration is doing some behind the scenes stuff. To those who accused his administration of corruption, he recently responded that he is "coming up with anti-corruption plan". This statement is problematic in itself. If after 6 years as president he is still does not have an anti-corruption plan, it is a clear indication that his government is rudderless on that issue. Nonetheless, he is being forced to tell Nigerians why he should be reelected, something that would not have happened if we did not have a viable opposition as before.

On the part of APC, they are being forced to do things they may not have done before. In the past, Buhari never worried about the perception of him as a religious fundamentalist. As such he rarely addressed that issue. But he has been forced to answer that and even begin to soften his image by the way he dresses. He now tries to defend his record when he was in power for two years and when he headed the PTF. He has been forced to start telling Nigerians how he would govern apart from just saying he would fight corruption.

Bottom line is that no matter what political spectrum Nigerians are in, no matter what political camp they pitch their tents, they should be delighted that a new era is emerging in Nigerian politics: An era of competitive presidential politics where one party can no longer take them for granted. This guarantees that the presidential candidates will listen more to the people and try to do more of the bidding of the people if elected. Having viable opposition is the first step towards getting where Nigeria needs to be.

Economic Downturn Pulling the Rug From Under Nigerians and Businesses

Just a few short months ago, Nigeria's currency exchanged at one dollar to 160 naira but as at the time of writing this article, the dollar is worth 208 naira. Nigerians should really be worried!

Here is an example of how the unbridled economic downturn is affecting people in Nigeria: Mr. Okonkwo (not his real name), is an assiduously working teacher in Nigeria. He has been a teacher for many years. One of his goals is to build a small bungalow where he will retire with his wife in the village. To meet this goal, he and his wife have continually denied themselves of a lot of conveniences, opting to save every penny that came their way. About 8 months ago, they reached their savings goal. Their bank account finally showed a total sum of 5 million naira. He and his wife were happy. Life seemed to be getting better.

Just as the Okonkwos started celebrating this milestone, the naira began its downward slide vis a vis the dollar. First of all, oil prices crashed and then the naira was devalued. The naira that was trading at about 160 naira to one dollar, when they celebrated their 5 million naira milestone, began an unbridled slide until it got to 208 naira to one dollar! This means that Mr. Okonkwo's savings which was worth about 31,000 dollars just a few months ago is now worth only 24,000 dollars. This represents a 23% loss of value in less than a year! Even though the Okonkwo's still have N5 million naira physically sitting in their bank account, the true value of that money is now only N3.85 million. To be able to build the bungalow of their dream, they now have to save some more because inflation engendered by devaluation of the naira has raised the cost of the building materials they need as well as the cost of labor in an unprecedented way.

This is not just a problem for people in the lower rung of the economic ladder in Nigeria. This problem is also effecting the rich and famous. Yesterday, I read a piece about Aliko Dangote's seeming misfortune. "The slump in oil prices, the consequent devaluation of the naira and the downturn in the capital market have seen Africa's richest man, Alhaji

Aliko Dangote, lose half of his fortune, according to the latest ranking by Bloomberg Billionaires."[Punch, Feb 13, 2015]. The Punch further stated, "… the billionaire, who was estimated by Forbes Magazine to be worth $25bn in February last year, has now lost $12.2bn to the economic headwinds". If Africa's richest man has lost half of his fortune as a result of this sordid national tragedy, how about the middle class businesses that actually sustain Nigeria's economy. Their plight may not have been printed on the pages of the newspapers or talked about on TV but that does not obviate the dire nature of the situation they face.

If this situation is not arrested with some sound economic policies and programs soon, Nigeria's economy will be in a very precarious situation. In fact, it already is. Many small scale businesses that import goods into the country, using dollars purchased from the Foreign Exchange market, are in danger of collapsing. With the precipitous change in value of the naira, the capacity of some of these business concerns have changed immensely. A company that was hitherto capitalized with 50 million naira for business, just a few months ago, now only has an equivalent value of N38.5 million to work with. Some of the companies will be forced to reduce staff, import less stuff, or try to sell their goods to Nigerians at cut throat prices to make up. Some are already complaining that they can no longer afford to repay the Nigerian banks they borrowed money from because they borrowed at a time the naira was stronger and now have to repay at a time the naira has weakened by 23%. When one adds the bank interest rate to the mix, it becomes a terrible situation to contend with.

There is another ramification: for many years, Nigeria's economy has been partly sustained by the funds that Diaspora Nigerians repatriate to and save in Nigerian banks for building houses, purchasing goods and sustaining their relatives. A diaspora Nigerian that saved N10 million naira in the bank now complains that his money has depreciated to just N7.7 million. So now he wonders why any sane Nigerian living in the Diaspora would want to save their hard earned money in naira, in a Nigerian bank, knowing that inflation and devaluation would wipe off their savings. That sentiment is gaining ground. Many Diaspora Nigerians now say they are no longer interested in saving their money in Nigerian currency, in Nigerian banks, but would rather keep them where they reside to forestall devaluation. Even individuals in Nigeria, like Dangote, may soon decide to keep their money in overseas banks for fear of devaluation. This will trigger capital flight that will further complicate an already terrible situation.

The problem is that there are no easy solutions. The oil cash cow that Nigeria depended on for so long is sliding in price and is no longer able to provide the cushion in external reserves that was used to shore up situations like this. Furthermore, United States has stopped buying Nigeria's oil and that is another blow. The next couple of years, as Minister Okonjo Iweala stated, will be very difficult economically for Nigeria. Whoever Nigerians decide to install as the helmsman, come March 28, must be able to set a new course for the nation financially. It must be a course that will steer Nigeria away from over dependence on oil. It must encourage strong internal generation of export goods to earn more foreign exchange. It must stress self-sufficiency. May God Help Us.

RE-Nigeria's Economy Tanking As US Oil Exports Dry Up – December 1, 2014

The above is the caption of an article that appeared on NBC website today, November 27, 2014. Penned by one Robert Windrem, the article alerted the world to the fact that seven years ago, the United States was importing 40 million barrels of oil from Nigeria but by April of this year, that number had gone down to 4.5 million barrels. By July, "not a single drop of Nigerian light, sweet crude arrived in the U.S. - all of it replaced at Gulf Coast refineries by fracked oil from fields like the Bakken formation in North Dakota and Eagle Ford in Texas[NBC News website, November 29, 2014]

To worsen an already bad situation, global oil glut caused the price of oil to tumble to its lowest level in many years. This means that the projected price of oil, upon which Nigeria's 2015 budget was predicated, is now invalid- a scary situation! Currently, Nigeria is scrambling to find an answer to this disconcerting but predictable development.

The minister of Finance, Dr. Okonjo Iweala tells Nigerians not to panic. She recently spoke to reporters in Abuja "assuring" them that the Federal Government was putting in place a series of austerity measures to help cushion the effect of oil revenue shortfall. She stated that the measures include, "introducing surcharges on certain luxury goods, not only to raise additional revenue but to ensure that the richer members of the society contribute a little bit more to easing the pain resulting from the existing economic challenges. Clearly, Nigeria cannot depend on an unpredictable and unsteady income stream to help balance her budget. Corruption and bribery in the country make it possible that the so called luxury items could be imported and yet the government will not be able to track all of them to collect the tax. This is a place where for the right amount of bribery money, anything could be forged. I am essentially saying that Nigerians should not place their hope on luxury good tax to help in balancing the budget.

Aware that Nigerians would be wondering how the so-called austerity measures would affect the common man, Dr Okonjo-Iweala stated during her speech that even as the government cuts down certain aspects of the 2015 budget, some infrastructure projects that the common man would benefit from like, "the Lagos Ibadan expressway, the second Niger Bridge, rail and power projects, etc which will create jobs and enhance the comfort of our people will go on."[The Guardian, Nov 27, 2014] This seems like a promise that will be broken soon. I fully understand the predicament of the coordinating minister. As the helmsperson on financial affairs, she cannot be seen to be instigating panic amongst the populace by stating how dire things are. However, the truth is that the minister cannot guarantee the promise she is making. If the United States does not resume the importation of Nigeria's oil as before, if oil prices continue to plummet because of global glut, if China and India do not step in to fill the oil import shoes vacated by America and if the world continues its seeming affinity for electric and hybrid cars as the technology gets better, all bets are off. Nigeria may never recover enough to sustain these multi-billion naira projects considering that we currently depend on oil revenue for almost 80% of our expenditure. Dr. Okonjo-Iweala says she has a new strategy, "to raise an additional N480 billion ($3 billion) over the 2014 base in the next three years and has launched a 10-year capital market master plan (2015-2025) to elevate the course and position it(Nigeria) for alternative wealth creation" Is this a case of too little too late? Only time will tell.

Already, the naira has been devalued by 8% because Nigeria no longer has enough money in reserves to continue to cushion the effects of oil revenue shortfall. With naira devalued, private importers will pay more to bring in goods and will sell them at exorbitant prices. Furthermore, the Central bank raised interest rates sharply. Of course this will affect the borrowing capacity of small-scale business concerns. All in all, there is no good news in all this.

Unfortunately, some of what Dr. Okonjo-Iweala is trying to do now should have been done many years ago but our leaders failed us. They instead spent their time in doling out oil blocks to their friends and families, making people like General Danjuma so rich that he, "did not know what to do with the $500 million he got from oil!" As oil flowed and the nation became awash with dollars, instead of investing in full diversification of the economy, encouraging industries that source materials locally and hence lessen dependence on importation while providing employment, our leaders continued to spend our funds like drunken sailors. In 2008, the nations' external reserves stood at about $63 billion! Today, it is down to half that amount. The chicken has now come to roost and the nation's Finance Minister is trying to do in one month what should have been done over the years by the administrations past. She says that the "common man" will be cushioned against the effects of the austerity measures she will put in place. The real truth is that the ordinary Nigerian will be hit the hardest in many ways. First, whether they say it or not, very soon, probably after elections, oil subsidy will be removed in its entirety because there is a good case for it now. Once that happens, the average Nigerian will be hit because transportation cost will go up and even the market person will increase their prices correspondingly.

In spite of all these, I applaud the efforts that the minister of finance is making because as she said, Nigeria cannot just throw up her hands and buckle because inaction would be more catastrophic. However, it is important that the plight of Nigerians in the lower rung of the economic ladder is always considered as we emplace austerity measures. So, in addition to some of the things that Dr. Okonjo-Iweala is putting in place, there are some other short -term measures that could collectively help somewhat. As I write, Nigeria has a presidential air fleet of 10 costly airplanes. The "combined estimated value of the PAF is $390.5m (N60.53bn)[Punch, October 23, 2013] When you add the cost of yearly maintenance and payment of pilots, this cost becomes a chart-buster. Wikipedia says that, "Nigeria happens to be one of few countries of the world with a large PAF". Why does Nigeria need 10 airplanes for one president?! The austerity that Dr. Okonjo-Iweala mentioned should start with the presidential air fleet. Reduce it to two and sell off others. Plow back the huge savings into our nation's austerity coffers.

Another area is motor convoys of elected officials. When one person is travelling, the convoy is almost a mile long with new vehicles all lined up. The reader should note that these are not just ordinary N10 million vehicles. They are hundreds of millions of naira bullet proof vehicles. Are all these vehicles necessary? Cut down the number of vehicles and sell off the rest. This will net for Nigeria several millions of naira that can be put in the austerity fund purse. Little drops of water make a mighty Ocean.

When our president and legislators travel, they go with a retinue of staff both needed and unneeded. Each and every one of these sight-seeing/delegates collect estacode in dollars for going to sight-see. Billions of naira can be saved by drastically trimming down the number of people that follow these elected officials out of the country. We can also reduce the number of cabinet positions because some of these folks really do not have much to do. The PDP former chairman was given a political patronage for agreeing to step down by being made a minister at large! He was collecting money for being at large. Go figure.

Currently, Nigeria ranks in the top of nations that pay the most to their legislators and elected officials. A Nigerian legislator receives an annual salary of about $189,000. Compare that with what legislators earn in more prosperous nations like Britain - $105,400 yearly, United States -$174,000, France - $85,900, South Africa -$104,000, Kenya -$74,500, Saudi Arabia -$64,000 and Brazil -$157,600. [The Economist] Nigerian legislators even get additional monies for "constituent projects" and the like even though they spend it on themselves. Dr. Okonjo Iweala's austerity measures need to affect Nigerian legislators too. As far as this writer is concerned, they are worth only half what they are currently paid so their salaries should be revised downwards and the savings plowed into the austerity fund.

There are many other little things that Dr. Okonjo-Iweala should do in addition to other macro and micro economic policies that this writer is not schooled in. It is a pity that Nigeria had to wait to get to the precipice before reacting. There will obviously be a lot of hardship in the horizon for the common Nigerian but it is possible that we will get things right this time.

Independent Corrupt Practices Commission Tells Nigerians That Former President Cannot Be Probed
– Is This Presidential Cover-up?- August 11, 2002

The chairman of the Independent Corrupt Practices Commission(ICPC), Justice Mustapha Adebayo Akanbi, shocked Nigerians a few days ago when he announced that his commission could not probe Nigeria's former president, General Ibrahim Babangida [Guardian, August 9, 2002]. He made the statement during a keynote address at a seminar organized by the commission for anti-corruption prosecutors from Ghana and Mali. According to him, his commission could not probe Babangida because the anti-graft law which came into effect in June of 2000 "had no retroactive or retrospective provisions". In essence, the Justice was telling Nigerians that if they were still expecting this government to ask the General to explain the source of his enormous wealth, that they were wasting their time.

This type of scenario also played out during the Oputa Commission hearings. Justice Oputa whet the appetite of Nigerians when he summoned the past heads of State to give account of human rights abuses perpetrated during their regimes. Nigerians were jubilant and expectant. They thought that a courageous judge had finally emerged to force the powers that be to come before the nation and give accounts of their misdeeds. The heads of state refused to show up as requested by Justice Oputa. The Justice threatened them with jail terms if they failed to obey his orders but they still did not show up. Instead of carrying through with his threats, thereby sending an unmistakable message that would have resonated around the world, he sent "special invitations" to them, begging them to come and tell Nigerians how the country could move forward! They still snubbed him anyway and so in one swoop, the Justice made a mockery of a process that would have brought forth a lot of good for Nigeria. Justice Mustapha has now gone the same way. Yet, the Corrupt Practices Commission was established by somebody and the mandate was established by somebody. If we seriously and honestly desire to look into IBB's financial deals, the commission's mandate could be expanded and extended. This whole process has left Nigerians wondering if IBB is just being given a pass by his army friend.

It must be remembered however, that right after Obasanjo's inauguration, he went on a crusade, emphasizing zero tolerance for corruption. He told a hopeful nation that there would be no sacred cows in his bid to rid Nigeria of those who may have contributed in one way or the other, to the economic woes that the nation is presently in. Nigerians welcomed this stance and wished him well. Before long, he descended on the Abacha family with the full might of the federal government. We felt that a messiah may have come after all and we were all expecting that gradually, the probes would expand to include every past leader.

Nigerians have to remember how this issue of probing previous administrations came about. After the establishment of the ICPC and subsequent commencement of the probing of General Abacha, as time passed, it became clear to Nigerians that President Babangida was not even being mentioned as a possible candidate for probe. As a result, citizens started speaking up and started calling for the inclusion of Babangida. At first, Obasanjo ignored all these calls until pressure increased to an unprecedented level from the populace in newspapers, on the internet. In response to the calls, Obasanjo told a disappointed nation that he would probe IBB "only if someone brought forth evidence" Many cried foul! The president's attention was directed to the fact that it was not the citizens that provided him with the evidence for the Abacha probe, so why would he want the citizens to bring evidence in the case of another former head of state? Obasanjo turned his back on all these and did nothing. Now, the ICPC decided to tell Nigerians that the mandate of the anti-graft panel is not retroactive. All Nigerians of goodwill must reject this shenanigan in its entirety.

The million-dollar question now is, why is the commission's mandate not retroactive? One would think that the goal of the anti-graft panel would be to investigate and find out what put Nigeria into this financial mess and then find a way to avoid a repeat. If the country fails to find out how she got into this financial mess and what part our public officials played, how would we establish a credible way to rectify the situation?

Even Abacha's probe has been bungled. Nigerians were told that the government entered into a deal with the Abacha family to return some of the money they were accused of stealing in exchange for dropping further prosecution. Obasanjo noted that by doing so, he was saving the country from expending a lot of legal fees. That is preposterous! Any public official suspected to have engaged in corruption, must be prosecuted to the fullest extent of the law to serve as a deterrent to potential others. The deal that Obasanjo made with the Abacha family has created a terrible precedent: corrupt public officials would even become more brazen because they would hope to cut deals with the government if caught.

As it stands now, Nigeria is being blacklisted financially overseas for various financial offenses ranging from corruption in the country to scam activities. One would think that our president would be in the forefront aggressively condemning, controlling and checking these crimes. He talks the talk all right but has woefully failed to walk the walk. So, how would Obasanjo be able to deal with 419ers who are destroying the country's image abroad when he has not dealt with those who committed even more heinous financial offenses?

When my commentary titled, Mr. President, Please Save Diaspora Nigerians from The Scourge Of Nigerian Scam (419) Artists! was published, I got a dizzying number of emails from Nigerians from all over the globe. In the emails, Nigerians overwhelmingly stated that 419 was a scourge that needed to be expunged to save our image. Many recounted the terrible embarrassments they had suffered as a result of the 419 activities in their various places of abode in the Diaspora. But some stated that there are 419ers in high places in Nigeria. They pointed to the fact that those who looted our treasury have practically gone scot-free and had become chiefs and kingmakers, living ostentatious lives. This ostentatious living, they argue, has enticed the younger generation into going the way of 419 scams to see if they could live like their role models. 419ers they say, are simply emulating corrupt public officials even though they are targeting their crimes on the international community. They believe that if Obasanjo cannot bring corrupt public officials to book, then he has no moral right to even attempt to speak against 419ers and their horrendous crimes. The readers feel that only when we have cleaned house in high places would we be able to start convincing the criminals writing 419 letters to cut out the stupidity.

Sometimes I find myself wondering why it is that even though Obasanjo made morality the mantra of his administration, he has failed to demonstrate this practically? For a president who had to commune with God before he decided to run again; for a president who invokes the name of God in everything he does, why does he find it difficult to really call a spade a spade? Does the president not understand that by looking the other way and not investigating all corrupt public officials, he is not living up to the promises he made to Nigerians? Does our president not know that by inviting IBB to chair his re-election announcement gathering, even when Nigerians are still asking questions about IBB's riches, he may have lost his moral locus standi to question anyone else in Nigeria?

I read with interest the article written by Laolu Akande and published on Nigeriaworld.com on July 10, 2002. The article was titled, "How Obasanjo blocked the recovery of IBB's $25bn loot". Just take the paragraph below excerpted from the article for instance which says: "specifically and most significantly, investigations have now revealed that the Obasanjo administration refused offers by the experts, including those from UN sources, to trace monies looted from Nigeria during the Babangida regime, but encouraged the pursuit of Abacha stolen funds" If all this is true, then it infers that Obasanjo may not have been telling the truth when he said that he has no evidence to probe IBB. Another paragraph of great interest in the article goes thus, "According to the expert, Nigeria's wealth is just sitting down there primarily in UK and all efforts are not being tapped to fully recover them. There are ways and options that are not being pursued. Even the UN has offered to help. But Nigeria's president's message to the international community was that you can go after Abacha, but not IBB's money."

I will end this piece with a quote from Obasanjo's message to the Commonwealth Parliament Association at Wilton Park, West Sussex, England on June 12, 2002. He said, "having realized that no meaningful progress could be achieved without curbing the scourge of corruption, my administration has initiated measures to stem its tide and punish perpetrators."

Well readers, judge for yourselves, is he living up to this quote?

Six Months Before Elections, Nigerian Senators Pardon Their Indicted Colleagues- Who Will Save Nigeria?- September 15, 2002

Not too long ago, while browsing through the information superhighway, I dabbled into a report which shocked me to the core! The Nigerian Senate had nullified the reports produced by Idris Kuta panel and Victor Oyofo Harmonization committee [Guardian Online, Sept 12, 2002] The implication of this singular act is not immediately apparent until one recalls that the Kuta panel investigated cases of alleged mismanagement of funds and impropriety by members of the Senate. After its investigations, the Kuta panel indicted some members and prescribed punishments which ranged from ordinary sanctions to actual removal from major responsibilities in the Senate. Protests by some of the indicted members led to the establishment of another panel, headed by Senator Victor Oyofo, to review the Kuta report. After deliberations, the Oyofo panel not only upheld the verdict rendered by the Kuta panel, but even recommended that harsher penalties be imposed on some of the already indicted members. These two reports formed the basis for the removal of Dr. Chuba Okadigbo as Senate president and sanctioning of other members like Senators Florence Ita Giwa and Gbenga Aluko.

After the errant Senators were sanctioned by their colleagues, the nation rallied around the senate body for having the uncommon courage to check themselves in a world where cronyism has replaced probity. It was felt, therefore, that they were worthy of the esteemed responsibilities entrusted on them by the nation. However, the indicted senators were concerned about how the indictments would affect their election bids as elections are around the corner. They, particularly senator Aluko, sought to be cleared of the indictment so that they would not constitute obstacles to their reelection hopes.

On September 11, 2002, during a plenary session, senate members reversed their stand on the issue of Kuta and Oyofo reports. It all started when one of the indicted Senators, Gbenga Aluko, representing Ekiti South, moved a motion to nullify the two reports, set aside any charges preferred against the errant Senators and absolve them of all wrong doing. Here is how Aluko put it: "Distinguished Senators, we are about six months to go. There is need for us to leave the senate at least the way we came, preferably better.... it would be unfair to condemn certain senators to perpetual indictment as no set of senators after us would be in any better position to revisit the matter" Senator, Arthur Nzeribe, seconded the motion and the senate body granted it. In moving the motion, Gbenga Aluko, said, "In the spirit of reconciliation that currently exists in the senate, the senate should absolve all senators indicted in both reports."

What came to mind when I first read about the motion to nullify the reports was that a counter investigation might have unearthed evidence showing that the indicted senators were innocent of the charges leveled against them. I therefore wondered what would now happen to someone like Chuba Okadigbo who lost the senate presidency as a result of the panel reports. But newspaper accounts showed that the reports were quashed, not because the senators were found innocent of the charges against them, but "in the spirit of reconciliation" as Gbenga Aluko put it, This created the impression that in Nigeria, as long as you are well-placed or wealthy, no matter how egregious an offense you commit, it would be forgiven or expunged. Senator Aluko was worried about the upcoming elections and how his constituents would perceive him since he was also indicted in the report. He wanted to be given a clean bill of health so that when he goes back again to ask his constituents for another mandate, the indictment would not be an obstacle. The same goes for the rest of the senators. By absolving themselves of transgressions for which they were duly indicted and punished, the senate body is demonstrating that it could not be trusted to represent Nigerians. They have set a precedent for incoming senators that no matter how much they misbehave, at the end of their tenures, their dirty slates would be wiped clean to pave the way for re-election. The senators have sacrificed the interest of the nation on the altar of cronyism and that is an outrage. The nullification of the reports forced me to conclude that until this generation of power-drunk and self-serving Nigerian politicians move on and out of the way, Nigeria may not witness any tangible progress.

The big question now is: what are the repercussions for financial mismanagement or outright corruption in the Senate? The answer is a resounding, NONE. The second question is what constitutes a deterrent to other Senators who may be tempted to go the way of Dr. Okadigbo, Gbenga Aluko and Florence Ita Giwa? The answer is NOTHING. There is no deterrent and so the usual Nigerian revolving door of corruption continues.

The Guardian further reported that after the motion to nullify the Kuta report was tabled and upheld, the Senators were all jubilant and went around embracing themselves. Obviously, they feel that what they did was camaraderie but in my humble opinion, it was shameful then and it is shameful now. At best, it is political quid pro quo.

What ails Nigeria today is that leaders do not lead by example. They tell citizens to refrain from corruption but when citizens are not looking, they engage in corruption. They say they would fight corruption but they are corrupt themselves so cannot see clearly to fight it. They ask citizens to refrain from violence but when citizens are not looking, some of them engage hooligans to perpetrate political violence so that they would continue to remain in power. They tell you to reject ethnicity but by their words they incite ethnic tensions. In this case, some of the Senators violated public trust. They were duly sanctioned for it but when the public was not looking, they voted to expunge their dirty records.

The President is not doing his job and we have an inept, if not corrupt, house of legislature. We have a Senate filled with over ambitious politicians so they pay more attention to power succession rather than cleaning up Nigeria and moving her forward. So who would actually be the custodial of our nascent democracy and its ethos? Who would save Nigeria from vices that have become so ingrained in our social fabric that our fledgling democracy is being seriously threatened? If we are relying on this entire group masquerading as lawmakers, senators and president to uphold democracy through their actions, words and deeds, I deign to say that we are doomed to fail. Nigerians must use this upcoming round of elections to look deeper and reject inept and corrupt politicians. The question is: do we have the will to reject electioneering bribes from moneybags when they start doling them out?

And So Gobir Died: A Victim of Election Violence in Kwara State - July 24, 2002

"I cannot replace my son. The grief they caused me, I will carry for the rest of my life. His father died in 1993, and he had been taking care of me since then. Now they have killed him, Who did this to me?"

That was the supplication of a grieving mother in Kwara State, Nigeria. Her 29 year old son, Gobir, a fashion designer and a supporter of "one of the front-line political heavyweights in Kwara state"[Guardian, July 12, 2002], was killed.

Trouble started earlier that day on June 29. It was the day for the creation of new councils in Kwara State and predictably, the political atmosphere was supercharged. Gobir was at a wedding party that night when 12 members of the Gbosa gang arrived at the hotel where the party was being held. They were armed with guns and machetes. They alighted from two unmarked buses and one of them lured Gobir outside where they read him his supposed offenses. The sum total of his offense was "his support for a political chieftain." He was then shot at point blank range! And so Gobir died, a victim of Nigeria's rising politically-motivated violence.

Cases of political violence are now springing up in many nooks and crannies of all 6 geopolitical zones of Nigeria. This is all happening as Nigeria prepares for local government and general elections. About three weeks ago, after the Delta state PDP party secretariat made public the results of the 16 out of 23 council primaries they allegedly conducted, armed thugs drove around the town precluding residents from going about their businesses. Those who ventured out had their vehicles snatched from them while the thugs released gun shots into the air.(Guardian July 03) In Rivers state, "violence occasioned by bitter jostling for party tickets disrupted local council primaries in Okrika" [Guardian, July 02]. During the violence, 5 people were abducted and scores maimed. At Azuzu, ward four, Mbaise road, Owerri, election was suddenly halted by people, mostly youths, suspected to be thugs hired by some defeated aspirants. The list goes on and on and the most troubling part is that because it has not become politically expedient, the current administration has not pragmatically addressed this issue which by right should be high on the priority list.

Tired of and frightened by increasing cases of political violence, in a Guardian opinion poll in 24 states, Nigerians overwhelmingly called for tough punitive measures against people who embark on political thuggery. They know that if left unchecked, this problem will derail a peaceful transition from one civilian administration to another, a perpetual monkey that Nigeria has not been able to get off her back.

The hallmark of a civilized society is the freedom to support any political entity and candidate(s) one chooses. In an atmosphere replete with fear where individuals are intimidated, harassed, maimed and even killed for holding political beliefs or for supporting candidates of their choice, democracy is bound to fail. The result of this uncivilized behavior is that law-abiding citizens would not go out and vote for fear of getting caught in politically-motivated violence. Recently, thugs precluded law-abiding citizens from going about their businesses in Asaba during the council primaries. On that day, in broad daylight, thugs alighted from their vehicles and started shooting sporadically into the air. Frightened citizens ran for their lives and were hence deprived of the ability to exercise their civic rights or to peacefully go about their daily businesses.

The issue of thugs bearing arms openly and using it to intimidate people begs the question: since when did Nigeria permit her citizens to bear arms openly? It should be of serious concern to the police and the Obasanjo administration that this is happening. Should the police not be scurrying around, impounding these weapons and charging culprits with appropriate offenses? How do we know that these thugs are not conducting dress rehearsals in readiness for 2003 elections?

On July 17, in London, General Obasanjo told the world at a Business Summit on Nigeria that his administration "will use everything within its executive power to ensure that the outcome of the elections will not only meet international standards, but also satisfy Nigerians for stable, good and purposeful government."[Vanguard, July 18] What Obasanjo said sounds good on paper but with the killing of people like Gobir and the menace of thugs during local council elections, one can tell that political violence has already started engulfing the nation and may worsen before the 2003 general elections.

In an apparent response to the rise in politically motivated violence in Nigeria, on June 24, the police high command announced that it had set up an "elite unit of well-armed and better motivated men of the Police Mobile Force" to combat political thuggery[Guardian, June 2002] Police spokesman, Mr. Haz Iwendi explained that it was part of the eight-point program embarked upon by Inspector General of police, Mr. Tafa Balogun. It sounds great on the surface until one remembers that it was the same eight-point program that gave birth to operation "Fire for Fire", which many, including this writer, hailed at its inception because of some immediate results realized. Since then, operation Fire for Fire seems to have fallen by the way side. With this type of record for operation Fire for Fire, why would anyone believe that the so-called elite police group would do any better at checkmating political thuggery?

It is not to say that political violence has not always been present in Nigeria. It has actually remained the most potent force in derailing peaceful democratic transition since Independence. It has also been the reason which the military cite for intervening into Nigerian politics instead of staying in the barracks and performing their supposed task of defense of the nation. Be that as it may, political violence has become more deadly than it has ever been. Where thugs used batons and machetes to harass people in the past, now they wield Uzi guns and AK 47s. Where they simply slapped opponents around in the past, now they shoot at point-blank range gangster style. Where their activities used to be somewhat uncoordinated in the past, these days, they have emails and cell phones to coordinate their activities and carry them out with military precision and dispatch. Where the members of the gangs were matured men in the past, now we are dealing with angry youths who carry out orders without minding whose ox is gored. This has therefore made this problem a national emergency and must be approached as such. Simply raising elite policemen who are also susceptible to corruption is just tackling the symptom of the ailment rather than the root cause.

So how do we curb political violence in Nigeria to ensure a free and fair election and peaceful transition from administration to administration? Let us first take a critical look at those who foment the violence. Some statistics, no matter how suspect, suggest that they are youths of ages 16 to about 25, often without any visible means of income and sometimes work in gangs. It is this age range that shot Gobir. This is the same age group of kids who commit cult-related crimes in our schools of higher learning; it is the same breed of kids that kill and dispossess people of their belongings. There is therefore a common thread that binds perpetrators of political violence, armed robbery and cultism together. It is their age. These young men seem to have lost hope in Nigeria and are now drifting towards any direction that would give them a sense of belonging and purpose, no matter how deadly. I agree completely with a writer who stated: "feelings of hopelessness, despair and anger turn into rage and lead the youth of Nigeria into doing bad things"

The feeling that the nation holds no hope for the youth is overwhelming them and most who would, under normal conditions, make something out of their lives, are now engaged in lives of crime. If a youth is unemployed and has no immediate hope of finding gainful employment, if a powerful politician approaches the youth with promise of money and other accouterments, the youth is most likely to do the politician's bidding and become a thug. If an undergraduate youth is sent on forced vacation as a result of teachers' strike, he finds himself in idle isolation and as they say, an idle mind is the devil's workshop. Hence, if armed robbers approach the kid to join them, there is some chance that he would at least contemplate it. The same goes for cultism. Let us reason together a little further: what is the probability that a young man with gainful employment would become an armed robber, a political thug, a cultist or an area boy? How much chance is there that a young man in the University who looks forward to a fruitful life after graduation, would join a cult and throw it all away? What is the chance that a gainfully employed youth or one who has hope of finding employment, would become a henchman or thug for a politician? The chance is very slim.

As an undergraduate at the University of Nigeria in the late 70s and early eighties, we had fraternities, but because we had hope of settling into productive and fruitful lives, the fraternities were just social gatherings for planning parties and being merry. I never witnessed violence or heard about one throughout my academic sojourn in that school.

Obasanjo must start sorting out the current economic mess Nigeria is in and encourage enterprise that would provide jobs for our youth and give them lasting hope. That way, they will begin to look away from crime, from political thuggery, from cultism and armed robbery and set their sights on bigger and better things. That is when incidents like the unfortunate murder of Gobir would cease to take place or at least minimized.

I Wish That Nigerians Listened To Gani Fawehinmi While He Was Living– September 13, 2009

When the news of the lung cancer diagnosis of Nigeria's foremost civil rights activist broke about a year ago, it was clear that the situation was grim. Lung cancer, which was the same disease that ended the life of the famed news anchor in the United States- Peter Jennings, was deadly. Gani's situation was even exacerbated by the fact that it was not caught early. I recall that the late Chief Fawehinmi lamented the fact that he had been having certain symptoms but every time he went to the hospital in Nigeria, they either told him it was pneumonia or just cold. It took going to London for Gani's condition to finally be diagnosed. It was then too late.

In spite of the grim diagnosis at the time, this writer, like many other Nigerians, had hoped that by some miracle, the life of the man some call Nigeria's conscience, a man who had given so much to the nation un-coerced and selflessly, would be spared. It was the hope of many that he would live longer to complete the crusade he had started or at least motivate enough Nigerians to step into his large shoes and continue where he stopped. It was therefore a shock when news came that Gani Fawehinmi had succumbed to the aggressive ailment. I took time to ponder the situation, wondering what would become of a nation that had become adrift since the ascension of Umar Yaradua to office. I wondered what would happen now that Nigeria's lone voice in the wilderness had been silenced forever. Things had fallen apart and the center had become wobbly.

As encomiums poured in for Gani from Nigerians across all political and social spectrum, I was struck by some of the people that had the temerity to show their faces in the public talking about the man, albeit in praise. These were the same people that figuratively cried for his head on a platter for years because of his belief and utterances. Rather than go bury their heads in shame for failing to listen to this man when they should have, they had the temerity to hypocritically rush to the man's house or release messages extolling him to high heavens. Even though a Latin phrase says that one should not speak ill of the dead, I was not prepared for the level of hypocrisy that some of these Nigerians have exhibited since the announcement of Gani's passing. Some were tripping over themselves to visit his house while the newspapers were crowded with sycophantic elegies for the man they hated his guts in life. Chief Fawehinmi called a spade a spade. He called out errant politicians and military goons that hijacked Nigerian government, her resources and her people for their personal gains. He never blinked in the face of threats of arrests from these political and military harlots that merely wanted Nigeria's resources in their pockets. For these, they abhorred him. How then could they have thought that Nigeria had forgotten, so fast, the roles they played and suddenly start seeing them as democracy-loving, Gani-agreeing people?

In 1986, Dele Giwa, the prominent and vocal Newswatch magazine editor was brutally murdered in his home via a letter bomb. Because it was basically the first incident of its kind in the nation, Nigeria was thrown into confusion. Citizens panicked and withdrew into their shells; no one knew who would be the next victim. Many were afraid to speak their minds in public about who may have perpetrated the dastardly act because Nigeria was under military rule. Instead of joining the masses in their timid stance, Gani Fawehinmi damned all consequences and reacted. Not only did he react but he also took up the dangerous responsibility of representing Newswatch magazine as their attorney. He spoke openly about the case, pointed accusing fingers at those he felt had the means and motive to commit the heinous crime. Even though no one was ever charged for the murder of Dele Giwa, because of Gani Fawehinmi's outspokenness, several other Nigerians became emboldened to talk about the case. Because of all that, some military men have become outcasts in Nigeria's political landscape because Gani and others pointed accusing fingers at them.

I was surprised when I read Babangida's reaction to Gani Fawehinmi's death. Considering that he was one of the military men that put Gani in jail many times, I expected Babangida to be bold and forthright enough to say, "I hated this man's guts when he was alive". He did not do that. He simply said that Gani kept all governments in power on their toes. It is possible that if Sani Abacha were alive, he would also be mourning the passing of Fawehinmi too. I have even read statements by men who openly taunted him when he was alive, talking about immortalizing him. Their hypocrisy is dizzying! It shows that in spite of this man's many incarcerations and manhandling by the governments in power, they knew deep down that he was fighting a just cause; they knew he was doing the right thing. They knew that he was not just a radical wing nut ready to say no to everything but had legitimate reasons why he opposed them. The question that then begs for answer is why they failed to heed his admonitions.

Gani Fawehinmi may be gone but he gave Nigeria his best. For that, he was arrested several times and incarcerated more than 30 times. Between 1994 and today, he was placed in jails under deplorable conditions as much as 5 times even though he never committed any crime. He complained many times about the conditions of the jails he was placed in, the food, the air, the environment and the likes but because of their sadistic tendencies towards him, the government paid no heed. As I write, some Nigerians have begun to ask for investigation into how the lung cancer that eventually led to his death started. They attribute it to the environmental condition he faced in some of the jails, inhaling polluted air. Even though this is a difficult case to prove because of its circumstantial nature, it is worth pursuing. If not for anything, it may in future discourage Nigerian lords masquerading as leaders to stop mistreating innocent people.

One of the questions to ask, as Nigerians bid final farewell to Chief Fawehinmi, is how much effect his crusade may have had on Nigeria. From this writer's perspective, the biggest effect it had was keeping governments in power on their toes. However, the leaders were not deterred from corruption and selfishness. Clearly, they did not listen to Chief Fawehinmi.

For many years and in many instances, Fawehinmi called for universal but qualitative education for all Nigerians. He reasoned that universal and qualitative education would pull the nation out of economic doldrums and poverty. It was his considered opinion that the masses would be empowered and the issue of social stratification along educational and economic lines would be blurred enough to create a virile nation. The powers that be ignored his noble call, neglected our schools. Today, Nigeria has a collapsed educational system. We now have university science graduates without any practical or laboratory experience in their fields of study because of the absence of equipped and modern laboratories. As I think of how backward our educational system has become, with some affluent Nigerians sending their children to Ghana, South Africa and other nations for good education, I cannot help but wonder what would have been had Nigerian leaders listened to and heeded the admonitions of Gani. They would have spent a big chunk of Nigeria's oil money on updating and rebuilding schools, from elementary to tertiary, providing modern laboratories that would keep students in tune with modern advancement in all works of life. If only they listened to him, our teachers would not be owed months of salary arrears. How can a teacher that is owed for months put forth his or her best?

Gani Fawehinmi called for poverty alleviation and jobs for all but the leaders ignored him. Now we have a country full of people that cannot feed themselves. Many university graduates roam the streets in search of non-existent jobs. They have done their part by staying in school and acquiring university education but there are no jobs to go to. When a 29-year old university graduate has no job and still has to depend on his or her parents for financial support, it should be anathema and Gani pointed that out all the way but no one listened.

The effect of joblessness can be felt all over the nation today. Nigeria is now a nation gripped in fear. People are afraid to go to the banks to withdraw their hard-earned money because of the possibility of being waylaid and dispossessed of the money or even killed. Bank robbery is so rampant now that banks in some parts of the nation have shut down their services for weeks. Prominent people and their relatives are afraid to freely move about in the nation for fear of being kidnapped for ransom. In Anambra state, a prominent actor was recently kidnapped but later released. When he regained his freedom, he said that his captors were all well-educated and spoke good English but complained that the reason why they were in the illicit business was because of joblessness. Nothing justifies armed robbery and kidnapping for ransom but if the government had listened to Gani and provided good and sustainable jobs for our teeming masses, may be, just may be Nigeria would have been a better nation today with respect to security.

Gani Fawehinmi fought fiercely for transparency in government. He noticed, just like most well-meaning Nigerians, that corruption had permeated all facets of the government. He called for the ouster of corrupt public officials and decried the activities of military men who seized power to line their pockets. Again, he was persecuted for his opinions and activism and jailed. They did not listen to him. Even Nigerians, the masses he was trying to help, did not provide enough support by way of vocally stating that enough was enough. Today, we see the consequences of corruption in official places. Government treasury has been looted to the tune of billions by individuals. We have billionaires that never worked for one day except get involved in politics. The money they stole could have been used to make Nigeria a better country. There are many projects that are not moving forward for want of funds. We have some of the worst roads and they cause premature death of citizens and slow down commerce. During the rainy season, it is difficult to go from one point to the other in a nation where oil flows like water. Electricity supply is just about 10% of the demand. The result is that industries do not thrive. If they listened to the man who was light years ahead of the so called leaders of Nigeria, the situation would have been different.

Chief Fawehinmi campaigned against constant military intervention. They did not quite listen but in the end, he and other patriots prevailed and democracy has come to stay. The only problem is that it is almost late now. Military rule did not benefit Nigeria otherwise the nation would not be in the state of poverty it is in today. In the time of Gowon in the early 70s, Nigeria was a rich nation with the wherewithal to be a great nation. That opportunity was lost because of continued intervention of the military through coups and counter coups. That has thrown Nigeria into one of the poorest with a population it cannot sustain.

Gani campaigned for individual rights and liberties. He deplored the idea of harassment of citizens for unsubstantiated reasons. He spoke in favor of freedom of speech and association. Again, at several points, he was persecuted for his beliefs and outspokenness. Today, even the president that seems benign in his look, is doing nothing even as security agents harass bloggers. A United-States based blogger was seized at the point of entry to Nigeria and detained against his will all because of his writings. Truthful journalists are still harassed albeit furtively. It makes Nigeria a perpetual third world country and hampers development.

Finally, when all failed, Gani tried his hands in politics. He founded the National Conscience Party in 2003, hoping to engender change from within. Nigerians were too timid to flock to him to lead them. In a nation where money was the main qualification that put politicians in power, he was sidelined because he could not match the deep pockets of other politicians feeding fat on Nigeria's treasury. The opportunity that Nigerians would have had to see him in action was lost. In the end, the people he was fighting for failed to rally around him to help make a difference. We are still suffering the consequences.

Only if they listened to Gani, Nigeria would have been a land of milk and honey with provision for all and sundry. Only if they listened to the civil rights crusader, the image of Nigeria as one of the most corrupt on the face of the earth would not have been. Only if they listened.

In spite of all these, Gani's legacy will endure. May his soul rest in peace and may God help us all.

Tribalism and Ethnocentricity Hampering
Prospects of a Better Nigeria - February 16, 2009.

January 20, 2009, was hailed by many as a turning point in the annals of history. In the United States, what seemed improbable as recently as only a few months ago came to pass. Barack Obama, the son of an African immigrant, became the 44th president of the United States. Before then, nobody believed that they would live to see a person of color emerge as the president of the United States but this country proved, once again, that it is a land of positive surprises.

The reaction from people around the world to Obama's victory was overwhelming. CNN carried images of people in remote countries around the world glued to their TVs and watching history being made. When I got to Nigeria last December, I was stunned by the level of interest and joy that most expressed that the son of a Kenyan immigrant had given them reason to hope. They were not expecting Obama to perform wonders for Africa but the symbolism of the removal of what seemed like a glass ceiling for the black race meant a lot to them.

Like many have said, the greatest significance of this development is that the dream of the young black child or any child of color in the United States would henceforth know no bounds. My children can also dare to dream about being whatever they set their minds on in the United States of America. If, for some reason, they fail to reach their God-given potentials, it may no longer necessarily be because of the absence of opportunities but it will have more to do with the level of effort and determination they put in. Inotherwords, they can dare dream and possibly reach the pinnacle of the political pyramid in the United States. That is awesome!

As if not to be outdone by ordinary citizens in their appreciation of what happened in the United States, Nigerian politicians, both past and current, some of whom were said to have shed tears of joy, were full of effusive praise. They openly noted that the word racism was on its way out of the world lexicon because it would no longer be needed. They freely quoted Martin Luther King's "I have a dream" speech and jubilated that the dream of a land where people would no longer be judged by their race but by the content of their character had been realized. The unbridled joy of some of these people, about the Obama phenomenon, made good press but as I watched them, I marveled at the hypocrisy of their actions. They needed to be reminded about the biblical admonition that one must remove the log in one's eyes to see clearly to remove the small speck in the eyes of one's neighbor. They were jubilating about what was going on 6000 miles from them when Nigeria still had a giant political glass ceiling for people from certain parts of the country. In spite of their theatrics and grandstanding about Obama's victory, Nigeria was still a nation where someone's political success at the federal level depended on that person's region or tribe of origin. You have better chances of becoming the president of Nigeria only if you hail from certain regions or tribes. This has been the case for almost 40-years.

In the beginning, Nigeria was really a disparate group of people in terms of tribe and language, coexisting loosely. In 1914, for ease of governance, the colonial masters amalgamated the Northern and Southern protectorates and one Nigeria was born. Using indirect rule, a form of governance where indigenous citizens were used to enforce the policies of colonial masters, the amalgam was kept together. Attempts to resist the British system, at various times, were met with crushing blows in various places. But as soon as the British left in 1960, inter-tribal suspicion, which never went away, reared its head again in various sections of the more than 250 ethnic groups that made up the nation. Several coups, counter coups and massive pogroms in Nigeria culminated in the 30-month civil war chronicled in my book - Surviving in Biafra, in which more than 2 million people died.

In January 1970, at the end of the Biafra War, the then head of state, General Yakubu Gowon, declared that there was no victor and no vanquished. This declaration gave hope to the people of the eastern region. The hope was that Nigeria would become a nation where everyone had equal access in all respects. It is mind-boggling, therefore, that almost 40-years after that epoch declaration by Gowon, the presidency has remained in the hands of members of a few tribes and regions. Talk about political glass ceiling! General Gowon, a northerner, was overthrown by another northerner, Murtala Muhammed in 1975.

Later, under unfortunate circumstances, the mantle fell on General Obasanjo, a South Westerner, who then handed over to Shehu Shagari, another northerner. Muhamadu Buhari, a northerner, forcibly took over from Shagari but his tenure was short-lived when a fellow northerner, Ibrahim Babangida, took away the helmsmanship from him. Under fire for annulling a supposedly free election that would have put Moshood Abiola, a south westerner in power, Babangida handed over to a south westerner, Ernest Shonekan before General Sani Abacha, another northerner, snatched it away from him. When Abacha mysteriously and suddenly died, General Abdulsalam Abubakar, a northerner, took over and eventually handed back to Obasanjo, a South Westerner. Before leaving office, Obasanjo handed back the presidency to another northerner - Umaru Yaradua. Haba! I am sure that this is sounding like a chess game between the north and southwest to the reader but it truly is the position that Nigeria is in as I write.

In a country that boasts of many regions and tribes, the baton of the presidency is being passed back and forth, sometimes forcibly, amongst the same regions. The question that any person of goodwill should ask is this: where are the rest of the regions in this presidential equation? Are they less intelligent than the rest of Nigerians? Are they less hard working? Are they less ambitious than others? Do they contribute less to nation building than the rest of Nigerians? If the answer to my questions are no, as I know it is, then someone has to call the situation what it is- a political glass ceiling for other regions for the presidency. There are those who have argued that it is no body's fault because when the army was in charge, there were no senior officers from other regions to head Nigeria. For the sake of argument, I will briefly entertain that argument but then my question would be: how about during the many democratic experiments that gave Nigeria General Obasanjo when Alex Ekwueme was craftily edged out and then Shehu Shagari, Abiola and now Umaru Yaradua? The truth is that if you are not from certain sections of Nigeria and you dare to nurse presidential ambition, you are seen as a joke or unrealistic person. In light of this, people from other regions have turned into political lackeys and harlots, always aiming to join political parties headed by people from more privileged regions for a shot at the corridors of power not the helm.

In the 2003 election, Dr. Chuba Okadigbo, a well read and well-traveled politician, threw his hat into the presidential race. His eloquence and political savvy was unquestionable. However, being challenged in his party for the presidential nomination by General Buhari, someone from one of the privileged regions, Chuba Okadigbo knew that he was at a disadvantage so he fell behind Buhari as a vice presidential candidate. He did what he felt was necessary to at least get into the corridors of power even though I disagreed with him.

Then there is Orji Uzo Kalu, the former governor of Abia State. During the 2007 elections, he also threw in his hat for the presidential race even though he knew that the odds were very much against him. To compensate for that, he started doing what he felt was necessary to placate the king makers in the north to at least take a second look at him. He touted the fact that he attended the University of Maiduguri in the north and the fact that he built a mosque for northern Muslims in Abia state. Seeing that it was not working for him, he offered an apology to Nigeria for the Biafran war even though that was not the position of Easterners. The young man was looking for a way to bring the northern king makers to give him a chance. His actions were pathetic but calculated politically to suit the reality on ground. This is not to say that he was the best candidate that south easterners could have put forward, but his case is referenced to show what the political equation in Nigeria has turned some into. Inspite of all the groveling, he did not register any win outside the South East.

In the past, some have tried to address my concerns above by saying that after a war, the winner takes home the spoils or booty. To them, the triumphant regions are keeping the presidency of Nigeria as part of the spoil of war. I have even heard people, including silly internet bloggers and politicians opine that the Easterners should be glad that they are included in government at all. To them, perpetual subjugation is the penalty for fighting a war. Their assertions have been acted out recently at the Nigerian Mission in Washington DC. Nigeria's ambassador to the United States, Rtd General Oluwole Rotimi, has just been relieved of his job by Nigeria's president. This was because he refused to subordinate himself to and take orders from his boss, the External Affairs minister, Ojo Maduekwe. The more outlandish thing is not that Gen Rotimi refused to respect Ojo Maduekwe but had the temerity of writing to Maduekwe, boasting, "I have dealt with people like you in the past. I was the Adjutant General of the Nigerian army that thoroughly defeated your ragtag Biafran army."[ThisDay, Feb 14, 2009]. From his statement, he seems to be one of those that believe that easterners such as Maduekwe should remain in perpetual subjugation and should never rise politically. What this despicable man wrote epitomizes how some still feel in Nigeria but cannot utter openly. I am glad that he committed his opinion to paper and I would say to him, good riddance!

Let me for a moment agree with the people like Oluwole Rotimi, who feel that some of their fellow Nigerians should be happy with political crumbs that fall off the table of people like him because he defeated their "ragtag army". The big question that begs for answer is this: On what moral pedestal do the Oluwoles stand when they boisterously say that the last political barrier in the world, for blacks, have been removed with the election of Obama? What happened to the barrier that currently exists in Nigeria and which people like him routinely uphold? How could Rotimis of Nigeria be pointing elsewhere for the shattering of political glass ceiling when a bigger and tougher ceiling exist in Nigeria? Rather than talking about shattering of glass ceiling in the United States and pretending that all is well, Nigeria should use the opportunity presented by Obama's victory to seek true inclusiveness where everyone, regardless of tribe, would have equal political access. It is refreshing, though, that Yaradua has sent an unmistakable message to would-be Rotimis that insubordination stemming from tribal jingoism is unacceptable.

The incident about Oluwole Rotimi is not unique. It is rampant in government. During Babangida's regime, Commodore Ebitu Ukiwe was the second in command for a period of time. Suddenly, he was dismissed from the military without telling the nation why. How about the current second in command in Nigeria, Dr Jonathan Goodluck? Here is how his current situation was described in a recent newspaper article: "According to investigations, the situation is so bad in the Villa that the Vice President, Dr. Goodluck Jonathan, has been schemed out of the main events in the government and his responsibilities virtually entrusted to some of his sub-ordinates. The Vice President whom investigations revealed had by his role been having only a little direct personal contact with his boss is now completely alienated and his aides often have to scamper for every fresh memo from the office of the President just to see if there is anything for their boss" [Online Tribune, Feb 7, 2009] Some just believe that the northern "king makers" do not want him to develop any ambitions so that after Yaradua, the presidency will remain in the north.

When we talk about tribalism, the tendency is for some to think that it is a scourge endemic only amongst Nigerians living in Nigeria. This is far from the truth. In my two decades of sojourn, outside the country, I have had the opportunity of meeting and associating with a cross section of Nigerians from all walks of life. My observation is that in spite of the many years some have spent outside the country, they have not shed the tribal cloak they left the country with. They still support, at least tacitly, political glass ceiling for Nigerians from certain tribes. Some still see it as a payback for the Biafra war. If you ever confront them on the issue and remind them that it is destroying Nigeria's chances at a more perfect amalgam, they seem to say: "get over it".

I used to believe that for Nigeria to develop to her fullest potential, her citizens living in western nations would play leading roles. This is because they live and work in successful multi-racial societies and must have realized that diversity carries with it a lot of advantages including diverse talents that spur national development. I had hoped that they would use their experience to help alter the attitude of Nigerians who still exploit tribal differences to dominate and subjugate. It has dawned on me, though, that some will never change. In the western countries where they live, they still preach tribalism for Nigeria, ever so furtively.

The irony is that Diaspora Nigerians that tend to favor ethnocentricity and political glass ceiling in Nigeria, seem to be the first to shout discrimination when things go sour for them where they live. They passionately hate to have a taste of their own bitter medicines. They always complain about discrimination in the work place, in school, in their professional practice and on and on. Not long ago, I shook my head in disbelief when a Nigerian in the United States, who once professed her belief in tribal separation, attributed a problem she had here to discrimination. It was ludicrous and in my mind I screamed hypocrisy.

For how could someone who sees nothing wrong with discrimination in her country of birth accuse others of discriminating against her? Her hypocrisy is so palpable that I am almost certain that on January 20th, she must have been glued to her TV, cheering wildly about Obama's victory and mouthing off about how it "has broken racial barriers in the world". My question for her is: what about the barriers people like her have erected in her country of birth because of petty tribal differences? We profess to be God's children and hope for equal treatment from God and yet work hard to block the paths of fellow humans. Oftentimes, people like this would be the first to quote copiously from the bible and talk about salvation without reference to the biblical admonition of love thy neighbor as thyself. One advice I have for people of this nature is that before they can accuse others of racism or talk about the breaking of racial barriers elsewhere, they need to remove the log in their eyes so they can see clearly to point at the perceived speck in the eyes of another. If Nigeria and Nigerians must have a superior moral pedestal to talk about the so-called glass ceiling that has been broken elsewhere, we better break down the bigger barriers we have erected in Nigeria.

Ideally, a gathering of Nigerians should be a very fertile ground for the exchange of ideas on how to develop the nation. Why not? After all, the country boasts of some of the best minds on the face of the earth. It was with great optimism that the advent of internet chat rooms was received in Nigerian circles. The thinking was that it was an added opportunity for her intellects to meet virtually and kick around ideas from the comfort of their homes. Unfortunately, they have failed to make good use of that opportunity because our so-called best minds, especially those in the Diaspora, still refuse to shed tribal sentiments and pull their God-given talents together. The chat rooms have become avenues for the bellicose exchange of hate. Organized in cliques along tribal lines, participants spew venom on and amongst themselves, using every opportunity to display their tribal leanings by defending or demonizing corrupt politicians depending on their tribe of origin.

When the memo written by Brigadier Oluwole Rotimi to Ojo Maduekwe, boasting about his defeat of the "Biafran rag tag army", became public, one would have expected universal condemnation of the man's insensitivity in the various Nigerian chat rooms. That was not to be. Except in very few cases, it was mostly Yoruba for Rotimi and Igbo against him while the Hausas stoked the fire of the lunacy in gleeful exuberance. The idea that everything in Nigeria has to be looked at through a tribal lens, even by Nigerians in western countries who should know better, is most unfortunate. A reader of my commentaries wrote to me to say that I should not have condemned Rotimi because I did not know what transpired between him and Maduekwe. He was invariably saying that under certain circumstances, Oluwole's insensitivity was acceptable. That type of shallow-mindedness baffled me. I tried to explain that the outrage against Rotimi was not about the feud between him and Maduekwe but about Rotimi's attempt to rub salt into an open wound that a whole tribe still bears. For the record and for someone who lost loved ones during that war, if Rotimi's memo did not mention Biafra the way it did, I would have cared less about that feud.

Going back to the reaction of Nigerians in the chat rooms, I was disappointed that the level and type of criticism that Nigerians level against elected officials depend on where they come from. It boils down to the fact that there is no consistency in the way we judge elected officials. What we see as bad today could be adjudged as good tomorrow when the hat is on another head. No wonder why we cannot rid the nation of corruption and corrupt officials. We have different barometers for measuring it's destructive effects on the nation depending on where the perpetrators hail from. With this type of biased national outlook, I am sad to observe that Nigeria is going nowhere fast as far as development is concerned.

The Minister of Information, Prof Dora Akunyili, has just embarked on what she calls re-branding of Nigeria. That is all well and good but the term re-branding makes me uncomfortable because it sounds like putting a new cover on an old product. In the midst of his murderous escapades in the 90s, Abacha sent out emissaries to try to portray Nigeria in good light. He failed woefully. For a lasting change, Nigeria must first embark on an introspective journey, culminating in general attitude adjustment. If we do not do away with tribalism and ethnocentricity, Nigeria will be difficult to re-brand because a lot of her problems revolve around that vice. For example, in government circles, you find people in high places doling out contracts to inept contractors because of tribal affinity instead of to qualified persons. The result is that shoddy roads and infrastructure, needing constant maintenance, are built. This leads to wastefulness. We have read stories of some members of the media who are so ethnocentric in their mindset and outlook that instead of doing the job of the press, they put out skewed opinions. Tribalism is the culprit in the demise of organizations set up in the Diaspora to address Nigeria's problems. As I write, Nigeria's presidency is "handed down" to people who do not even understand what Nigeria's problems are let alone knowing how to solve them all because they belong to privileged regions or tribes. The result is that ineptitude runs wild. Dora Akunyili was successful with NAFDAC and if she wants to get anywhere close to that type of success in her re-branding effort, she must first put the issue of tribalism on the table for honest and candid discussion with an aim to developing a way forward. She must help bring about a less tribalistic and ethnocentric Nigeria where a crime is a crime in the eyes of all regardless of who committed it. She should work towards a Nigeria where corruption is corruption in the eyes of all regardless of the perpetrators.

As part of re-branding Nigeria, Akunyili should embark on a nation-wide education tour to talk to ordinary citizens who vote during elections based on tribal sentiments. Get them to understand that voting for someone just because of where they are from rather than what they can do for Nigeria does not help anyone. Part of re-branding should also include making every Nigerian feel like they have a stake in the country. I routinely hear Americans say that they are ready to die for the USA because they love her. I am yet to hear Nigerians say the same. The truth is that you can only want to die for a nation you love. To love a nation, you have to have a stake in it. That stake must be complete and unconditional. A Nigerian once said that every time the American national anthem was played, he would see Americans shedding tears, a sign of their affection for America. Then he said, "When the Nigerian anthem is played I do not feel the same emotion because I still feel like an outsider" There are many that feel that way and it is very unfortunate.

When I was a kid, the worst thing a fellow kid could do to you was to say something bad about your mother. Even the gentlest child would fight for that reason. Why? Because a mother provides succor and protection to her kids and loves them without favoritism. Children return the favor to their mothers, ready to fight and even die for them if necessary. While I am not a believer that government has the solution to all problems, a country should be a lot like a mother to all its citizens. She must not condone tribalism or ethnicity. She must seek to provide a level playing field for all so that those who work hard and play by the rules can be rewarded accordingly. A country should not make some to work extraordinarily hard just to get by while some are virtually given the key to the government coffers to enrich themselves at will. A country that gives all of her citizens a fair sense of belonging and purpose is the kind of country citizens want to die for. That is the country that Akunyili must seek for rather than try to cover up Nigeria's bad sides just to give her a new image.

The greatness of America lies in her diversity. People from all over the world converge in the United States with diverse and unique talents and push the envelope of development every day. Nigeria is also an amalgamation of various tribes. Inspite of the differences in tribe and tongue, Nigerians of various tribes bring unique talents and gifts to the amalgam or union.

As Nigerians enjoy the moment regarding Obama's victory, they must now determine whether they want to follow the sound example that the United States has set and work towards a country where all children, regardless of tribe, can believe that if they work hard and play by the rules, they can have a decent shot at the presidency or other high national office. A more perfect union will come when the presidency and all elected offices go to people who have the intellect, the experience, the temperament and the skills to lead the nation. At that time, citizens would be proud to have come from Nigeria. Then, even though tribe and tongue will still differ, all Nigerians will stand in brotherhood.

Obligations of Nigerians Under The New
Democratic Dispensation – August 9, 2001

Democracy is back in Nigeria but the journey to this point has not been smooth nor easy. The fight for democracy wreaked havoc of unimaginable proportions on the nation and her citizenry. Many people like Chris Anyanwu lost their freedom, Gani Fawehinmi was tormented beyond belief and Dele Giwa, Kudirat Abiola and others paid with their lives. We must therefore rise as one nation and with one voice and pay tribute to the champions of democracy in Nigeria, living and deceased, known and unknown, vocal or quiet. Hopefully, this time around, democracy has come to stay.

So what does this pleasant turn of events mean for Nigeria as a nation? As Americans would say, "now what"? It simply means that Nigerians have once again become the architects of their destiny. The hackneyed expression: "As you make your bed, so must you lie on it", has become even more relevant in the Nigerian political context. To sustain our nascent democracy, we must nurture it and treat it like a new bride. We must handle it like a basket of eggs and play by the rules envisioned by the forerunners of this noble ideology. If we fumble and blow this God-given opportunity once again, we may never get another chance.

Many years ago, I listened to a sermon in church. It was delivered by the resident pastor at the height of President Shehu Shagari's administration. The sermon, which was delivered with a lot of passion, had prophetic significance. The pastor was lamenting the state of affairs in the country. He talked about the vices that had enveloped Nigeria at the time and wondered why our democracy seemed more like a counterfeit rather than a true one. He said that democracy yields dividends only when practiced as should and added that rather than practice true democracy, Nigerians had become "DEMON-CRAZY." With melodrama, he described the destruction of Sodom and Gomorra and asked all to pray so as to avoid consequences akin to what Sodom suffered.

The pastor was right. At this time, corruption, favoritism, bribery, ineptitude and mediocrity, had taken center stage in the country. Our law-makers that were paid to make laws for the nation practically derelicted their duties, turning their living quarters at the infamous "1004 building" in Lagos into a haven where young girls paraded at odd hours of the day. Not long after the reverend's sermon, General Muhammadu Buhari and his Deputy, Brigadier Tunde Idiagbon, took over the reins of power in a bloodless coup!

The intervention of the military brought a catastrophic end to a democracy that was still struggling to take hold in the face of civilian mismanagement and corruption. Coincidentally, General Buhari cited the state of affairs in Nigeria as the primary reason for their intervention. For the next 15 years or so, the military took turns at mismanaging the nation's coffers, spewing forth their destructive influence as far afoot as they could reach.

Insinuating that Nigerians were incapable of policing themselves, the army instituted the War Against Indiscipline (WAI) program where soldiers flogged people mercilessly for such infractions as dropping thrash on the streets and jumping queues in post offices, banks and petrol stations. They bullied people into submission and suddenly, places like Lagos began to turn into clean cities. If you dropped thrash on the street, people would nearly lynch you and if you jumped a queue, people would almost burn you alive. Even the police stopped asking for bribe brazen-facedly but continued more discretely. A friend of mine who came into the country at the time, oblivious of the WAI program, was flabbergasted at his encounter with customs officials at Murtala Muhammed airport. The customs official simply asked him cordially to open his bag and dutifully searched his baggage after which the officer closed his bag and said: "welcome to Nigeria sir" without asking for bribe. A lot of people liked the results of the WAI program but loathed the modus operandi of the military.

Since the demise of the WAI program, some nagging questions have continued in my mind: if Nigerians are capable of decency, why did they need the military to treat them like animals before they displayed their goodness? Why did they allow the army to flog them like horses before realizing that they should not drop thrash on the streets? Why did we need to be reminded to wait for our turns in queues?

Now that we have another democracy, we have another chance to correct the mistakes made in the past. We have the chance to don our cloaks of decency and demonstrate that we are capable of doing good voluntarily. We must look at some of the things that made a mockery of our democracy in the past and work to stamp them out altogether.

As we speak out against the excesses of our current and past leaders, as we condemn the unforgivable atrocities perpetrated on us by the military, we must remain cognizant of the fact that in a democratic dispensation, the citizenry has obligations too: the obligation to conform to the rule of law and do what is right.

Take the issue of bribery for instance: a democracy that condones the bribing of law enforcement agents will fail because law enforcement agents cannot be relied on. The police is already corrupt but the citizenry aid and abet this abhorrent practice. The idea of bribing the police force has become entrenched in our national psyche so much so that people set aside money for bribing police even when they have done nothing wrong! I was recently told by a contemporary that if you do not offer bribe to the police when they stop you on the road, they will intentionally delay you, hoping that you would capitulate and do their bidding. We should not be encouraging this practice because the police plays a pivotal role in the furtherance of the ethos of democracy. They should be enforcing the laws and fighting crime. In fact, their mere presence should be acting as a deterrent to crime.

Bribery should be discouraged in all forms. It is a culprit in the appointment of unqualified people to government positions culminating in mediocrity; it is a culprit in the award of road construction contracts to incompetent contractors resulting in construction of bad roads; it is a culprit in examination malpractices leading to graduation of functional illiterates; it is a culprit in the importation and distribution of fake and expired drugs to unsuspecting citizens. The list goes on.

The judiciary is the third arm of government in a true democracy. If an election process goes awry, the judiciary is relied upon to sort things out; if couples can no longer coexist, they turn to the courts to settle things; if someone's rights are violated, the person turns to the courts for redress. The military came close to bastardizing the judicial process in Nigeria with their kangaroo courts and tribunals but thanks to the unrelenting efforts of some courageous Nigerians, they can be said to have failed. As a first step towards sanitizing the judicial system, the President must ensure that all the draconian decrees promulgated during the military era must all be repealed. Court officials must watch their public statements and avoid being embroiled in politics so as to maintain their independence and moral authority to dispense justice. Backlogged cases must be cleared up in courts to make way for new ones.

One of the greatest fruits of democracy is the protection of the rights of the citizen to free speech, freedom of association, peaceful co-existence and the like. There are some signs that human rights record of Nigeria may have started improving under President Obasanjo. Some say this is because Obasanjo suffered human rights abuses under General Sani Abacha. However, it must be emphasized that human rights abuses come in very many forms. When a common man's rights are trampled upon by the rich and powerful, it is abuse; when leaders take advantage of their positions and deny people of things that are due them, it is a form of abuse. This must be addressed.

The tax burden in any democracy falls on all citizens and is usually graduated so that people pay in accordance with what they make. This is part of the money the government depends on for societal upkeep. In Nigeria today, the burden is still lopsidedly distributed so much so that mainly civil servants, whose salaries cannot be hidden, and big companies, whose accounts are audited, pay the bulk sum. Some very wealthy individuals still pay very little. Wealthy Nigerians should start giving the nation as much as they are getting out of the nation. If they want good roads and electricity; if they want the menace of robbers to be curtailed by equipping police with better weaponry, they must pay their fair share.

Recently, the Minister of Information - Jerry Gana, while commenting on the policy of 100% inspection of goods at the ports was quoted as saying: "Nigerian importers are conniving with foreigners to defraud the country". He accused the businessmen of collaborating with unscrupulous Lebanese and Indian businessmen to ruin the nation's economy by making false declaration of the content of their containers to evade taxation. Wao Nigeria! Where is the spirit of patriotism? How can we be encouraging strangers to ruin the nation? We must change this type of unpatriotic attitude if this nascent democracy must survive.

Discipline and civility are proverbial oils that lubricate the wheel of democracy and make it run smoothly. The habit of jumping queues in banks, post offices, petrol stations and even in traffic do not augur well for the nation. Excessive speeding, drunk driving, driving on shoulders and other irresponsible behavior in traffic, which contribute to road accidents, must be changed.

Advance fee fraud activities (419), drug peddling, importation of expired or fake medications, petrol bunkering and the like are all things that give Nigeria a very bad name in international circles. We must change all these for a better Nigeria.

Press freedom is very important in any democracy. Our press, however, has the responsibility to avoid irresponsible reporting or jaundiced journalism. Reporting must come from exhaustive investigative journalism and once the truth is unearthed, it must be reported without fear or favor. The press must keep the masses abreast of issues and remember that their reports are capable of building or tearing down our democracy.

The rate at which the cost of foodstuff is rising is alarming but as citizens, we must depend less on the government and start helping ourselves. In the past, families may be poor but they never lacked food to eat and that was because each family engaged in small-scale farming (subsistence). They planted cassava for making garri; planted yam, maize and cocoa-yam. Some reared goats and chickens. These provided them with sufficient food all year round and cases of hunger were either non-existent or just occasionally heard of. These days, everyone seems to have abandoned farming in search of non-existent "golden fleece" The result is that those that are wise enough to continue farming and rearing livestock sell their products at cut throat prices because too few goods are being chased by a lot of money. Today, several fertile former farmlands have been cleared and replaced with real estate and if we do not proceed with caution, we would even run out of fertile land for family subsistence farming. I was happy to read that the Federal Government has approved a six billion naira special food program to facilitate the development of rural communities and reduce poverty among farmers. This is part of effort to boost food production in the country. It is indeed a welcome development.

Finally, it is the citizens of Nigeria that will make the nation what it will be. All hands must be on deck.

PART 3

Infrastructure

My Flight into the not-so International Port Harcourt Airport - Jan 15, 2006

My family and I chose to fly into Nigeria during our 2005 Christmas visit via the Port Harcourt international airport. It was a conscious decision based purely on convenience and its proximity to our final destination- Nnewi. Prior to December 2005, I had never been to that airport but always imagined a well-maintained airport with modern amenities and facilities. Who would blame me for thinking that way? After all, the strategic location of the airport, in oil-rich Port Harcourt, makes it the airport of choice for rich oil sector multi nationals operating in the area. Furthermore, it has become one of the major gateways into Nigeria. It was with all these in mind that one assumed that the airport was being maintained as needed to sustain its international appellation. I was wrong!

Our plane touched down on the airport tarmac just before 5:00PM on that muggy December 15 evening. There was still ample daylight when we touched down so I had the opportunity to survey the tarmac through the window while the pilot made last-minute maneuvers to bring the wide-bodied airbus to a final stop. I kept peering out the window to the inconvenience of one of my kids sitting next to the window. In a very short while, the plane jerked to a final stop. Most of the passengers quickly rose to their feet and began to remove their carry-on bags from the baggage compartment. Disembarkation followed shortly.

My first disappointment came as I walked through the aircraft door. I did not see any enclosed gangway leading directly from the aircraft door into the airport building. Passengers just disembarked onto the tarmac and then proceeded, in a very disorderly fashion, to a walkway about 800 feet away. That walkway eventually led into the arrival hall. While standing on the aircraft stairs, I quickly surveyed the airport precincts and noticed that there was an even bigger problem. The airport did not have any real perimeter fencing around it. This must be the reason why cows easily strayed into the tarmac, a few months back, nearly causing a plane accident, I thought. I pondered this laxity and it dawned on me that just as cows freely strayed into the airport tarmac, arriving passengers could easily stroll out of the airport tarmac, into the city, without undergoing security or immigration checks in the "arrival hall". In this day and age of terrorism, when every nation wants to know and identify every in-coming visitor, the Port Harcourt airport had obvious loopholes and no one seemed to care. I was shocked.

The reader might be wondering what security has to do with the international status of the airport. Well, as an international airport, Port Harcourt airport has become a direct gateway into Nigeria. Foreigners could directly enter the country via the airport. It is therefore imperative that the airport have tight safeguards against unwarranted and undocumented entry, whether by terrorists or others.

My kids seemed exceedingly happy to be back in their country of origin. They were all over the place, freely gesticulating in response to what they were seeing. As for me, I was overcome by my civil engineering instincts. My attention was focused on the tarmac and I was not pleased with the condition of some parts of it. Some of the joints between the individual concrete slabs (pavements) that make up the tarmac had deteriorated. At some locations, due to differential settlement, some of the concrete slabs had settled a little bit and were no longer flush horizontally with adjacent slabs. This created undulations not healthy for a tarmac. Although it is good for tarmacs to be slightly textured to create and maintain friction between aircraft landing tires and the tarmac (pavement). It is however suicidal for appreciable undulations to exist on the pavement considering the warping speed at which airplanes touch down. Little undulations on the tarmac are capable of ripping aircraft tires to shreds on impact.

Engineers with airport pavement experience should be dispatched to fix this problem. Remedies may include grinding down those parts of the concrete slabs that are not flush with one another. It may even be necessary to remove portions of the slabs completely to ascertain the suitability and bearing capacity of the soil beneath. If unsuitable soil is encountered, it is removed, replaced with suitable soil and compacted before a fresh concrete slab is cast.

When we finally entered the arrival hall, I was even more disappointed. Nothing in that room made me feel like I was in the arrival hall of an international airport. Bags, probably from previous flights, were scattered all over the place. I looked up and saw a sign that read something like, "In the event of fire, go this way". I followed the direction of the arrow with my eyes, hoping to see a clear egress to the outside. What my eyes met was a wall. The fire sign seemed to be there only perfunctorily. In a real fire emergency, passengers would run in the direction of the arrow only to meet a blank wall or at best a louvered window opening. That would spell disaster.

Passengers had now crowded around the conveyor belt, sweating bullets because the overhead fans did not seem to be having any appreciable effect. The whole place was enveloped with the odor of stale air and perspiration. I watched other passengers nervously waiting for their luggage to materialize and kept wondering why a nation as rich as Nigeria would find it difficult to install a working air conditioner in an airport that is as strategic and important as Port Harcourt International.

We eventually retrieved our suitcases after sweating it out for close to 60 minutes in the baggage area. Then it dawned on us that baggage carts were essential commodities of sorts because there was none in sight. Other passengers had already taken the few in the airport. I was still looking for a cart when a man, dressed in a custom uniform, asked if we were looking for carts and I said yes. "Follow that man going out, when he unloads his suitcases into his car, you can take his cart", he advised. I appreciated the man's advice but it was rather stunning that to get a cart for use in an international airport, I have to follow a passenger outside, to the parking lot, wait for him to discharge his luggage into his car before getting a cart for my use and walking back into the arrival hall. Assuming I was traveling alone, who would keep an eye on my bags while I trailed a passenger to get a cart? From my perspective, that was appalling. What would it cost Nigerian authorities to provide a bank of baggage carts that passengers could use for a fee? Simply calculate the maximum number of passengers that could land in that airport on a peak day concurrently. Provide carts that would service at least 80% to 90% of the passengers at the same time. All they need to do is stack the carts in one secure location inside the arrival hall. Passengers would pay to use the carts. This would generate money for maintaining the airport, replenishing old worn-out carts and paying the salaries of the people that man that process. The arrival hall needs to be expanded to accommodate a location for stacking the carts though.

On the way to the place where we spent the night in the city, I noticed that a lot of construction work was going on. All manners of road construction equipment, vibratory compactors, graders, dozers were lined up. The name of the construction company was Stemco. I asked my relative, sitting beside me, if Stemco was a foreign company and he laughed. "It belongs to Stella Obasanjo", he quipped. "The wife of the president, are you serious?", I asked. "Positive", he intoned. "Was she a contractor too?" I pressed further. "Apparently so", he responded as our bus made its way into the Port Harcourt dusk.

The drive from Port Harcourt to my hometown the next day was very uneventful. When we got home, we still had ample energy and daylight left to move around.

The Christmas vacation went by rather quickly and before we knew it, it was time to head back again so we traveled back to Port Harcourt, en route to the United States. Our aircraft was billed to depart the Garden City for Germany by 10:50PM but we were at the airport at about 6:45PM. As our vehicle approached the airport building, I was surprised by what greeted my eyes. Long lines of people outside the airport building! But for the suitcases that were lined up beside them, I would not have known that these were passengers waiting to be admitted into the airport building for check in. Apparently, the departure hall of our "international airport" building was too small to accommodate passengers so they had to stand outside. It was a sorry sight for an international airport.

After settling into the line, out of curiosity, I strolled over to the beginning point of the line. It was chaos of the first order! The line led to a glass door where two Lufthansa staff members were stationed. One of them, a young lady, was telling passengers to come in, one after another, but it was not working. I stood there for a while, trying to understand why people were struggling and sweating profusely. It soon became clear to me that the long line was not being respected and the Lufthansa staff were doing nothing about it. Periodically, passengers who were not standing in the queue would come in from the side, whisper something into the ear of the young lady and she would instantly let them in to the obvious chagrin of the other passengers. What she was doing was unacceptable to the people in front of the line and they continued to protest to the lady but she maintained a straight face. Occasionally, she tried to explain why a passenger, not in line, was allowed in. At a point, she said that a passenger had a medical emergency and had to be checked in immediately. The passengers standing in front were amused by that shallow explanation. This was because the departure time of the aircraft was 10:50 PM and the time was only about 8:00PM or so. What good would it do a passenger with a medical emergency to be checked in by 8:00PM for a flight that was to depart in 3 hours? If it were real medical emergency, by the time the aircraft would lift off three hours later, the passenger would have died or become incapacitated. If it were a real medical emergency, the right course of action would have been to call an ambulance and take the passenger to the nearest hospital. Clearly, the medical emergency story was mere excuse to douse the anger of the passengers who were screaming and tugging at her from all directions. The lady's attempt to explain her actions merely angered people more and chaos intensified. While all these unfolded, I kept thinking to myself that a bigger building was the answer.

As the passengers began to settle down, after the emergency check-in uproar, a Caucasian man who had just been dropped off in front of the airport, casually walked to the front of the line, straight to the glass door and started talking to the Lufthansa lady. For a brief moment, the other passengers looked on in silence but the moment it seemed like he was about to be allowed into the departure hall, one of the passengers forcefully stepped towards the front and accosted him. "There is a line behind you and you decided to bypass it and go straight to the front. If it were in your country, would you do the same?" He angrily queried. "I- am- just- trying- to- ask- the- lady- a -question", the stunned man stuttered. The irate passenger was not satisfied; he was clutching a couple of blue-colored passports which indicated to me that he must be residing in the United States. "When we come to your country, we respect your rules and regulations but when you come to ours, you disrespect it and you are being aided by Nigerians", the man said. Then he turned to the Lufthansa official, "If you let this man in now, we will all move in simultaneously and see how you handle that".

I was surprised at the effect that his last threat elicited. The Lufthansa lady asked the man to turn back and then turned to the rest of the passengers and announced that the problem had been taken care of. At that time, most of the passengers had become so exasperated that they were not impressed by what the Lufthansa lady said. I kept thinking to myself that merely having a landing space should not be the sole arbiter in determining which airstrip becomes an international one. The convenience of passengers and safety must be considered. Port Harcourt airport is very strategic as an international airport and its international status must be maintained but more needs to be done to make it live up to that name "international." The root of the problem we were having was that people had to queue outside. If the airport had ample space and people queued inside and merely walked up to a counter to check in, all the hassles, the tugging, the sweating, the cursing and altercation going on would be non-existent. An airport where passengers have to queue outside the building and be let in one after the other like they were going to slaughter is simply unacceptable.

By the time we got past the glass door and entered the building, my shirt was soaked with sweat. My kids then started telling me how they were pushed and shoved as they tried to assert their rights to be in the long queue and be checked in. They talked spiritedly about how they shoved others back and maintained their positions. I did not see all that action because I was in front. In a funny way, though, I was happy that they did not capitulate in the face of the shoving and pushing that was going on. To an extent, they had realized that in Nigeria, unfortunately, it was every man to himself and God for us all.

After this, our suitcases were weighed in, on a big red scale. While one of the officials stood idly by, watching what was going on as though he was not part of the staff, the other was lifting and placing the suitcases on the scale. Another young lady was dutifully punching in the weight of each baggage into an antiquated calculator she had in her hand. It was not clear to me why she was doing that. The aim of weighing the suitcases was to ensure that they did not exceed a certain weight. Why then did she need the calculator to punch in the numbers? Was she trying to convert the weights from one unit to the other? I could not tell but was glad to leave that station and go to the one where actual check-in was being done at the Lufthansa check-in counter.

We went through the rest of the nerve-racking rigmaroles and then came to the point where suitcases were to be searched. There must have been as much as 15 people in different uniforms standing behind a long stretch of table, poking into passengers' suitcases, ransacking them, one after the other. It is important to state, at this juncture, that this writer has no problems with thorough baggage search. The September 11 experiences have shown that one can never be too careful about searching passengers and their belongings. I therefore welcomed the searches. It did not however take long for me to realize that all these men and women, dutifully standing behind the long table, seemed more interested in something else. They were more interested in the boxes that housed foodstuffs, as attested to by their reactions every time they found one. Some were openly asking passengers if they had foodstuff and then zero in on the box that had it.

After going through my family's several suitcases that housed inconsequential items and books, they were getting dismayed. Finally, the last box was placed on the long table. Immediately the thick aroma of foodstuff filled the air. The custom man that had been standing there with a dejected look on his face suddenly broke into a hearty smile. "Na this one carry the gear box, the engine and all the accessories", he said to the delight of the others within earshot. They all turned and all attention was focused on that singular suitcase. I gingerly opened the box and the nightmare began. From what I saw from that point on, I hasten to caution the Nigerian authorities that what these men and women of customs, Nahco, airline staff, that stand behind the long table do is far from what is important. They are more interested in extorting money from people carrying foodstuff than do their job. If they find foodstuff in a passenger's suitcase, they would recite a little known edict to you. It states that before you can travel out of the country with food stuff, you need to get the foodstuff tested by a lab and obtain a certificate attesting to the fact that the foodstuff has been tested and that it does not have any communicable diseases. Now, the reader should tell me how many Nigerian passengers would first take their foodstuff to a laboratory and obtain clearance certificates before traveling out of the country. What this edict has done is provide an avenue for bribery and corruption because as soon as they recite the edict to a passenger, the passenger is bound to capitulate and wallow in bribery. The only alternative is to forfeit the food items.

I am sure that the reader is wondering what all the above have to do with the status of Port Harcourt as an international airport. Well, Nigerian airports must not be seen, by the outside world, as lax in searching for and intercepting unwholesome items like narcotics and the likes before they get to overseas countries. If the people who should be checking and intercepting these unwholesome items fail to do so, because they are more interested in foodstuff, in attempts to make some quick money, then airports outside Nigeria will be intercepting these unwholesome items. The corollary is that they would be questioning and looking down on Nigeria. The government must review the foodstuff edict and if it must be continued, then they need to mount cameras at the points where officials take advantage of passengers. It may help keep their eyes on the ball and reduce bribery that goes on at that point.

I had just finished checking in and was giving final departure instructions to my kids when a man walked up to me. "Are you not Alfred Uzokwe of Nigeriaworld", he said politely, stretching out his hand toward me for a handshake. "I am," I said, reciprocating his gesture. "I read your column and have in fact communicated with you, by email, in the past after reading your articles" Thanks, I said, a little surprised. I was surprised because people always tell me that I look older in the Nigeriaworld picture and that they would not have been able to recognize me using the picture. I have always reveled in the anonymity that that provided me. I guess I may have finally caught up, in age, with my image on Nigeriaworld. Anyway, after exchanging pleasantries with the man, my family and I walked over to the waiting lounge, all hungry for something to eat. I looked around and saw a poorly made sign that read: "restaurant". We still had a little time so we all went straight to the restaurant. The interior of the restaurant was less than appealing. If I were not traveling with kids, I would have gone back out. The ceiling was falling apart in some locations and you could see what seemed like water damage on some parts of the walls next to the windows. We pulled some chairs together and beckoned on the waitress. Can we get your menu?" I asked. She looked at me like someone who had not heard the word "menu" before. My child, Jennifer, who has a penchant for injecting humor into any situation, quickly said, "here is the menu". We all looked toward her and she was holding up a small paper with the word "EVA" written on it. It had the picture of bottled water on it. Just then, the lady said that they were out of food and had just started boiling rice. We all started laughing. Jennifer was right after all. They were out of food and probably had only EVA water to sell. I then asked if they had any "chewables" and the lady said no. I ended up ordering fruit juice for the kids and before they could start drinking, the departure announcement was made. Again, this is an international airport. A restaurant in an international airport should have some measures of class. The environment must be clean and the enclosure itself should reflect its international status. A visitor who enters the country via that airport and goes into that restaurant is bound to develop a poor impression of the country.

When we finally lined up to check into the aircraft, I was somewhat impressed by the security check. Just like in any international airport, carry-on bags went through scans and passengers were frisked. But then after the scanning and frisking, we went back out into an open tarmac instead of stepping into an enclosed gangway that should have led us directly into the airplane. A gangway, in this day and age, helps with security. Once you are checked into a gangway, there is no other entry into the airplane. While on the tarmac and before boarding the airplane, we went through yet another carry-on bag search. It was at that time becoming inconveniencing, yet, this writer does not feel that the goal was accomplished because as our bags were being checked again, there were people milling around behind the checkers. A determined bad person, who sneaks into the airport via its many open perimeter fencing, could also enter the aircraft with dangerous objects, eluding security.

Before I end this piece, let me state that the aim of cataloging my experience at the Port Harcourt International is not to make Nigeria look bad. It is to point out potential dangers that need to be rectified. Some of my points border on passenger safety and others have to do with passenger comfort. Others merely deal with burnishing Nigeria's image and presenting her in good light to foreigners. They are all important.

Our leaders travel overseas all the time. They touch down on well-maintained and safety-conscious airports and they love it. Why is it difficult for them to replicate those things they love in those overseas airports in Nigeria? Why can't they make the safety of passengers paramount?

Must an accident occur before someone repairs the deteriorating tarmac in Port Harcourt airport? Must a herd of cows cause a major accident before safe perimeter fencing is installed? Must a real fire emergency take place before a reasonable fire evacuation strategy is established? Must a passenger suffocate and slump before the air conditioner in that airport is made to work or the building expanded to accommodate passengers? A government of the people, for the people, by the people would not wait to be told before rectifying the shortcomings in this airport.

A parting question for our leaders is this: How would they feel if an accident happens as a result of their inefficiency and then they find out that their own loved ones are involved? At that time, it would be too late.

Build A Second Niger Bridge Now - Lives Are On The Line! - February 8, 2009

For years now, Nigerians have been hearing that a second Niger bridge would be built in Onitsha, in Anambra State to connect the eastern part of Nigeria with the western part. Unfortunately, that promise has largely remained a mirage because of political shenanigans, a factor that has been the bane of many worthy projects in Nigeria. As I write, the current bridge is getting older, structurally deficient, functionally obsolete and the lives of many motorists are in danger.

This project, which was conceived many years ago, has seen many administrations come and go and for some reason, they talk about it and do nothing in the long run. The former Nigerian minister of finance, Dr. Kalu Idika Kalu, recently stated in an interview that he appropriated the funds for this project more than 14 years ago and wondered why the project has not started. Nigerians would really like to know the answer to Dr Kalu's question.

Just before he left office, looking to get votes for the People's Democratic Party(PDP) in the South East that he neglected throughout his presidency, General Olusegun Obasanjo hurriedly arranged a photo opportunity in Onitsha and announced that the construction of a second Niger bridge was about to start. Hopes were raised and motorists looked forward to the reprieve that the project would afford them when completed. General Obasanjo has now been out of office for almost two years and nothing has happened. It was after his departure from office that the details of what really happened began to emerge. Apparently, Obasanjo, in his characteristic style coerced the governments of Anambra and Delta states to agree to contribute billions of naira, which they did not have, towards the second Niger bridge project. He called it a public-private partnership where the federal government would contribute some of the funds and the states would contribute some while other private ventures would chip in.

At the time, there was talk about using toll system to recoup the money spent. The toll part sounded like a good idea but what was not considered was the fact that the state governments did not have the money to contribute. Now that Obasanjo is no longer in power, the Anambra and Delta State governors have announced that they do not really have the money to contribute and so would withdraw from participating in the project. This, to me, means that unless a miracle happens, the project will again remain dormant during the administration of the current President, Umaru Yaradua. This should not be allowed to happen again. This issue must be kept in the front burner by every means because time is not on the side of the current aging and excessively loaded bridge. With every excess load that the current bridge is forced to carry, with every additional vibration that the bridge is subjected to and with the passage of time that continues to see the concrete piers spall and the iron bars delaminate, the situation continues to get more dire.

The refusal of the federal government to take complete ownership of the proposed second Niger Bridge project and build it from start to finish beats the imagination of this writer. Some people have posited that if that bridge were located in the north, it would have been built and commissioned long ago. Others see the dilly-dallying as a ploy to delay and eventually cancel the project because projects located in the South East never attract the interest of the Federal Government. Whatever the case, it must be borne in mind that the Niger Bridge spans a body of water of national significance and commercial-cum-historical importance and is located on a major federal roadway linking the West to the East. These factors qualify the project for hundred percent federal takeover.

As recently as January 29, 2009, during a public hearing of the Senate Committee on Works, the Minister of Works and Urban Development, Dr Hassan Lawal, again made the same type of promise we hear every day about the second Niger Bridge project. He said that the Federal Executive Council had approved the award of the contract and was getting documents for signing between the FEC and Debt Management Office when the Anambra and Delta state governments announced their withdrawal from the project. "The Minster disclosed that notwithstanding that development, the Federal government's 2009 budget had captured the project and that given the viability and bankability of the project, many private investors would jump at the opportunity to partake if the two states indeed withdrew from the project"[Leadership in Nigeria, Feb 7, 2009]. My take on this is that if the federal government believes that the project is that bankable, what stops it from starting and completing the project and reaping the said rewards? The continued attempt to tie the states into a project that should be the responsibility of the federal government smells like a ploy to continue to do nothing.

We are told that the reason why the federal government is not going it alone is that it does not have money. That is balderdash! Nigeria boasts of 50 billion dollars in foreign reserves and on top of that, reaped the excess profits that came in when the price of crude sky-rocketed. That bridge can be built if there is the will.

Considering the age of the current bridge and the average daily traffic figure on which the design was predicated over 40 -years ago, I have always known that it is currently being overburdened by increased traffic. But after my visit to Nigeria, during which I took a trip to Asaba from Nnewi, it became clear to me that the problem was no longer just academic but a real issue that needs constructive action now. Our journey from Nnewi to Upper Iweka Road bypass in Onitsha, a distance of about 13 miles, took about 40 minutes. That was good considering that we had to deal with potholes in some sections of the highway as well as grapple with the surge of roadside hawkers that jammed the road as we entered Onitsha. When we got to the Upper Iweka bypass, heading towards the Niger Bridge to cross into Asaba, all hell broke loose. We were stuck in traffic for the next 2 hours, slowly creeping, slowly crawling like tired old turtles. As if the chaotic traffic congestion was not enough problem, vehicles were blaring their horns to the highest decibel and fumes from aging vehicles steadily wafted into the polluted and hazy afternoon sky. To add insult to injury, impatient drivers, erratically turning their vehicle steering wheels in an attempt to escape the nightmare, continued to bump into other cars, creating fender benders here and there to the chagrin of law-abiding road users.

As we snaked our way forward, I kept looking around in all directions to see what was causing the hold-up but could not see any accident or obstacles on the way. It was all vehicles, old, new, rickety, heavy and light, heading towards Asaba. We were already at the bridge head when my epiphany occurred! The problem was the Niger Bridge itself!

I would use an hourglass analogy to describe to the reader what I saw. Imagine what happens when an hourglass, with grains of sand inside it, is placed on one end. Immediately, all the sand will start rushing downwards. But once they get to the constricted part of the hourglass, the downward movement of the sand slows down appreciably, almost to a halt. At that time, few grains of sand, at a time, start emerging slowly from the other side of the constriction. Just as the constricted part of an hourglass restricts the flow of sand because of the small opening at the constriction, so does the current Niger Bridge restrict the flow of traffic because the capacity of the bridge has become too small for the number of vehicles trying to go through it. The number of lanes on the bridge deck no longer matches the unbelievable number of vehicles competing for access through it.

Traffic bottleneck at the Niger bridge head.
Picture by Alfred Uzokwe

When we eventually got onto the bridge deck, I thought that the traffic would speed up a little but I was wrong. It was a bumper to bumper affair all the way. An aerial photography of the bridge, at the time, would have given the impression that it was a parking garage rather than a bridge. That, in itself, poses great danger to motorists.

Every bridge is designed to carry a certain amount of dead and live loads with some factor of safety. If this total load is exceeded and the factor of safety used up, that bridge becomes susceptible to failure. By allowing vehicles, both heavy and light to pile up on that bridge deck for hours and crawling slowly, we are pushing the envelope of its structural tolerance. Nigerian authorities may think that they have all the time in the world to continue playing politics with the second Niger Bridge project. With the way the current bridge is being stressed, they better think again. Not quite long ago, I used to visit Minnesota here in the United States three times a year or so on official duty. While there, I used to drive through the I-35 Bridge without thinking twice about it. It was a shock to me when that bridge came tumbling down, claiming the lives of many motorists. Of course the first thing that came to mind was that I could have been driving on it when that happened. Later, an investigation revealed that overloading was part of the reason why the bridge collapsed. If this could happen in Minnesota, then we need to worry for the Niger Bridge that rarely sees inspection and routine maintenance.

During a session that the Minister of Transportation had with Senate Committee on Works, she said that "maintenance records for the bridge were non-existent, since no maintenance had ever been carried out before the current intervention [*ThisDay*, Nov 5, 2008]. That says it all. A bridge whose capacity has now been oversubscribed traffic-wise has never even been maintained in the 40 years of its existence! Nigerians of goodwill must send unmistakable messages by phone, email and other means to the federal government that we can no longer accept the delay of a second Niger Bridge because the current one is an accident waiting to happen.

As it is today, the current bridge has a lot of problems. Some heavy vehicle drivers who use it have reportedly complained that it vibrates as they drive by. Bridges are designed to experience and absorb a certain amount of dynamic forces during use but when the movement becomes very pronounced, it is usually an indication of serious problems. Excessive movement of the structure, as occurs with the current bridge, has led to bolts loosening and coming off from gusset plates that hold the trusses together. It has even been reported that the concrete piers are showing signs of cracking and spalling. All these are indications that the bridge can no longer withstand the load that it is being forced to carry. If the government does not want to build another bridge, for the sake of the lives of motorists, they should inspect the bridge, determine what its residual strength is and rate it. Rating means assigning the maximum weight of vehicles that can safely use the bridge and then put a weight restriction on it. That will at least buy some time without putting the lives of people in danger. This will be silly to do, though, because that route is a major artery for commerce and if heavy vehicle drivers are deprived from using it, it will cause them a lot of hardship and increase cost of goods invariably.

Another issue that bothers me about the current bridge is the phenomenon called scour. A bridge over water is supported from under by a series of pillars called piers. The piers are founded below the river bed. As the river flows, depending on the speed of flow, sand and other sediments are gradually eroded from around and under the bridge piers. This is called scour. If the problem is not addressed, over time, substantial amounts of the sand could be scooped away from around and under the piers and make them unstable. Usually, most bridges built over water and with susceptibility to scour are inspected periodically by divers and remediated if need be. Now, the Niger Bridge spans a river and has piers. We have read that pier 2, one of the piers that support the Niger Bridge, now has a shallow caisson foundation. It was originally designed to stand on land (land pier) but because the Niger River has slightly changed course over the years, pier 2 is now inside water, in a shallow foundation, making it unstable. Need I say more about the urgency of a second Niger bridge? As if this was not trouble enough, during her session with the Senate Committee, Mrs. Madueke "said that the design and drawings of the bridge's substructure were missing"! [*ThisDay*, November 5, 2008] It is laughable that the drawings of an infrastructure of that magnitude and importance are missing and we are not ashamed to say so. In civilized nations, multiple copies of drawings of this import are made and archived in several locations. What happened here? Some again have cried sabotage but one is willing to call this ineptitude. The problem is that without the substructure drawings, trying to inspect that bridge and coming up, with certainty, how to remediate it will be problematic.

My contention here, as experts have also said, is that the Niger Bridge is getting old and being overloaded. Even Mrs. Madueke said it herself that "Further model simulation of the(bridge) trusses showed that some members (of the bridge trusses) were overstressed due to overloading.

It is not clear whether the second Niger Bridge has actually been designed but to truly serve its purpose, it must be designed to accommodate the chaotic traffic that streams towards Asaba from Onitsha every day. Provision must also be made for the expected surge in number of vehicles that will be using the bridge when the Asaba airport is completed. At a minimum, the bridge must have three lanes in each direction for a total of six lanes. Each lane must at least measure 12 feet or 3.6 meters and clearly delineated with raised pavement markers. There should be enough shoulder space on both sides of the deck for vehicles in distress to pull onto.

The statement by the Delta and Anambra state governments that they are pulling out of the project is the wrong one. Even if they do not have the money to contribute, they have other non-financial contributions to make. They should increase pressure on the federal government to get to work on this project. They should be in the forefront agitating for the project.

Hazardous Asbestos Ceilings are Health Hazards During Building Remodeling - October 29, 2007

Prices of building materials are rising in geometric progression making the construction of new buildings almost the exclusive preserve of the well-to-do. For example, the price of a bag of cement, in a very short time, rose from twenty naira to one thousand three hundred naira. The implication of this is not readily apparent until one considers that a teacher earns as little as 15 thousand naira a month! With one month's salary, a teacher can only afford as few as 10 bags of cement!

As a result of the above trend, the building sector is slowly experiencing a radical change. In lieu of the construction of new residential buildings, the average Nigerian now settles for rehabilitating existing ones. This is most prevalent in the villages where most people have older houses inherited from parents. Instead of demolishing the older houses to build new ones, they now settle for remodeling existing ones for far less money. Where a new one-story residential building could cost as much as 12 to 15 million naira to build, the rehabilitation of a comparable existing one-story building could cost as little as 2 to 3 million naira with new amenities like modern toilets and bathrooms and long span aluminum roofing sheets.

The issue of remodeling existing homes has brought with it a very unique challenge. Most homes built in Nigeria before the 1990s were built with asbestos ceilings. That was before Nigerians became aware of the negative health effects of asbestos. This situation is somewhat similar to what happened in the United States where asbestos materials were used for fireproofing buildings since the era of world war II. It was not until the seventies that the negative health effects became apparent. Till this day, many older buildings in the United States facing rehabilitation or demolition have asbestos. They are therefore subjected to remediation before demolition or rehabilitation. The same issue now confronts Nigerians when they decide to remodel existing buildings. Unsuspecting laborers are saddled with the job of going room by room and stripping the asbestos ceiling boards. There is usually a latent price to be paid by the laborers and I will explain below.

The process of removal of asbestos ceilings often entails yanking out the panels or saw-cutting through them and pulling them off the ceiling. As the panels are saw-cut, bits and pieces of the material become pulverized into fibers and float like powder in the air. In that state, the laborers doing the removal, as well as those observing the work, without the benefit of masks or other protective gears, continually inhale the fibers into their lungs. This was also the case when some of the ceiling panels were installed in the buildings many years ago during construction. Even though the panels came in standard sizes, sometimes, it was necessary for the workers to saw-cut the panels to fit irregular spaces in the ceiling. During that process, most inhaled the deadly fibers.

Asbestos fibers are harmful when inhaled over a period of time. Two major lung cancers - asbestosis and mesothelioma - have been linked to asbestos fiber inhalation. When the fibers are inhaled, they travel to the lungs and because they are not degradable, they stay there. After a while, sensing that foreign objects have invaded it, the lungs begin to make and secrete acid to "break down" the asbestos fibers. Instead of breaking down the asbestos particles, the acid begins to attack the lung tissues, commencing an irreversible lung damage that culminates in metastasis and cancer. The process takes place over a period of time so victims do not often know when the damaging health effect began.

In the USA, where the use of asbestos in buildings has basically been outlawed for years, the lingering effects of exposure can still be seen in the many asbestos-related deaths. A report published in 2004 by Medical News Today noted: "In the USA about ten thousand people die each year from diseases caused by asbestos." This is an alarming number for a nation that has taken positive steps to end the practice of using asbestos as an insulating material in buildings. One therefore wonders what the death statistics is in a developing country like Nigeria where most buildings have asbestos ceilings which were installed by unsuspecting workers without masks many years ago. Causes of deaths, from specific diseases, are not tracked and recorded in Nigeria. It will therefore be difficult to know the extent of havoc asbestos has caused in Nigeria. All we know is that there are many cases of pulmonary-related deaths but no one has been able to trace these deaths to the exact cause.

The problem of asbestos fiber inhalation does not only rest with the workers who do the removal of the asbestos boards or those who installed them years ago. During building remodeling, when workers saw-cut and yank out the asbestos panels, the fiber particulates float into the air and later settle like dust on the walls of the house being remodeled. If the walls of the house are not properly cleaned, it will be the turn of the occupants of the house to be exposed to asbestos.

The safest approach when remodeling an existing house that has asbestos ceiling boards is to hire the services of hazardous material (Hazmat) remediation experts. One is unsure of how many of these experts Nigeria currently has. Before they commence the removal of the asbestos panels, they encapsulate the enclosure with special drapes that preclude the escape of the fibers into the air. Some sophisticated experts, like those in the western world, have specialized equipment with a form of vacuum suction. As the asbestos panels are saw-cut and yanked out, fibers that float into the air are suctioned directly into the equipment and disposed of properly. Those doing the removal also have special oxygen masks they wear to protect themselves and avoid inhalation. At the end of the removal, the whole building is completely wiped down before remodeling work proceeds.

Critics, I am sure, would opine that the cost of this type of remediation would be too prohibitive, especially for someone trying to save money by remodeling an old house instead of building a new one. The question is: how much price are you willing to put on your life?

Open Letter to Governor Peter Obi of Anambra State about Substandard and Crumbling Infrastructure in Nnewi– January 28, 2011

This last Christmas period, I was in Nigeria and spent most of my time in Nnewi, Anambra State. I have been undertaking this pilgrimage of sorts for the past several years. The visits have enabled me to closely follow and monitor the pace and progress of development in the town. Many times, during my past visits, I have had cause to cheer because of positive developments, but at other times, I have had reasons to become concerned. This past Christmas, there were reasons to cheer but I also saw many opportunities for improvement. This is why I am writing.

First, it is worth noting, to the credit of your administration and the good people of Nnewi, that a town that was teetering on the verge of becoming a "no-go" area, security-wise, is gradually returning to normalcy. Although it is too early to say that the battle has been won, but most residents I chanced upon during my visit freely moved about their businesses, to banks, markets and social gatherings without palpable security concerns. Even churches held their Yuletide services in relative peace. Whatever steps your administration and the indigenes of the town put in place to make the town livable again should be lauded by all.

Other developments that warmed my heart include several erstwhile dusty and pothole-laden roads that have now been tarred. While there are more roads that need attention, the projects executed so far indicate that more will come.

Last year, I had the opportunity of seeing a master plan developed by UN-Habitat at the behest of your administration. The master plan is a blueprint for the infrastructural development and revitalization of the three major urban centers in Anambra State: Awka, Onitsha and Nnewi. When implemented, this has the potential of stemming the tide of urban sprawl and unplanned development that is creating pockets of slums in these towns. The development of that master plan is a very bold first move and one cannot wait for its implementation. I realize that because of the sheer size and complexity of the project, implementation will take years to complete. I am however hopeful that your administration will take steps to give legislative teeth to its implementation. That way, when your tenure expires, your successors will not abandon the plan as is common in Nigeria where change of administration often means change of priorities and abandonment of even good projects.

I could not help but observe, again to the credit of your administration, that several of the new road projects now have roadside drainage gutters. These gutters, as you know, play the important role of draining storm water or runoff away from roadways, preventing premature roadway failure. However, as an engineer, I was concerned that because the gutters are the open types, their effectiveness will be reduced or even stymied very soon. As I write, several of the gutters have already become repositories for debris and are half-full with banana peels, water plastic sachets, plastic bottles, wood chunks, rubber, burlaps, human waste, empty cans of beverages and other difficult to discern items. Once these open gutters fill up with debris, they become useless. When the rainy season comes, concentrated runoff that is supposed to flow into the gutters will by-pass them and start pooling on and around the roadways. Gradually, the standing water seeps into the roadbed, weakening it. As the roadway weakens, vehicle tires start depressing their path of travel, creating potholes. As the potholes widen, more runoff seeps into the subgrade and eventually start breaking up and washing out the asphalt.

Clogged open gutters also create health risks to the citizenry because the storm water they carry stagnates and become reservoirs for green, algae-laden, disease-infested and putrefying pools. The malaria parasite-carrying female anopheles mosquito thrives well in these types of stagnant water. Furthermore, as the organisms that breed in the stagnant water break down the contents of the gutters, toxic and noxious gases like sulfur and methane, both by-products of decomposition, are released into the air and cause health problems when inhaled.

From an engineering standpoint, the concealed underground pipe drainage system, although more difficult to clean out, is better. It is not only out of sight and so will not be a dumping ground for trash, it also lasts longer and does the job better. Sir, I am mindful of the unfortunate nature of the fact that residents have chosen to use gutters as repositories for trash. However, since there is as yet no practical way of enforcing good behavior within the ranks of the citizenry, keeping the gutters out of view will help deal with this problem. I am therefore suggesting that for the areas where open gutters already exist, long sections of removable concrete panels, interspersed with cast-iron inlet grates, should be used to cover them. The openings in the cast-iron grates will allow water to flow into the gutters but will keep out debris because of the closely spaced iron grates.

Open roadside gutter now clogged and useless – now a trash bin. Picture by Alfred Uzokwe

The long sections of reinforced concrete panels could be removed, when necessary, to clean out the gutters. For new road projects, I suggest underground pipe networks with intermittent inlets at curbsides.

Several times during my visit, I plied the Edo Ezemewi Road. This road is flanked on both sides by major banks in Nnewi. It used to be a tarred road but is currently characterized by the presence of ubiquitous potholes and craters. Cars routinely break down on the road because of its condition and then block the road for other motorists, creating traffic hold-ups. From my engineering judgment, the absence of drainage system must have contributed to the speedy crumbling and washing away of large sections of the asphalt. I suggest that your administration add this road to your rehabilitation priority list. I am also hopeful that work on the road will include the installation of a sound drainage system to make the road last longer.

Then, there is the old Nnewi-Oba Road. The section of this road in front of the Nnamdi Azikiwe Teaching Hospital is also pothole laden with large sections of the asphalt washed away, leaving craters that motorists frantically strive to avoid. I was astounded that storm water that pooled in some of the potholes during the rainy season had not dried out on the 23rd of December! That tells how deep these potholes are.

Consider that this is the roadway that leads to the Nnamdi Azikiwe Teaching Hospital where patients in medical distress are taken to in emergency. A seriously ill patient being conveyed to the hospital with all manners of galloping and jarring might become even worse before getting to the hospital. Furthermore, dust emanating from this road, as vehicles jockey past one another, settles on the exterior and interior of the hospital buildings. Sir, you very well know that filth, in the form of dust, is not good for a hospital where critical surgeries are routinely performed. There are other road projects that need attention but I just highlighted the above because of their critical locations and attendant importance.

Another problem along the old Nnewi-Oba Road, near the Teaching Hospital, is the issue of trash. There is a section where trash dumping is threatening the roadway itself. The trash bins located in the area have filled up and people have resorted to dumping trash on the bare ground. It has become an eyesore. Again, it is unfortunate that the presence of trash bins has not deterred people from dumping trash on the ground but here is my opinion: It may be that people dump trash on the ground because the bins are routinely full. In that case, provide more bins commensurate with the amount of trash generated in the area. Or, the frequency of removal of trash from the trash bins could be increased so that at every point in time, there will be space in the bins.

Thrash-dumping by the roadside next to the teaching hospital – an eyesore and public health issue. Picture by Alfred Uzokwe

Another issue that needs urgent attention is the persistent burning of trash along the new Oba-Nnewi–Okigwe Road, at the section referred to as "ugwu akpati ozu". Since 2004, every time one visited the town, mounds and mounds of trash would be seen burning along that road with plumes of smoke wafting upwards into the sky. A constant haze of dark grey cloud now hangs perpetually over the horizon. In fact, a review of satellite pictures over the area, taken by Google earth shows plumes of smoke in the southern part. Your Excellency, I realize that some of these issues are the responsibility of the Local Authority and the citizens but I am also aware that your administration has oversight jurisdiction and can make a huge difference by intervention. The health implication of people constantly inhaling by-products of thrash incineration makes this an issue that cannot wait another day for jurisdictional determination. Anecdotal evidence shows that cases of pulmonary diseases like asthma, COPD (Chronic Obstructive Pulmonary Diseases) and allergy are on the rise in Nnewi. We do not, as yet, have a specific scientific study linking trash incineration with the rise in pulmonary diseases but it is reasonable to assume that someone that breathes in methane and Sulphur on a daily basis will become susceptible to pulmonary ailments. I cannot count how many times, during my December visits, that I sat in a gathering where this issue came up. People are concerned for their health and will appreciate your coming to their aid on this issue.

Thrash burning creating health hazard. Picture by Alfred Uzokwe

Sir, you are aware that there has been an upsurge in the problem of erosion in the town. In some areas, erosion has started creating huge craters. 40 years ago, erosion was nearly not a major issue in the town. The town was forested and there were fewer buildings. Rainwater had sufficient pervious land mass to seep into. Also, many families dug and maintained what we called "umi" or rainwater catchment pits in the compounds. This was where excess rainwater (runoff) was channeled into. Furthermore, there were natural and manmade swales or "uzo ide" which were shallow channels along which storm water traveled without disruption of the whole landscape. That was then.

These days, because of population explosion and unbridled real estate development, the forests are gone and large portions of the landscape are occupied by buildings and road networks. The buildings create impervious areas that do not allow rain water to seep into the ground. As if that is not bad enough, most compounds today are paved with concrete or interlock pavers. The pavements are impervious to the infiltration of rain water. The result is that during storms, huge amounts of runoff are generated in the compounds and the water has nowhere to go but farmlands and roadways. In other words, runoff from these compounds flow out and merge with storm water from other compounds, increasing in amount and velocity. Increase in velocity of flow provides the force necessary to erode farmlands and roads. If practical steps are not taken to deal with this issue, huge craters will continue to develop and cause damage not just to the landscape, but to the roads that your administration is working hard to construct.

What am I hoping that your administration will do? Well, work with the local authority and citizens to put a practical policy in place to require that owners of paved compounds do the following:

Build underground catchment basins, within the compound, where runoff generated in the compound will flow into. The catchment basin is a hole dug in the ground. The top of the catchment basins will be covered with reinforced concrete panels with grated cast iron opening. Storm water flows into the basin through the iron grate inlets. The size of each basin will be directly proportional to the surface area of the paved area in the compound. Engineers in the Local Government council can help citizens calculate the size of catchment basin needed for each compound. The goal of this is simple, after each rain event, all runoff from each compound flows into the catchment basin located in that compound and gradually infiltrates into the ground.

Also, require that henceforth, before approval is granted for the construction of any new building, where the compound will be paved, the plan of a catchment basin must also be shown for attenuating the storm water generated within that compound. In the same light, mandate that residents no longer block manmade or natural swales or uzo ide.

Interlock pavers in a compound in Nnewi. Picture by Alfred Uzokwe

As you know, the good citizens of the town are responding to the clarion call by government to embark on self-help projects. They are establishing factories of all sorts and creating hundreds of employment opportunities. We appreciate the support your government has been giving to them. Clearly, because of the absence of a master plan and through no fault of the factory owners, several of the factories are located within residential neighborhoods. We welcome industrialization and in fact rejoice about it but it is clear that if waste by-products of the activities like chemicals and gases are not disposed of in a responsible manner, the lives of residents will be threatened. A majority of the factory owners seem to be practicing safe and responsible disposal of waste-products. If safe disposal is not practiced, liquid waste-products migrate into adjacent lands, slowly leach underground and with time harm farmlands and pollute ground water (bore hole). It is my fervent hope that guidelines for the disposal of waste by-products are being adhered to by existing and new factories.

Just as I was rounding up this letter, I read that your administration has set up Anambra State Road Maintenance Agency. This is the right step in the right direction. Even a well-built road is susceptible to wear and tear and if the wear and tear are caught on time and repaired, less money will be spent rebuilding from scratch.

Nnewi is a great town and we need to bequeath that greatness to the generation to come. One of the ways to achieve this is by implementation of your UN-Habitat master plan. I am optimistic that if that is done, much of the perpetual issues enumerated in this letter will be reduced appreciably. But while the modalities for implementation of the plan are being hashed out, something that will take a while, it is my fervent hope that you will give urgent consideration to attending to the issues outlined above. Like I stated earlier, I realize that jurisdiction over the remediation of some of these issues may reside with the local authority and even citizens. However, regardless of who has jurisdiction, I am hoping that with your administration in the lead, these issues that are threatening to stagnate the holistic development of a burgeoning and boisterous town will be arrested. Nnewi needs you.

Unreliable Power Supply and its Negative Ramifications on Nigeria-December 17, 2007

One of the major aspects of General Obasanjo's manifesto, as he ascended the office of the presidency in 1999, was that he was going to fix the problem of "epileptic" power supply. As part of Obasanjo's effort to make good his promise, or so Nigerians thought, he handed over the responsibility of power generation and distribution to an outfit called Power Holdings (PHCN). Unfortunately, eight years after the promise of constant electricity was made, the situation has worsened! Throughout the period I was in Nigeria, in 2006 for the Christmas holidays, I do not recall any day that we had electricity from the so-called Power Holdings for more than a few minutes. The irony was that they never wavered in sending in bills for non-existent power usage. If you failed to pay up, they would gladly send their foot soldiers to "cut your light". For me, it was a very miserable experience.

I had gone straight home from Lagos, after arriving Nigeria, because I wanted to temporarily escape the hustle and bustle of city life and have some serenity for a change. That turned out to be a pipe dream for me because even in my village, every evening, individual electric generating plants hummed all over the place until the wee hours of the night. The annoying humming sounds were complemented by thick clouds of black smoke, streaming upwards into the evening skies, adulterating and fouling one of the loveliest gifts that nature bestowed on mankind- clean air to breathe.

General Obasanjo made unplanned and unmanaged effort to revamp electricity generation in the country. It is a shame that after wastefully disbursing billions of taxpayer money, raising the collective hope of Nigerians that the monster of epileptic power supply would be tamed, in the final analysis, he threw up his hands with no substantive accomplishment. In a feeble attempt to justify why he failed, he told surprised Nigerians that at the time of his inauguration, when he made the promise of constant power supply, he was not fully aware of the enormity of the problems involved. Inotherwords, if he had understood the magnitude of the problems, he would not have made the promise.

Nigerians were surprised because the statement was coming from a man that was once the head of state for three years or so. Seeing that Nigerians were not buying his flimsy excuse, he followed it with another one. He told a bewildered populace that some people were sabotaging his efforts and as such he was not able to meet the electric generating goals he set for himself and the nation at the time of his first inauguration. Sadly, therefore, Obasanjo left office with the situation worse than he met it. That was then, this is now.

Nigeria's change of guard, at the helm, has been in effect for almost 7-months now. The man that stepped into Obasanjo's shoes also promised, at the time of his inauguration, to solve the problem of electricity supply. He sounded more serious about solving the problem than Obasanjo did. He told Nigerians that he was going to declare a state of emergency in the energy sector if nothing meaningful was done to correct electric supply problem. By declaring a state of emergency, he would have the authority to enlist the help of any competent outfit, including foreign nationals, to solve the problem. Unfortunately, seven or more months after President Yar'Adua's inauguration, the situation in the electricity sector has remained the same. The so-called Power Holding is the same as National Electric Power Authority (NEPA). Infact, people have argued that this outfit is worse. I recently read a news report that there was power blackout in the government house in Anambra State! This goes to tell how bad things have become in this sector under Yaradua.

Inspite of Yar'Adua's seeming failure in this sector, Nigerians have, until now, continued to look towards him and hope that he would do something dramatic. His latest pronouncement about the issue shows that he is gradually going the way of Obasanjo. A few weeks ago, Power Holdings (PHCN) told Nigerians that the problem of power outages would possibly continue. They blamed it on sabotage by faceless ghosts! Then came the bombshell: the man that Nigerians were hoping would fix the problem, president Umar Yaradua, "attributed the incessant blackouts in the country to the handiwork of a cabal sabotaging government's efforts at revamping the energy sector" *[Daily Champion, December 9, 2007].* Yaradua is telling Nigerians the same story that Obasanjo told them for which he failed to perform. The Federal government wanted an excuse to advance or someone to blame for giving up. They have found it in the idea of the existence of saboteurs. Now instead of spending time to look for meaningful ways to solve the power problem, they are spending valuable time looking for a "cabal". It is true that vandals do wreak havoc on public utilities. Even in advanced countries, they vandalize electric poles, guard rails and items they sell as scrap. What these countries do is institute a stiff penalty for such offences and put the police on alert. They do not go looking for a "cabal" to blame for their ineptitude.

Before going further with this treatise, it is important that I restate the obvious effect of government inability to provide constant electricity for the citizens.

The absence of constant electricity is seriously inhibiting the ability of Nigeria to attract foreign industries that heavily depend on electric energy to get their products out. It is ironic that would-be industrialists now take their businesses to more electrically stable countries like Ghana. The Rawlings-tamed Ghana is waxing stronger in all aspects of national development for it. As I write, many Nigerians are now establishing businesses in Ghana, building factories and private mansions there. Some even send their children to boarding schools there because the schools have better amenities, constant supply of electricity and a more conducive environment for studying. This is ironic because I still remember the late seventies to early eighties in Nigeria when Ghanaians left their country in droves to come to Nigeria because of joblessness. Then you could find Ghanaian college graduates working as bricklayers and many of their womenfolk settled inexorably in places like Lagos, doing jobs they would normally not do, just to survive. Now, because of proper and better planning, which included constant electricity, Ghana has reversed that trend and Nigerians are running over there. If Nigeria is serious about solving the problem of electricity supply, there are many experts in that field both in and outside Nigeria that could be brought in to help.

Another effect of epileptic power supply in Nigeria is that those factories that have decided to stay in the country now invest in expensive but reliable power generating plants. They try to recoup the business cost of the plants by hiking up the prices of their goods. No wonder why many "made-in-Nigeria" goods cost so much that one does not see the benefit of local production. It is those at the lowest rung of the economic ladder that suffer the brunt of the effect of steep prices of goods. For example, the commonest commodity that Nigerian factories churn out in all forms is the so-called "pure water" whether bottled or in plastic sachets. These items are not as cheap as one would expect considering that they are bottled in Nigeria. Talk to any of the proprietors of the local factories and they will tell you how much money they sunk into the generating plants they use as well as what it costs to maintain them.

Look at the aluminum-extruding factories that produce the long span corrugated aluminum roofing sheets used for roofing in Nigeria. They no longer rely on Power Holding (PHCN) for electric supply, instead, they have huge power plants in their premises to do the needed work. The generators cost millions of naira and they have to recoup the costs by hiking the prices of the aluminum roofing sheets. One is not saying that the steep prices are all the result of investment in generators but it certainly has a huge effect. This same problem has succeeded in fizzling out small scale to medium scale factories. Since they cannot afford large-scale generating plants for their businesses, they rely on Power Holding. After many cases of power failure with attendant destruction of production equipment because of power surges, they pack up the businesses. This is a national shame.

The environment has suffered greatly because of unreliable electric supply. Individual and factory-owned generators that litter the landscape, blanket the air with toxic fumes. People breathe in these fumes, day and night, and we wonder why all manners of respiratory illnesses have increased exponentially. Apartment dwellers even have portable generators. They place them on their balconies so that robbers cannot reach them. In a six-flat apartment, you could find as much as six different generators! Some of them are so old that once they come on, the surrounding air is immediately filled with black smoke. The toxic fumes find their way into bedrooms and other sleeping places at night. There have been many cases where families were found dead in the morning because they operated generators placed too close to their sleeping quarters.

The quality of education in Nigeria is indirectly being affected by the absence of constant electricity in schools. In the world of today, the internet has become an integral part of education and access to the internet is dependent on electricity. A kid with constant access to the internet will be able to conduct research and pull up information about so many aspects of education. I read about governors "donating" computers to schools. This is good but the million dollar question is: with what electricity will they make full use of the computers when generators are turned on around 6:30 PM daily and turned off by 9:30PM? To make full use of the computers, as well as the internet, the kids need all day access.

There are other areas where the absence of constant electricity is doing a lot of harm to Nigeria and Nigerians. Hospitals depend on instruments like ultra sound, kidney dialysis machines, CT scan equipment and more to save lives. These instruments are powered by electricity and so it is imperative that a constant source of electricity is provided in all hospitals. We've heard about cases where patients were turned away from certain hospitals because the generator broke down and certain life-saving services could not be offered.

It is surprising that the Yaradua government has started throwing up its hands about epileptic power supply. If there truly exists a cabal that is sabotaging the energy sector, and the government knows those involved, why can't the government move in and have all the culprits arrested and tried while plowing ahead with solving the problem at hand?

What now for Nigerians? This Christmas period, many will be headed to Nigeria from all over the globe and all works of life. They will go in to face another Christmas period of constant humming of generators and poisoning of their lungs. They will face an uncomfortable Christmas period where you sweat through the night and suffer sleeplessness because you cannot operate a simple fan to alleviate the December heat. They will go through another Christmas unable to do the things that people on vacation do to make it worthwhile. In this day and age, this is not what Nigerians should be experiencing.

I insist that Nigeria has tons of experts that could help untangle the mess of electric supply. We must not continue to wallow in constant blackouts. The Yaradua government should know that the stakes, as outlined above, are just too high for this problem to be left as it is. Yaradua must begin to match his seeming uprightness with substantive action that includes providing constant electricity in Nigeria. Many of the general problems he has to grapple with, like joblessness and the like, will significantly fade away if he lives up to his promise of providing constant electricity.

Industrial Buildings in Residential Neighborhoods May Be Posing Health Risks – November 5, 2001

Recently, the Nigerian Institute of Architects released a communiqué urging the Federal Government to mandate the development of master plans for all cities and rural areas in Nigeria. They also proposed the imposition of sanctions on companies whose activities are detrimental to the environment.

A master plan is the blue print by which a city, municipality or suburban area is built. It is developed after a careful study of the environment with particular attention to the landscape and socio-economic make up of potential inhabitants of the area. A master plan subdivides a city or rural area into a series of mapped zones with each zone assigned a use. The zones are typically residential zones, multifamily residential zones, commercial zones, industrial zones and more.

The absence of master plans for most cities and rural areas in Nigeria is the reason why industrial buildings are found in areas where residential buildings exist. Most industrial buildings or factories produce waste which is the incidental by-product of the industrial activity. Some of the wastes come in solid form, some in liquid form while others come in the vapor form. Some of the wastes may be harmless but others are harmful to humans, plants or organisms. Because of poor environmental regulation, some of the factory owners discharge the wastes right into the environment where they are located without pretreating it to minimize or remove toxicity. The vaporized wastes are discharged into the air. When the factories are located in residential neighborhoods, people breathe in the fumes all day with attendant health consequences that include respiratory diseases like asthma, COPD, lung cancer and allergy. If cigarette smoke is adjudged to be hazardous to health, and has been linked to thousands of cases of lung cancer, one cannot discount the potential lethality of industrial fumes especially when the factory building is in the person's backyard.

The liquid wastes are sometimes discharged into adjacent land or onto swales and they slowly seep into the ground, destroying farmlands by starving them of essential nutrients for plants and the ecosystem. Where boreholes are located, they slowly seep in, affecting the quality of water again with attendant health implications.

Not long ago, someone I designed a residential building for had to travel home to the village in Nigeria to commence construction. The building was to be constructed on the land which he inherited by birth from his parents. When he got home and walked over to the site the next morning, he discovered that a new single-story building had been erected next to his land. He could hear a constant humming sound emanating from the general direction of the building. On a closer look, he noticed that a chimney stack, unobtrusively tucked into a corner of the building, protruding through the long span aluminum roof, was emitting plumes of dark-colored smoke. In his words, "you would occasionally see plumes of smoke coming out of a chimney unobtrusively tucked into the side of the factory building during the day". He later found out that the building was a small-scale factory.

According to the client, he does not know if the fumes are toxic or not but he noticed that the leaves of the cassava plants behind the building were all unusually brownish in color. He surmised that the cassava plants were whittling away because of the fumes or the wastewater that was being discharged from the building into the adjacent farmland. He changed his mind about building his family house next to the building because he wanted to err on the side of caution. Currently, he is looking for a different parcel of land to build his family house on. The question that begs for answer is why a factory should be built in a residential neighborhood. Did the building go through review by the local government and duly approved? One could aver that if a master plan existed that zoned the area purely residential, the owner of the building would be breaking the law by building a factory, no matter how small, in the area and could be prosecuted, fined or the building demolished. But because of the absence of a master plan delineating land use, it would be difficult to push a case against the factory owner.

In discussing this issue with a contemporary of mine, he felt that my client was crying wolf. He went on to say that many people in Nigeria live in family houses near industrial buildings but "have not all died!" This underscores the mindset that makes it difficult to institute positive change in Nigeria. Because my contemporary has not specifically seen people dying because of inhalation of toxic fumes emitted by factories, he does not feel that this is an issue. Yet, in Nigeria today, there has been an unprecedented upsurge in respiratory diseases that were hitherto unheard of in the country. Commonsense simply dictates that when a human is constantly breathing in fumes that are by products of factory production, it can never be healthy.

In the villages, this issue of zoning is made somewhat difficult by the fact that people tend to make the argument that they could build what they want on their land. That may be so but the good of the majority should always supersede that of the individual. That is why we have the doctrine of eminent domain where the government can take a land considered needed for public good. Also, one realizes that industries create jobs and help minimize the issue of unemployment in the nation. However, we must not do that at the peril of the lives of inhabitants of our great country. The call by the Nigerian Institute of Architects for mandating master plans for cities and even rural areas is in order and should be implemented. It is equally important to have laws that sanction those who flout the land use zoning or discharge industrial wastes into the air or land where they should not.

Nigerians in rural communities should become more aware of what is happening where they live or want to build residential buildings. Ask questions about the industries located too close to where you live like: Is this factory permitted to be located there? If so, what does the industry manufacture or produce? What are the by-products and wastes and are they toxic? Where are the wastes discharged? Did any environmental regulation agency visit the site and given the okay?

PART 4
Aviation

Nigeria Needs a National Airline -May 2, 2005

Douglas(not his real name) is a hard-working Nigerian living in the United States. He was forced to take up a job as a nursing assistant in one of the hospices close to his apartment. This was after an exhaustive but fruitless search for work in his area of expertise. He hoped to save up some money and eventually bring his wife and their two young sons over to the United States. He was also looking forward to a time when he could bring over his aging parents for a visit. It would be an opportunity to get a doctor to attend to the nagging rheumatism that had debilitated his mother for a while, he felt.

The slim-built and gap-toothed man had just returned from work three hours earlier and was now sound asleep on his sofa bed. Suddenly, the shrill sound of the telephone sliced through the silence of the night like a knife would an apple. At the third ring, he blearily raised his head and peered in the direction of the wall clock. The bright stream of light emitted by the incandescent ring of neon light around the perimeter of the clock temporarily blinded him. He rubbed his eyes and looked again. As his tired eyes began to get used to the ray of pink-colored light, the numbers on the clock became clearer. He noticed that the long hand of the clock lazily idled over the number ten while the short hand rested over the number two. Ten minutes to two in the morning. Who must be calling at this ungodly time of the night? He wondered. The phone was not letting up though. The ear-piercing sound propagated in every direction of the room, bouncing back towards him and in the process scuttling any attempt he was making to ignore the sound and get back to sleep.

Rubbing his eyes again, Douglas rolled out of bed and sauntered towards the phone. It was balanced on the stool next to the lamp stand. He grudgingly picked it up. "Hello", he crooned in a very raspy voice. There was an eerie silence at first, but then the near-trembling voice of the man on the other end responded, "The unthinkable has happened", the man said. Douglas' heart missed a beat and then began to race at what seemed like a thousand miles per minute. He composed himself, or so he thought, and then asked, "Who is speaking and what happened?"

155

The emotionally laden voice responded, "Father is in the mortuary". The bones in his body seemingly began to crumble just as his knees began to cave in. Involuntarily, he sank onto the bare but carpeted floor and thus began an ordeal that would pose to him the greatest challenge he had ever encountered in his life. He had just been informed, by a close relative, of the unexpected demise of his father in Nigeria. The man also told him that his father would be buried in four weeks in accordance with the native tradition. The burial time frame did not leave him with much time to make any planning. He was certain of one thing though: he was going to be in Nigeria to pay his final respects to his father, a man he adored in life and would miss dearly.

The fog of the whole nightmare had not completely dissipated in the morning when Douglas decided to temporarily shed the grief that had engulfed him and start making some important decisions. First, he called his office and asked for some time off. With that out of the way, he directed his attention to the next important task - that of purchasing an air ticket for his travel. With tears still coming down his cheeks intermittently, he began to place calls to several airlines. He was trying to get the best deal there was for his proposed journey to Nigeria. By the time he went half way with the calls, he began to doubt whether he was going to be able to afford the airfare. The prices that he was getting from the airlines were very exorbitant. Some quoted airfares as high as three thousand dollars with the least price pegged at two thousand two hundred dollars!

By the end of the whole exercise, it was clear to Douglas that he could not afford the amount of money that the airlines were asking from him. He had already earmarked his next paycheck for funeral expenses and with very little money in the bank, the only option he now had was to fall back on his credit card, which thankfully had a limit of $4000. He was going to charge the ticket with his card and pay gradually when he returned from Nigeria.

Eventually, he settled with the airline that gave him the lowest fare of two thousand two hundred dollars. The lady on the other end of the line took his particulars and after punching them into the computer, she began to read his itinerary to him. "You will depart from your city on flight xyz and head to Chicago. There will be a three-hour layover in

Chicago after which you will board another plane, flight xyz. The plane is an airbus and will take you into Europe the next day. Your final leg of the journey to Nigeria will begin four hours after you touch down in Europe and airbus flight xyz will be your carrier."

As the lady rattled off Douglas' itinerary, he was bothered by the amount of layover time he had to spend in-between flights, especially in Europe. At this point, he thought about the seeming equivocation of the Nigerian government in establishing a national carrier or at least commissioning an established airline to fly directly to the country. If Nigeria had her own airline, just like it had Nigeria Airways in the 80s, why would he be flying around the world and spending an inordinate amount of time in Europe, just to get to Lagos? He could easily have boarded a direct flight from New York or Atlanta to Lagos. It was very unnerving for him but he had no choice.

Douglas thought that his biggest headache was the fact that he had to travel through Europe and spend needless time in the airport there. He was therefore unprepared for the next shocker he was to face. When he told the airline lady that he was going to pay with his credit card, the lady demurred and then said, "We cannot accept credit card. You will need to go to the closet travel agent or go to the airport and pay with cash or check". He was dumbfounded. He tried to protest but saw that it was leading to nowhere so he asked the lady for the name of the closest travel agent. He was asking for the information, knowing that he had no way of raising the amount of cash that was involved.

With the address of the travel agent in hand, it was time to decide how the cash for his fare would be raised. After ruminating the issue for a while, he decided not to swallow phlegm in the name of decorum and called some of his friends. In the end, they were able to raise some money with which he paid for his ticket. He continued to wonder why he could not use his credit card to buy his airfare just like he could do if he were traveling somewhere other than Nigeria. This would not be happening, he felt, if Nigeria had a national carrier of its own. An airline that would depart the United States via New York or Atlanta and head straight for Nigeria. Clearly, if Nigeria had a national carrier, most of the airlines that treat her citizens like dirt, knowing that they have no choice, will be compelled to compete for the business of her citizens.

They would be forced to treat Nigerian citizens with dignity. The above is reason enough for Nigeria, Douglas felt, to expedite action on the deal with Virgin Atlantic to provide direct flights to Nigeria from overseas countries.

On the day of Douglas' departure, he drove the short distance to the local airport and then at check-in, after reviewing his documents, the lady behind the counter went over his itinerary while looking over his passport. Suddenly, a worried expression enveloped her face. There is no transit visa on your passport", she said. "That's right", Douglas responded. "I am not stopping anywhere. I am going to Nigeria". "Your flight will stop over in Europe. You need a transit visa or the immigration officials over there will not let you into the airport." Douglas could not believe what he was hearing. "When did this start?" he asked, half screaming at the woman. Obviously, the lady was unaware of the pain he was going through since learning of the sudden death of his father. Again, he re-iterated the fact that he was not stopping over the European city by choice and had no business there. "Sir," the woman said with emphasis, "the policy is that any passenger that will stop over in this European city needs a transit visa unless the passenger carries an American passport." "Even if the passenger is merely changing planes in the city and not setting foot on the soil?" He asked. "Yes", the woman said. At this point, Douglas had become sick of the run-around he was getting.

"What do I do now?" he asked the lady as he dabbed the tears that had involuntarily gathered in the corner of his eyes "I am afraid you will need to get a transit VISA". He began to explain his circumstance to the lady. She showed some sympathy but maintained that she could not flout the airline rule and that even if she let him go through, he would not be allowed to go through the European city. Slowly, he started removing his bags, which had already been loaded on the weigh scale. He placed them on a trolley and dejectedly started in the direction of the airport ground transportation. He was headed back to his apartment disappointed.

The next day, after obtaining the transit visa for which he was denied travel earlier, Douglas called up the airline and asked for a change in his travel date. For a fee, the airline assigned a new travel date to him. He had to use part of the money intended for the funeral to offset the unanticipated expense.

On the day of his travel, he first flew to Chicago O'Hare airport. Two hours later, he boarded a wide-bodied aircraft and 8 hours after that, his plane touched down in Europe. After the customary activities that usually follow the touch-down of an aircraft, they began disembarkation. He would now have to board another aircraft for the third and final leg of his journey to Nigeria.

As soon as he stepped out of the airplane and into the transit airport lounge, he met a long line of people. They were passengers who had disembarked before him. When he looked further down the line, he noticed that they were lined up in front of two immigration officers. The immigration officials asked for each passenger's passport, reviewed it and then handed it back to the passenger. When it came to his turn, one of the immigration officials, a man of no more than 26 years, took his passport from him and immediately whipped out a magnifying glass from his pocket. The man began to examine the portion of the passport where his picture was. Soon after, he moved the magnifying glass to the section that bore the transit visa and started looking it over, occasionally raising his head to look at Douglas. He kept wondering if this was happening to him because he was a Nigerian. He had earlier noticed that passengers who had passports from other nations spent less time in front of the man. He did not feel that travelers should be treated that way, especially when they were involuntarily stopping over in the country. It would have been a different case, he thought, if he were coming into that country specifically for a visit. In that case, the immigration would be at liberty to look him over as much as they wanted. All he wanted was to travel to Nigeria and be with his grieving mother and then pay his final respects to his father.

Douglas could not understand what the man was trying to find. He understood that 9-11 gave unfettered rights to countries to scrutinize travelers but what he was witnessing was the extreme, he felt. "If Nigeria had a national carrier, this insult would not be taking place", he muttered under his breath. "Were you talking to me?" the immigration official said in a heavily accented English as he finally handed his passport to him, "No", Douglas lied and walked away. He headed for the duty-free shop to look around and "kill" some time since the Nigeria-bound plane would not be taking off immediately. He hated spending all these hours in transit but had to deal with it. By the time he was done looking around and filling up his stomach, boarding time was only an hour away so he set out for his assigned boarding gate.

As he approached the boarding gate area, he noticed that a man that looked like an airport security official was addressing passengers who were lined up behind the boarding counter. He was telling them that once their boarding passes were taken from them, they would go into a cordoned off lounge and stay until the door to the airplane was opened. At that time, they would have to board the plane. He warned that once a passenger was in the cordoned off lounge area, he would not be allowed back into the general lounge area.

Douglas glanced around, specifically looking at other boarding gate areas. He did not see any cordoned off areas next to those gates. Why were Nigeria-bound passengers being subjected to a two-tier security check and then confined to a cordoned off lounge? Was there something special about Nigeria-bound passengers that he did not know? He wondered.

After standing in the line for a while without appreciable movement, Douglas decided to go to the front and find out why it was so slow. There, he noticed that people who were carrying two hand baggage were being asked to hand over one, regardless of the sizes.

One of the passengers was protesting to the lady behind the counter. "You are treating us this way because we are Africans". "I am merely doing my job", the lady said. "These bags you are taking away from us were all duly checked, went through security and allowed at our point of departure in the United States. The bag you took away from me contains a few harmless but perishable things as well as my hygiene items. The one you left me with contains my baby's diapers and his food items. Why are you doing this?" The woman asked angrily. The lady behind the counter did not respond but merely placed a red tag on the hand luggage she took away and put it amongst the pile of bags that had accumulated there.

"Look at how you people cordoned off this boarding lounge with metals, refusing to allow people out even if they had to use the bathroom, unless they were willing to go through boarding checking again. How come passengers going to other countries, who went through security like the rest of us, are moving about freely in the general lounge and do not have cordoned off areas next to their boarding gates? And you say you are doing your job?" the woman further asked. The lady pretended not to hear her.

As Douglas listened to the above conversation, he felt that the angry Nigerian was actually speaking for all the Nigerian passengers there. In most other airports, once you go through security and get into the boarding lounge, where all the boarding gates were located, you were free to move around, buy things from duty-free shops or use the bathrooms. In this case, they were being confined to a cordoned off lounge as if they were animals. Was it all because of September 11, 2001, or had someone found an opportunity to mistreat Africans in Europe? He wondered.

Three hours after Douglas entered the European airport, the Nigeria-bound aircraft finally departed, with him on board. Before drifting into a restless sleep, he hoped that someone would bring the plight of Nigeria-bound passengers, in Europe, to public attention. It is unconscionable, he felt, that they should ask passengers to obtain transit visas just to fly through their country. Then they treat them like animals at their airports.

The remedy for the above embarrassment for Nigerians, Douglas thought, was for Nigeria to quickly consummate the deal with Virgin Atlantic or any other airline to provide direct flights from the United States to Nigeria. That way, Nigeria-bound passengers would be spared the agony of passing unpleasant time in European countries that they had not asked to visit or spending unnecessary time in transit. A direct flight from New York to Lagos would take less than 8 hours. Going through Europe, the passenger has to be willing to spend 20 to 24 hours on the whole. That is sad. Sad indeed.

Danger Lurking In Our Skies
- November 9, 2009

About a week ago, I read about the reaction of the passengers of a chartered aircraft that was conveying the governor of Akwa Ibom State from Calabar to Lagos in Nigeria. Here is how the incident was reported by the Director of Protocol of the state governor: "the aircraft took off at the Calabar Airport en route Port Harcourt to Lagos. As we were going above the airspace in Port Harcourt, which is the air route, we began to experience a sudden drop of about 5000 feet in a split of a second and from there problems started and we tried to go up and all to no avail. It was madness and everybody on board after that experience fell ill and the air hostess collapsed on the floor of the aircraft." [Daily Independent Online, October 31, 2009].

The surprise that this writer feels is not the fact that the aircraft lost 5000 ft of altitude in the split of a second. While abnormal, it does happen. Certainly, my surprise is not the fact that an air hostess, collapsed. Again, while that is not normal, she is certainly human and that may have been her first time in that type of situation. What is not normal is what caused the sudden drop in altitude of the aircraft. The co-pilot explained to the governor that, "while we were flying at about 24,000 ft above sea level, there was an aircraft which was above us which was coming towards Calabar. The aircraft decided to descend, and it was descending right inside our aircraft. At about 400 meters to our aircraft", the co-pilot further explained, "we made a mad descent because the upcoming plane was a bigger one, and was faster than ours. We were once again advised to go up and in that process, the plane got stalled and we had a free fall until the engine came up again." [Daily Independent Online]

The questions here are many but the most important one is this: Does this near-miss constitute an anomaly or is it something that pilots of aircrafts over our airspace have come to expect? Do airline passengers have to become concerned that every time they fly in our supposedly friendly skies they are gambling with their lives? Is there a latent danger lurking in the skies over our beloved nation? Though an accident was averted, many things could have gone wrong. A head-on collision could have occurred and lives lost in both crafts. Furthermore, the preemptive acrobatic maneuver that the pilot engaged in to avoid the oncoming aircraft could have resulted in complete and irreversible stalling of the engine, leading to a crash and attendant loss of lives.

I would like to believe that our skies are completely safe but considering the near- miss stories we read about all the time and notable crashes like the Bellview aircraft crash in October 2005, the Sosoliso crash of December 2005 and the ADC flight 53 crash of October 2006, one is truly concerned. My concern becomes even more heightened by the fact that the co-pilot of the plane ferrying the Akwa Ibom governor explained that a critical instrument that all aircrafts are supposed to have onboard, to detect impending collisions, are either lacking in some aircrafts or are not functional. Essentially, some of the pilots are flying blind! What is the Nigerian Airspace Management Agency (NAMA) doing about this malady or is the agency waiting for another crash before action? For the avoidance of doubt, this type of issue already caused an aircraft accident in Nigeria in November of 1996. The pilot of a Boeing 727 jet could not regain control of the jetliner after it took some maneuvers to prevent a mid-air collision. The jet went down at Ejirin and took with it 143 lives! Now, is this what we want in the skies over Nigeria?

Talking about flying blind, it did not help matters that a few days before the incident involving the aircraft that the governor of Akwa Ibom was in, the chairman of the board of directors of NAMA, Alhaji Kawu Baraje, told Nigerians that the Total Radar Coverage of Nigeria (TRACON) project was 95% complete. This is a project meant to cover every inch of airspace with radar to make the skies safer. He explained that the era of pilots flying blind was over. Alhaji Baraje felt that he was breaking good news to Nigerians but he was actually alarming them when he indicated that some areas are yet to be covered. The question this brings up is whether any of the accidents or near-misses we hear of, over Nigerian air space, may have been the result of this radar insufficiency or gap? Is anyone investigating to find that out? With the way Nigeria operates, where the government gives assurances that never come to fruition, how can one even be sure that the 95% radar coverage assurance is much of an assurance to believe in? These questions need to be answered to ensure that Nigerians would have rest of mind as they board aircrafts in the country.

The near mishap of the governor's airplane should be a wakeup call for NAMA to live up to expectation. It is important that all aircrafts are subjected to the right level of scrutiny to ensure that they not only carry the necessary flying instrumentation but that all onboard instrumentation are functioning at all times. Also, a very important part is pilot training for professional competence. Hiring a pilot from overseas does not automatically translate into competency. There are crappy pilots in Australia, USA, Britain, South Africa and the likes. Pilot records must be fully examined and needed flying hours reached before being unleashed into the Nigerian skies. Furthermore, the idea of a flight attendant collapsing is one for the records! It tells this writer that the flight attendant was not adequately prepared for the job. A flight attendant plays an invaluable role outside of food service. In most aircraft disasters where some passengers survived, there is always a correlation between the survival rate and the stoic resolve of flight attendants to guide passengers. If a flight attendant has to collapse, what would the passengers do, all die before the mishap occurs? This reminds me of the story of a man that resolved to be present at the birth of his first child. When his wife went into labor, he was called into the labor room and asked to hold and encourage his wife. When the spasms began and the woman started groaning, the man fainted and crumpled onto the floor. His wife had to ask the doctor to go and take care of her husband first.

Flight attendants should be well trained to withstand the stress and help douse tension in an aircraft cabin when things go awry. This writer has observed that as soon as there is sign of trouble in an aircraft, passengers start looking at the flight attendants for a clue regarding the seriousness of the event. If they look calm, that energy is translated into the passengers but if they look panicky, the passengers will panic too. A cool and calm attendant ensures that there is orderly evacuation in the event of a mishap and could mean saving of more lives.

Nigeria's Minister of Aviation, Babatunde Omotoba, has now put the blame of the near-miss on an Air Traffic controller. He explained that the Air Traffic Controller "mistakenly asked the two aircrafts involved to descend and ascend to the same 21,000 feet"[AllAfrica.com]. One hopes that this is not a case of passing the buck to a defenseless air traffic controller. There should be a thorough investigation to get to the bottom of what happened and emplace appropriate remedial and punitive measures.

As all manners of airports keep springing up in Nigeria, a welcome development one must say, strict adherence to all aviation safety rules, in the construction of runways and taxiways, emplacement of all necessary ground instrumentation and the training of air traffic controllers, must be sine qua non.

In the final analysis, the question that must be answered by NAMA is clear: Are our skies safe? Is there a latent or clear and present danger lurking in our skies, waiting to unfold at unsuspecting passengers? Does the absence of 100% radar coverage for all of Nigeria put aviation and passengers at risk? Do we have in place stringent policies for determination of competent pilots for the Nigerians skies? Do we enforce the emplacement of the right instrumentation on board to avert the type of near mishap that occurred over Port Harcourt skies? The time to honestly answer these questions is now.

Unfriendly Experience With Delta Airlines
On A Visit To Nigeria - January 28, 2008

A few days to Christmas of 2007, I left my house to board a Delta flight at the Harrisburg International airport. The flight was to take me to Lagos Nigeria via Atlanta Georgia. I departed my house at exactly 9:00AM even though the flight was to leave by 12:00 noon; I just did not want to take any chances.

The previous week, a colleague of mine who traveled the same route and with Delta airlines, had left a message for me saying that if I wanted to carry any excess bag, I should go to the airport with some money to pay for the excess baggage. According to him, he was made to pay for every pound and every baggage he was carrying beyond the allowable. As a result, several days before my departure, I went to Delta website and reviewed their luggage policy. A message on the site stated that a passenger was entitled to 2-bags free of charge. The caveat was that each bag must weigh 50 pounds or less. It also stated that each passenger was entitled to a carryon baggage not to exceed a certain size and weight. The website confirmed, to my utmost delight, that Delta also accommodated excess baggage. Each excess baggage weighing 50 pounds or less would be charged a $125 excess baggage fee. After reading through the website, I decided to travel with a total of three bags, all weighing 50 pounds or less. For the third bag, which would house the many gifts I was saddled with, I would pay the excess baggage cost of $125.

My wife and I got to the Harrisburg airport about twenty minutes after nine and I quickly disembarked and unloaded my bags. Because we could not park in front of the airport for obvious security reasons, I requested that she circle around the airport a few times with the car, verify that I had successfully checked in before driving back home. She had her cell phone at the ready to call me and vice versa. Inside the airport, I went straight to the Delta checking counter. Two ladies were already behind the counter. One of them explained that I could use the computer system to self-check myself in. I promptly swiped my card and got down to business, punching in the necessary information that the system was requesting of me. Things were going smoothly until Lagos popped up as my final destination. "Your check-in requires special handling", a message came on the screen. Unperturbed, I beckoned to one of the ladies. She took my papers and began to process them.

Half way into the processing, the lady asked how many bags I had. "I have three bags and they all weigh less than 50-pounds each", I said confidently. "I will pay the excess baggage fee on the third bag, in accordance with your policy", I added. "Wait a minute", she intoned frowning and then called over the other lady. She came over and as soon as Nigeria was mentioned as my final destination, the lady quipped, "we can only take two bags weighing 50 pounds or less". "I understand that", I clarified, "so I am paying 125 dollars for the extra bag just as your website stipulated". "No", she echoed nonchalantly, "we have a directive that we cannot accept extra bags for that destination whether the passenger is paying for it or not", she said. "I relied on information on your website to pack three bags and you changed the instructions without duly informing me?" I asked dejectedly. "I don't know what to tell you" she said without looking at me. By then, I could tell that she was feeling disturbed by the repeated questions coming from me. There was no single word of apology from her mouth as she just walked away muttering, "that is our directive and we cannot change it".

My issue was not with the policy because I strictly comply with policies. The issue was that they moved the goalpost midway into a game and did not have the courtesy to pass the information to the players. Now they were enforcing the policy change as though I should have known. The most upsetting part was that they never displayed any iota of remorse about the level of inconvenience the change would cause me. "What do I do now?" I managed to say to the lady that had my documents without showing the anger that was already bubbling up in me. She shrugged and then said, "if any of your two allowed bags weighs less than 50-pounds, you can transfer some stuff from the extra bag" At this time, a few other passengers had started lining up behind me, I did not want to hold them up so I pushed my bags aside to make way for them.

Knowing that I could not afford to leave behind all the gifts I had, I called my wife on the cell phone. She was still circling the airport.

"Are you done checking in?" she asked optimistically? "No", I crooned in anger. "They say I cannot carry three bags" "I thought you were going to pay for the third one?" she inquired innocently. "Yes, but they have now changed their story". I could hear her sigh. I then asked her to find a parking place for the car and come back in to help me sort things out. As I waited for her to come, I weighed my bags and discovered to my delight that they were all slightly less than 50 pounds. Apparently, the scale I used at home was off by a few pounds. I then opened all three bags and while other passengers watched, I moved a couple of things from the third bag into the other two and re-weighed. By the time my wife joined me, we were able to move over a few things to the two allowable bags but left others in the third bag. It simply meant that several people would not get any gifts from us because of the intransigence of Delta Airlines.

After the silly ordeal, I went straight to the departure lounge, sat down and began to contemplate the disappointment I had at the hands of the airline. Delta was a new addition to the string of airlines that recently started direct flights between the USA and Nigeria. I once wrote an article called "In desperate need of a national airline". In that article, I called for Nigeria to establish a national airline that would be plying between the USA and Nigeria to save Nigerians living in the USA the humiliation they suffer at the hands of the customs and immigration when they travel through Europe. A direct flight from USA to Nigeria, I had written, would mean reduced airfare for Nigerians. With this frame of mind, when Delta started operations, I was poised to patronize them fully. I saw their emergence as a partial answer to my prayers and those of most Nigerians for direct flights to the country.

As I sat in the lounge of Harrisburg airport, waiting to commence the first leg of my journey, which was from Harrisburg to Atlanta, I was no longer so sure about my decision to go Delta. I thought about the many gifts I left behind and how disappointed the unlucky ones, whose presents were returned, would be when I got to Nigeria. I Just felt that the first level of service that Delta had offered me, at the beginning of my journey, was not satisfactory nor acceptable. I wondered if they understood the implications of making such drastic changes and not communicating the information to passengers and causing them disappointment and inconveniences. What if my wife did not come with me to the airport, I thought, what would I have done to the baggage that I had to send back home? I kept hoping that the baggage issue would be the last of the inconveniences and disappointments. Soon, my flight was announced and within minutes, the small aircraft thundered into the clear blue skies and the first leg of my journey back to Nigeria began in earnest.

I must confess that I hate long flights. The feeling of confinement, watching the time as minutes slowly go by always get me disconcerted. To pass time therefore, I had brought along my lap top with me, equipped it to play the DVD -"The Last King of Scotland". I had other interesting DVDs to watch but the problem was that the battery in my lap top had a mere 2-hour life. But when I visited Delta website, before embarking on the journey, I had read that one could purchase a form of adaptor, through Delta Airlines. The adaptor would continually charge the battery in my lap top, making it easy for one to use the computer throughout the flight. The cost of the adaptor was about $125. I was ready to pay for it just to keep busy with my lap top during the flight. I had packed a total of three movies, hoping that watching three interesting movies would knock off about 5 hours from my flight time. I would then use the remaining 5 hours to read, do some drawings and writing as well. I had a plan, I thought and was bubbling with the exuberance of someone who had it all figured out.

My flight from Harrisburg to Atlanta was smooth. Soon we were back in the air, this time headed to Lagos. When we originally boarded the jumbo jet that was to take us to Lagos, there was an announcement to the effect that the flight was a full one. I therefore took up my window position in the three seat row and waited for the other two passengers to show up. Of course I was hoping for passengers that did not have strikingly annoying habits. I once sat next to a man that snored all the way from the USA to Nigeria. I had to endure the sound for so many hours, periodically nudging him to break the sound. In this case, I was hoping that none of that would happen. Then a lady came along; she looked young but dressed very shabbily. She had layers of uncoordinated clothing dangling from every part of her body. I am not a fashion guru by any standards but I have always felt that for someone traveling 6000 miles in an aircraft where one is supposed to sit in very close proximity with people you have never met, a little decency was in order. She sat on that row but on the aisle side. Then I waited and waited for the person in the middle row to show up. Not too long, the attendant announced that the aircraft door was about to be closed for departure. I was pleasantly bewildered! They had announced that the aircraft was full and now there was no one in the middle seat of my row and they were about to close the door and depart?. Then I undid my seat belt, stood up and gently surveyed the cabin. A few more rows had some empty seats. I was convinced that the flight was not really a full one as previously announced. It did not take long before the aircraft slowly lifted its nose in search of the African skies. Eager to purchase the so-called adaptor and start watching "The Last King of Scotland", which is a movie about Idi Amin and his tyrannical reign, I longed for the aircraft to ascend to cruising altitude so that the attendants would come calling to dispense duty-free items.

Meanwhile, I picked up a duty-free magazine tucked into a pouch in front of me and began to peruse it for any items I may like. Sure enough, I came across the so-called adapter and was assured that it was exactly what I wanted. When it was time, I called over a flight attendant and asked to purchase one of the adapters. She looked bewildered after I explained what I wanted. "Can you show it to me in the duty free magazine?" she requested. I obliged. She still had a startled look on her face; it was as though she had never seen or heard of it before. Then she beckoned another attendant and showed the picture to her. That one looked surprised for a while but then straightened up and said, "Oh, we do not have it in stock". I was again disappointed. "You advertised this on your website and duty-free magazine and you do not have it?" I said rhetorically. The lady was about to leave when I added sarcastically, "this is just the beginning of a ten and half hour journey and you are already running out of items you advertised?" Although this seems like a minor issue but remembering the disappointment I already had with my baggage, I began to wonder how serious Delta Airline was taking the Atlanta-Lagos flight. Most airlines would do whatever it took to keep their customers and here was Delta doing all it could to chase one away. It just did not make sense to me. I chose not to complain but swallowed my disappointment and took on plan B. I was going to watch the inflight movies.

I opened the monitor in front of me and pushed several buttons before coming across a movie selection menu. I followed all instructions and then came to the portion where you pay. In line with the instruction on the screen, I pushed my call button and after a while, one of the flight attendants came. I told her that I needed to pay for the movie I had selected and handed her my five dollars. She swiped a card and said I was ready to watch the movie and left. The movie started alright but the screen froze in less than two minutes. Well, I waited patiently hoping that it would return to normalcy but the minutes kept going by and nothing happened, it was still frozen. Without hesitation, I pushed my call button again. The same Lady that I gave five dollars came back. "What is it again?" she said trying to be funny. "This thing is frozen", I said. "Okay, I will go and reset it", she said and quickly left again. Not too long after she left, the monitor blanked out for a while and then a stream of letters and numbers started scrolling across, it was apparently rebooting. At the end of it, the original screen from which I had selected the movie came up again. I was happy so I made the same selection and hit enter. It went through the motions and then asked for the mode of payment and I entered cash, the same routine I went through before. Then it requested, again, that I call an attendant. At this time I was frustrated! Calling on the same attendant that was already feeling disturbed by me was not exactly something I was delighted to do but I already gave her money so I had no choice. Moreover, none of the anomalies was the result of anything I had done. "Ping pong", I pushed the button again.

None of the flight attendants responded for what seemed like eternity but I was patient, after all it was a ten hour flight. Finally, I looked up and saw the same flight attendant on the far corner, she had seen the call button light above me and, I may be wrong, but I felt like she was trying to sneak past me before I beckoned on her. She motioned that she was coming and I could see the frustration that had built up. She briskly walked over to my seat. "Now what?" she said. "The computer screen requested that I call you again but I thought I had paid you and did not need to go through the same payment motion again", I said, sounding serious. She did not say a word and simply swiped a card she had around her neck through a slit below the monitor. She did not even wait for the movie to come on but dashed off. Well, the movie came on but again, just a few minutes later, it froze. I had had it! I pushed the button three times in a row. Again, that very flight attendant appeared, took a look at the screen and as soon as she saw that it was frozen again, she did not even allow me to say a word and just took out the money that I had earlier given to her and handed it back to me. "There is nothing more I can do", she said as she made to leave. "Can I use the monitor in the middle since no one is sitting there?" I asked helplessly. "Its up to you", she muttered as she walked away. "Some customer service for an airline that I decided to patronize and help succeed", I muttered under my breadth. At this time, I stood up briefly and cast a sweeping glance. I noticed that there were a few other monitors that seemed to have error messages also. Some seemed like they were still rebooting. It was later that I found out that I was not the only one having problems with my monitor. Now what do I do to keep myself busy, I wondered. If I turned on my laptop that early, the battery life would soon be gone and when boredom really set in, I would have nothing to fall back to. I closed my eyes and promptly dozed off albeit briefly.

Resumption Of Direct Flight From New York To Lagos: A Welcome News For Nigerians In The USA- October 6, 2006

Since the commencement of direct flight from New York to Lagos by North American Airlines, I have received several emails from Nigerians living in the United States. They wholeheartedly welcome the development and feel that it will go a long way in easing the burden of those traveling from the United States to Nigeria. Some even feel that the positive development should be counted as a major milestone or achievement by Obasanjo administration. They therefore argue that since this writer is "always quick to criticize" General Obasanjo when things go wrong in Nigeria, that it was incumbent on me to quickly give credit to him for creating the "enabling environment" for the resumption of direct flight to Nigeria.

I agree that the development is a positive one but I would defer to another time the discussion of the issue of lauding the president for it. Nigerians must understand that elected officials owe them certain duties. When such duties are discharged, elected officials should merely be seen as doing the job they signed up for and for which they are paid. Ordinary Nigerians labor daily in their respective jobs to discharge their responsibilities. They do not wait around to be extolled to high heavens for doing the job for which they are paid!

The reader may be wondering why this writer was getting emails about the resumption of direct flight to Nigeria. I will attempt to answer. On May 28, 2006, an article I wrote, titled, "In desperate need of a national airline", was published. In it, I highlighted the suffering and humiliation that Nigerians living in the United States go through when they travel to Nigeria on European airlines. These airlines make stopovers in their home airports, en route to Nigeria and passengers end up spending countless hours at the airports waiting for their connecting flights to Nigeria. My commentary also talked about certain humiliating booking policies and restrictions that these airlines put in place just for Nigerian passengers. I believe that the article brought to light this writer's passion for the issue and most definitely triggered the emails I got when direct flight commenced July 20, 2006.

The implication of the direct flight development is that those who decide to fly North American Airlines to Nigeria would now spend as little as 11 travel hours! This is a far cry from the 20 to 24 hours that passengers hitherto spent with European airlines. I have always longed for the day that direct flights would start and that day has come. Forced stopovers in Europe with attendant inconveniences, exorbitant air fares and prolonged jet lag will hopefully be consigned to the limbo of forgotten things or at least will be minimized. At the risk of sounding like Oliver Twist, though, I hasten to say that Nigeria needs more airlines to join North American Airlines on that route. It will still be a monopoly of sorts if that route is plied by North American Airlines alone. Real competition will begin only when more airlines join in and the gains would include lower air fares, good on-board and counter services, treatment of Nigerian passengers with dignity because they have choices and more. Those airlines that have been practicing draconian reservation and booking polices towards Nigerians, like refusing to accept their credit cards for reservations, would be forced to either change their policies or forgo Nigerian passengers to their financial peril. It is my understanding that arrangements have been concluded for another airline to commence direct flight from Lagos to Newark sometime in December. If that comes to pass, it will not only be good for passengers, but will augur well for the Nigerian government financially.

Right after North American Airlines' maiden flight from Lagos to New York, I began a general assessment of their operation. First I called the customer service number that was displayed on their website. This was around July 22 or so. The first disappointment I had, came right after I dialed the number; it immediately entered into an automated line and a long wait began. I waited for more than 10 minutes and was about to give up when a lady came on the line. The first thing I said to her was that the waiting time was too long. "It's because of the volume of calls we have been getting", she responded politely. I was not impressed. To me, they should have expected that the new route would cause a spike in the volume of calls. Furthermore, they should have expected that having advertised a promotional fare of $1000 for that route, they would be inundated with calls. Anyway, that was not a very big deal for me but I hoped that the oversight was not a harbinger of more serious issues to come.

I then asked the lady what the New York-Lagos fare was. After a few clicks of the computer key board, which I could hear from my end, she said something like $1300. "That is not what I was told by a friend who called you earlier", I protested as if I was buying a ticket. "Your friend probably told you about the promotional fee of $1000 but that is sold out now", she said with an air of pride and satisfaction. "You mean that potential travelers have already bought up all the seats?" I asked. "Yes", she said. In a way, I was happy for them because I want any airline that would give the other greedy ones a run for their money to succeed. But then something came to my mind, I wondered if the tickets were actually bought by potential travelers or by "organized touts". "Organized touts" buy up airline tickets and when peak travel time comes, that is Christmas season, they start reselling them to actual travelers at higher rates. That practice is probably not illegal but it is just disconcerting. I quickly pushed this thought out of my mind and proceeded to verify other things.

"Do you accept credit cards for flight reservation?" I asked the woman. "Yes, of course", she answered. She must have perceived it as a dumb question. I did not find it necessary to explain to her why I was asking but merely moved to other questions. In general, it looks like the airline is making progress but I was disappointed when I called them a few weeks ago. I wanted to see if their fare had stabilized but found out that it was still climbing. Hopefully, the fare hike is just the result of high energy cost not an attempt to continue the fleecing of Nigerians.

This article may sound like an endorsement of North American Airlines. I am not quite ready to give them an endorsement until I have personally flown with them sometime in the next year or two. I am however mindful of the fact that it is the only direct flight we have so far and in my heart, I pray that they succeed.

At this juncture, I find it necessary to caution North American Airlines to be careful not to take the patronage of Nigeria-bound passengers for granted like other airlines did. For example, a ten minute wait before the phone is answered by their customer service is unacceptable! They must ensure that the treatment they mete out to Nigerians, during booking exercises and on board their aircrafts, is comparable to the level of service in other world class airlines. They must ensure that the food, snack and beverage they serve on board meet the standards that other international flights have. They should provide 800 numbers for people to call for reporting subpar treatment. On their own part, Nigerian passengers must not and should never shy away from letting the airline know, through complaint letters or phone calls, if what they are serving seem subpar.

Furthermore, the Airline must also ensure that it is keeping abreast with modernity as far as on-board conveniences are concerned. For example, the last time I traveled to Nigeria, the airline I used had already installed a wireless internet system. All you do is pay a fee and wirelessly use your lap top to log onto the internet in the air! To me, that was very revolutionary and exceedingly convenient. One of the things I dread during flights is boredom, especially when I am traveling alone. However, being able to surf the web during flight will make boredom go away. If a passenger is able to surf the internet for two or three hours, then watch the on-board movie for another ninety minutes before falling asleep, by the time the passenger wakes up, the airplane would be preparing to land in its final destination. I urge North American Airlines to equip their aircrafts for such convenience services if they have not already done so. They must not neglect such services just because they are dealing with Nigerian passengers.

The marriage between Nigerian passengers and North American Airlines or any other airlines that later joins the route must be a two way street. If Nigerians expect the operators of these airline to respect their rights, during flights or when they make reservations, then they must live up to certain expectations. Two important things come to mind here. When an airline states the allowable size and weight of carryon bags, Nigerians must strive to abide by it. Because of the culture of bribery in Nigeria, I have noticed that there are people who always try to flout this. They go to the airport with carryon baggage that are over the limit in size and weight. When the airline officials ask them to surrender them for check in since they cannot ask for bribe as is done in Nigeria, they become unnecessarily effusive, trying to foolishly assert rights they do not have. Passengers should ask for and carefully read the official policies of the airlines about baggage sizes and weight and abide by them. Respect is reciprocal.

The other aspect is cleanliness. The last time I traveled with my family via Germany, I was disgusted with some of the things I saw fellow Nigerians doing. The flight left from Philadelphia and touched down in Germany. When we were disembarking from the aircraft in Germany, the interior of the aircraft was still reasonably clean. Of course it was populated by non-Nigerian passengers. But then we boarded the Port Harcourt-bound aircraft. The population was 95% Nigerians. Alas, when we got to Port Harcourt and began to disembark, as I passed rows and rows of seats, the whole aircraft looked like a dust bin. Food wrappers, tissue papers, cups, you name it were all littered all over the place and for some reason the aircraft stunk! I kept wondering why the airline that took us from Philadelphia to Germany remained reasonably clean when it landed in Germany while the current one looked like a landfill. Of course, the answer was clear. Nigerians in the aircraft did not respect themselves. These are the things that could make Nigerian passengers lose the respect of the airline attendants and the repercussion cannot be overemphasized. If they feel we do not deserve respect, then they react accordingly. Nigerian passengers should ensure that when they generate thrash on-board an aircraft, they should hand over the trash to airhostesses as they make their rounds to pick up dinner plates.

I have children and I love them dearly. However, I have no right to inconvenience other people with my children. Nigerians must learn to take care of the children they travel with during the flight. It is wrong to leave them gallivanting up and down the aircraft aisle, bumping into airhostesses and other passengers. The flight attendants may not say anything for the sake of politeness but it is only reasonable to expect that they would be feeling irritated. It is the right of every passenger to periodically get up and stretch or use the toilet but no one has the right to be walking up and down the aisle as if they are the only ones in the aircraft.

Sometimes, there is this war about where people should put their carryon bags. The right thing is for one to put one's carryon on the bin directly above the person's seat. If people adhere to the carryon rules, this is possible but in rare cases that could become impossible. In that case, one should politely ask for permission to use the bin above someone else. There are people who deliberately refuse to do that. They place their baggage wherever they like and would be the first to try to reach for those bags to retrieve their items as soon as the plane is airborne. This is sometimes inconveniencing to the person sitting below and can generate altercation.

Finally, I make bold to say that there is a fine line between seeking one's right and being unnecessarily overbearing. A case in point is this: on one of the legs of my journey, the man sitting in front of me kept demanding for something to drink from the air hostess. I watched as the attendant gave him what he wanted twice. Within a very short while, he pushed the attendant bell a third time and made another request. The lady obliged but I could tell that she had reached her limit of tolerance. Not long after, this same guy pushed the button yet again! The lady went by him twice and never even looked in his direction. I could hear him fuming! "I paid full price for this flight and deserve to be attended to", he complained. To me, what he was doing was laughable, he was being inconsiderate and overbearing. If all the passengers on board pushed their buttons as often as he did his, the aircraft would need 50 more attendants! This man could have made all his requests in the first or second go around. He did not do that but instead wanted the attendants to jump whenever he pushed the button. We should be careful and remember the phrase that respect is reciprocal.

PART 5

Insecurity

Insecurity in Nigeria-Training and Intelligence Gathering Should Be the Operative Word as Foreign Assistance Arrives -May 14, 2014

Everyone knows it now; the news is all over the globe. The terror group that has plagued Nigeria unchallenged for a couple of years now has finally walked a step too far. Their dastardly act of abducting more than 200 innocent girls from their school in Chibok, Borno State, has caught the attention of the world. Nations that have found this unconscionable like USA, Britain, France, Israel and others, are now stepping in to help arrest what could become the new normal in the world if allowed to stand.

The United States is careful not to promise placing boots on the ground in search of the missing girls but would assist Nigeria with intelligence gathering, reconnaissance, training of Nigeria's security personnel and general support. All these are support measures that will, in the interim, help unearth the location of the abducted girls and eventual rescue. The video that surfaced a few days ago, showing the abducted girls reciting the Koran, as well as the purported statement by Boko Haram leader that he is willing to release the girls in exchange for the release of his comrades in crime, signifies to me that the heat is on. The international community has made a bold statement that the group will not be allowed to be running roughshod over Nigeria.

United States discloses that when it offered assistance to Nigeria in the past on matters of this sort, it was rejected. Many have wondered what basis Nigeria had for rejecting the offers but it may be that Nigeria was trying to assert her sovereignty or make a statement that it could handle her internal affairs. One can conjecture that had the assistance been accepted earlier and had the sect been declared a terror group earlier, maybe some of the lives lost since the group embarked on this macabre dance would have been saved. But this is not the time to apportion blame but to take stock of what happened in the past and avoid a repeat in the future.

After my last article about President Jonathan's dimming political prospects because of insecurity was published, a few readers expressed the opinion that it was unreasonable to ask why Jonathan was not acting fast to tame this insurgency. They insisted that he has a plan but keeps it under wraps for obvious reasons. The problem with this line of argument is that the insurgency did not start today. It has been in place for years now and the abduction of the girls is not Boko Haram's first foray into this sadistic display of heartlessness. If Jonathan had a viable plan, Nigerians are yet to see it and it is yet to work because these guys are still out there terrorizing the nation and seem to have become emboldened with each day. Clearly, acceptance of foreign assistance at this time by the government, albeit to provide intelligence gathering and training, shows that even Jonathan now agrees that he needs help.

In 2001, I wrote an article about Nigeria captioned, "I want Nigeria back". In it, I lamented the many ills bedeviling the nation and wondered when all the ills would be tamed so that Nigeria would return to some semblance of normalcy. One of the maladies I pointed to was armed robbery, which at the time was on an uphill climb. I saw armed robbery as a security threat then but little did I know that the nation was headed into more sinister times in terms of security. Sadly, the security challenges continued to rise, fester and even become more intractable.

In tertiary schools of learning, cultism began to incubate and take a life of its own often with gory consequences. Young men and women, sent to go and acquire education, suddenly started banding together in groups or cults and had no qualms with killing members of rival cults. Many parents reacted by sending their wards to schools in neighboring African countries because they did not want their wards to become casualties in inter and intra cult turf wars. There were even instances where professors, for fear of intimidation and harm by cultists, doled out unmerited grades to students that threatened them. All these combined to plunge an already plummeting standard of education in the country to its lowest level, a malady that the nation is still suffering from up till this day.

As if cultism was not bad enough, and as though the security of lives and property had not been threatened enough, slowly, the issue of kidnapping for ransom began to rear its head and take hold. It soon became a means of livelihood for some young men and women. The nation could no longer guarantee the security of citizens, and fear, which bestrode the nation like a colossus, became palpable. If you wished to visit Nigeria from the Diaspora, you would either be discouraged by relatives or some security arrangements would be made for you to be guarded by security, something that took away the joy of visits to the fatherland. The well-to-do ones in the country resorted to travelling in convoys guarded by armed police. It was not uncommon to see up to 10 policemen guarding just one person depending on their status. In addition to kidnapping, armed robbery and cultism, Boko Haram menace was injected into the mix and the nation became an undeclared war zone.

Since 2009, Boko Haram has committed a series of abominable crimes against the nation. The government of the day has equally tried to solve the problems by deploying more and more security personnel in the affected areas, declaring a state of emergency in three north-eastern states and reassigning security personnel. It is clear from the results we have so far that these measures did nothing to deter the sect, instead, they became even more brazen and daring. Most people now believe that the answer did not lie solely on the enumerated measures which one can sum up as being reactive. What we need to add to the measures is a good dose of proactivity. Proactivity would mean gathering and analyzing intelligence, using the intelligence information to disrupt cells before they have the chance to unleash their plans. Intelligence would tell when a sinister plan is being hatched and be removed before hatching.

The importance of learning how to gather intelligence, know what intelligence to gather, learn how to work with the locals in an area to gain their trust and in turn use them to infiltrate cells, cannot be overemphasized. It is a common discussion in Nigeria that when an armed robbery exercise is taking place anywhere, one would not see the police but just as soon as the operation is concluded, the police would show up and start asking, "wey them?, wey them?". This is not to trivialize the work the police do and one needs to recognize that many of them have died in the line of duty, but if the security apparatus is trained to know how to gather intelligence, decode the intelligence and work with locals to stay one step ahead of criminals and terrorists, it will help. Often, when armed robbers are captured, we read that they said that on the day of their operation, they spent time in bars, restaurants and hotels priming themselves for their sordid operations. When I read that, I often wonder why other people in the same bars, restaurants or hotels did not suspect or hear anything that could be reportable to the police so they can take proactive steps. We also read that some of these robbers go to native doctors to get charms and amulets for protection. These are leads that if properly exploited and harnessed by way of intelligence gathering, Nigeria would be better for it.

There is still a dispute as to who is telling the truth about what happened the day the more than 200 girls were abducted. Some say that security agencies were notified more than 4 hours before the attack. If this is so, the question is: what did they do with that information. Intelligence gathering and reconnaissance could help them stay one step ahead of the criminals. But the government also has to equip security personnel and train them on the use of sophisticated security gadgets that advanced nations now use

United States and other nations have entered Nigeria to help locate the girls by helping to gather and analyze intelligence. Nigerian security should use this as a huge opportunity to learn and become conversant with the various intelligence gathering means and methods, how to use information gathered, as well as learn all the new tools that are available for effective intelligence gathering. The government must spare no expense in procuring whatever Nigeria needs to be able to fight the security threat of insurgency and preemptively stop the attacks, but also extend that to tame the beasts of kidnapping for ransom, armed robbery, cultism and the like. It must be a concerted operation aimed at once again putting Nigeria on the mend with respect to peace, security and stability. It is a war that must be fought and won by the nation. It is a war that is worth expending Nigeria's considerable oil money on in a very intelligent way.

The time to put to a stop to the cold-hearted killings that have been going on in the country for some time now has come. It is a pity that it took the abduction of more than 200 girls for the awareness to get to the front burner but providence and serendipity have a way of converging for eventual good. In this case, they have and Nigeria must seize this opportunity and get it right. There is always a turning point for anything in life. If the young girls are rescued because of good intelligence, this period will go down in history as the period when Nigeria experienced a turning point in terms of security. Boko haram has shocked the collective conscience of the world and must now face what is coming to it.

"Anti-Bullet Charms" May Be Encouraging Armed Robbery in Nigeria -In December of 2003

A traditional "healer" was killed in Benue State of Nigeria while testing an anti-bullet charm he prepared for his client [BBC, December 17, 2003] The charm which was designed in the form of an amulet, to be worn around the neck, was prepared for one Mr. Umaa Ukor. To demonstrate its efficacy, the "healer", Ashi Terfa, placed the charm around his own neck and asked Umaa to shoot at him. Obliging Terfa's request, Umaa pointed the gun at his head and squeezed the trigger.

Of course guns and bullets are no respecter of persons. According to BBC report, on impact, the bullet shattered the man's skull and instantly brought a melodramatic end to an incident that would have made the record books had things gone the "healer's" way. This story is very instructive, it reveals the type of mentality that has permeated and pervaded the psyche of some Nigerians. To think that anyone would believe that an amulet would prevent a bullet from penetrating the human body is unbelievable. It is even more intriguing that the so-called healer believed so much in his charm that he had to use himself as a guinea pig. Is it possible that he had successfully demonstrated the efficacy of the charm in the past and was merely going through a routine exercise? One doubts it. This sort of absurd mentality has played a large part in creating some of the social problems that Nigeria continues to grapple with.

This incident should not just be waved off casually, there is much more to it than meets the undiscerning eyes. The incident should now serve to refocus the spotlight on a larger problem that Nigeria has unsuccessfully tried to deal with. One is referring to the problem of armed robbery.

No day goes by in the country without reported and unreported cases of armed robbery in one part of the country or the other. The cases usually involve the cold-blooded murder of innocent men and women. In some instances, the hoodlums waylay passengers traveling aboard commercial vehicles, killing and dispossessing them of their belongings.

In other instances, they brazenly enter the homes of unsuspecting Nigerians, killing them and looting their belongings.

These robbery incidents have generated a pervasive sense of insecurity among Nigerians. Citizens are afraid to venture outside of their often barb wired and fortified compounds as often as they would like to. People have become prisoners in their own homes while a good night's rest has all but been traded for eternal vigilance. Also, potential foreign investors who continue to hear about these robbery incidents have understandably kept away from the country to avoid becoming statistics. Of course their absence in the country continue to work against economic recovery.

The reader is probably wondering what armed robbery has to do with the anti-bullet charm incident in Benue state. Well, everything. Every time the Nigerian police apprehends suspected armed robbers, they also find assorted charms in their possession. This has happened so often that it is now more of the rule than exception; it shows that many of these hoodlums derive the temporary courage with which they wreak havoc on the masses from the charms they carry around. They procure the charms from diabolical men such as Teshi of Benue state. The charms give them false sense of invincibility and make them feel that they would never be caught and their bodies are impregnable to bullets for there is no other way to explain why they operate so brazenly, killing, maiming and looting.

Sometime in 1985/86, two notorious robbers, Anini and Monday Osunbor terrorized people in the old Bendel state, killing indiscriminately and taking away possessions. General Babangida ordered a massive manhunt for the robbers and the police went after them, combing every part of Bendel state where they were reportedly operating and living in. The whole nation was gripped with fear of the robbers and their daredevil exploits. Police manhunt failed to stop their activities, the more they were hunted, the more intensified their activities became. Some of the locals in the area even began to tell stories of their invincibility and for a while it felt like they were never going to be caught.

Finally, it took the courage of a police sergeant called Uyanroro to bring the nightmarish drama to an end. Acting on a tip-off from the locals, he went straight to the house where Anini was hiding and apprehended him with very little resistance. That was after Monday Osunbor was also captured. When Anini's hideout was searched, police recovered assorted charms, including the one he usually wore around his waist during "operations".

It was instructive that after Anini was captured and dispossessed of his charms, the man who terrorized a whole state and was supposed to be fearless and daring, turned into a lily-livered coward, making confessions as no robber had ever done before. When the news of Anini's capture broke, many were expecting to see a daredevil who would remain defiant to the very end. The reverse was the case, they instead saw a coward who acted sorry, felt sorry and looked sorry. So much for "Anini the great".

One of the things that baffled Nigerians, when the men were caught, was that the duo of Anini and Monday Osunbor never left their area of operation around Benin City. Even though they knew that the whole nation was looking for them and that the area was crawling with policemen searching for them, they stayed put and did not feel the need to run to somewhere else. The reason was because they believed in the efficacy of the charms they had. Anini was said to wear his own charm under his trousers before venturing outside for "operations". The charms made him feel invincible and impregnable to bullets.

Like Umaa of Benue state who was assured that Teshi's charm would stop bullets from penetrating his body, Anini and Osunbor must have been assured that with the charms, they could never be caught. With these types of assurances, they became unnaturally brave, callous and heartless but when their charms were taken away, their courage left them. They were both executed later. One can therefore aver, based on this anecdotal evidence that there is a direct correlation between the activities of armed robbers in Nigeria and the so called healers that prepare anti-bullet charms for them. Those charms provide the false courage with which robbers operate and kill. The charm preparers must therefore be seen for what they really are: accessories or accomplices. "healers"

The Nigerian police must cash in on this seeming relationship between "healers" and robbers and adjust their armed robbery fighting strategy. They should now become proactive rather than just reactive. The reactive approach where the police starts chasing after armed robbers after the fact has obviously failed. They must begin to take actions that pre-empt potential robberies. The "healers" who prepare charms for men of the underworld must now be put under police surveillance radar. In every community, the locals are very familiar with the so-called healers so the police should have no problems identifying them.

The healers should be brought into police confidence and made to provide information about clients coming to look for anti-bullet charms. With that type of information, the police could infiltrate the ranks of potential robbers, set up sting operations as they would do in drug operations, eventually nabbing and jailing them before they kill. Furthermore, any armed robber caught with charms must be forced to reveal the name and location of the "healer" that prepared it. Identified charm makers must then be taken into custody as accomplices and made to reveal the names and whereabouts of all the people they may have prepared anti-bullet charms for. These people would in turn be put under surveillance and suspicious activities preempted before innocent people get hurt.

One must caution here that identifying someone as haven taken delivery of anti-bullet charms does not necessarily make the person an armed robber. This is because out of naivety, there are honest Nigerians that would procure such charms in the misguided attempt to ward off the bullets of armed robbers. However, a trained police interrogator should be able to separate the wheat from the chaff.

Police Kill Youth In Apparent Extortion
Attempt - December 3, 2007

Inspite of the efforts that parents endlessly expend to ensure conducive and safe environments for their children to live long and reach the stars, sometimes, tragedy sneaks in. It strikes when parents least expect, leaving in its wake a trail of sorrow and heartbreak. It leaves shattered dreams, despair, hopelessness, and a gory tale of lonesomeness.

So was it for the parents of an innocent 15-year old boy in Ogidi, Anambra state. The life of Daniel Ofiaeli, an SS 2 student at the Ogbunike Secondary school, was snuffed out by a greedy policeman. On that fateful day, Daniel was in a commercial bus going back to school when the police tried to stop the bus for the mandatory 20 naira they unofficially collect from bus drivers. To the chagrin of the police man who was flagging down the bus, the driver refused to pay the money but drove away instead. In a fit of anger, the policeman opened fire at the bus. In the end, an innocent young passenger, a boy whose parents had been toiling to nurture his dreams to fruition lay dead in a pool of blood. He was a victim of police brutality, avarice and recklessness.

According to the [Sunday Champion, November 10, 2007], as soon as the policeman became aware of what he had done, he took to his heels, effectively bringing to a melodramatic but untimely end, the life of a young man. The Anambra State commissioner of police has confirmed the case and it is the understanding of this writer that the policemen at the checkpoint have all been arrested.

What would motivate a policeman who is supposed to protect citizens to turn against them instead? What would motivate a policeman to open fire at a bus full of innocent passengers? He did not even shoot to merely demobilize the vehicle by aiming at the tires, instead, he shot straight into the vehicle, knowing that the result would be deadly. Now that he has ended the life of a young man, who was not even part of his dispute with the bus driver, what has he gained?

This is not the first time that a policeman in Nigeria has ended the life of an innocent citizen because of money, insignificant amount of money at that. Every time that happened, one had hoped that the police would take strong measures to forestall a repeat. For starters, the idea that policemen go to checkpoints to collect money from bus drivers, in itself, is preposterous and should have been stamped out by police management long ago. It seems to me, however, that the checkpoint money-collection trend would be difficult to stamp out. I have been told that some corrupt higher-ups in the police force benefit greatly from the sordid act. At the end of the day, portions of the money collected by junior officers get to them as gratitude for posting the policemen to the check points. During a discussion, sometime ago, a colleague of mine noted that police constables have been reported to actually lobby their officers to be deployed at the check points because of its lucrative nature. At the checkpoints, the policemen menacingly brandish their guns at oncoming vehicles to intimidate commercial vehicle drivers and even private ones. They extort money from them one after the other and at the end of the day, they go back to their stations with Ghana-must-go bags full of 20-naira notes. What these constables do is sickening enough but to think that they share their booty with their "ogas" should be very disturbing to all Nigerians. My colleague even added that policemen who handsomely settle their officers at the end of the day are in turn rewarded by being sent to "more lucrative checkpoints".

One is sure that the reader is wondering what a "lucrative checkpoint" is. Some checkpoints are more lucrative than others because of the type and size of traffic that pass through them. For example, during the Christmas season, when Nigerians return to their various villages from all corners of the globe, certain check points that see a lot of traffic carrying returnees become lucrative and net a lot of bribe money for errant policemen. These policemen have come to depend on this illegal collection and would therefore kill anyone that stands between them and the illegal collection or refuses to give up the money. In my mind, the policeman that killed Daniel Offiaeli felt that his supplementary income source was threatened and so went berserk. To him, the refusal to give him the 20 naira was a denial of his "legitimate right." That must have sent him into a temporary insane state, leading to the most irrational behavior that could ever be, that of senselessly ending a budding life.

One seriously blames the policeman that shot Daniel and hope he would get a punishment commensurate with the crime he committed. In the same vein, culpability must be shared amongst the ranks of the police, including the officer that posted him and his colleagues to that spot. The police must institute an unbiased investigation to cover issues like whether the culpable policeman had ever sent part of his illegal collection to his boss or the person that posted him to the check point. It should include uncovering the extent of knowledge his boss had of what was going on at the checkpoint. Without an all-encompassing investigation to unearth answers to these troubling questions, Nigerians are bound to keep hearing or reading about tragedies like this.

It is worth mentioning here that policemen, at checkpoints, seem to be on their own and so do however they please. For example, when they break for lunch, some of them just go into the nearest roadside place to eat. Of course these roadside eatries have alcohol in abundance for sale. Some of the policemen get their fill in alcohol at the end of their meal before heading back to their posts. One could personally attest to this because in December of 2005, at one of the check points, I could smell the strong odor of alcohol in the breath of the policeman who stuck his head into the vehicle I was in, as he asked, "una nogo settle us"? A gun in the hands of someone impaired by alcohol is as dangerous as can be. In any organization, this is called drinking on the job and is an action that is punishable by dismissal. Because Nigeria has not yet advanced to the level where alcohol breath tests could be done, one would never know what state the policeman that murdered Daniel Ofiaeli was in. Was he under the influence of alcohol, drugs or was he even mentally fit to be serving in the police force? For what it is worth, these questions have to be asked as the investigation proceeds.

It is not my intent in this article to cast aspersion on the police force but anyone in position of authority like the police must be held to a certain standard of behavior. When members of the police force carry out heinous offences like shooting innocent citizens, it becomes even more important that certain codes of conduct be strictly enforced. It is frightening to learn that alcohol and drugs are not the only substances capable of altering behaviors and making people do bad things. Seemingly benign drugs like amphetamines or anti-depressants sometimes alter behavior in a very bad way. It is therefore imperative that the issue of substance abuse be covered as part of the investigation of Ofiaeli's death.

It is certainly heartening to read that the federal government has invited the British to come and train Nigerian police. Surprisingly, some Nigerians are already raising objections. Their contention is that it would be tantamount to colonialism. To this writer, that is balderdash! For 47 years since our independence, we have not gotten many things right, including the issue of nurturing a dedicated and corrupt-free police force. If what it would take to get us where we need to be and stamp out corruption, avarice and poor performance within the ranks of the police force is by inviting the British police, so be it. They should help institute an alcohol and drug testing program to ensure that the actions of men and women of our police force are always done with "clear eyes". They should also ensure a force that is anchored on integrity with selfless national service as their mantra.

What should now happen to the parents of Daniel Ofiaeli? Granted, no amount of money will bring Daniel back to life but a few things have to happen: The Ofiaeli family has to be compensated for the loss and attendant pain and suffering. A thorough investigation must be instituted and all those found culpable should be punished accordingly to serve as a deterrent to others.

Is Bribery a Necessity in The Nigerian Police Force?

My concern about the seeming dereliction of the Nigerian police force by the government was reinforced a few weeks ago. This was during a spirited but frank exchange between the rank and file of the police force and the Senate Committee on Police Affairs. Without mincing words, a representative of the police rank and file told the Senate Committee that they [the police] "demand bribe from Nigerians to augment the operational costs incurred in protecting lives and property" [ThisDay News, August 29, 2004]

This was a most audacious statement and most Nigerians are bound to recoil in disgust just like this writer did when I first read about the exchange. The first thought that came to mind was that the police force was now looking for reasons to justify their despicable affinity for bribery and corruption. But as I pondered the statement a little more, it dawned on me that the man was simply being candid about what obtains in the police force. I do not and will never condone bribery in any form, but when I hear that the rank and file of the police is made to use their personal funds to take care of the operational expenses concerned with the discharge of their duties, I wonder why the powers that be would let that happen. Is it possible that the management of the police force is aware of this and still let it happen? Or is it possible that they are not even aware of this? If the latter is the case, then through this commentary, this author is calling their attention to it.

The reader would probably be wondering how it was possible for the police rank and file to summon the courage to tell the senate about the vices in their camp without the fear of reprisals from the officers. Well, the David Mark Senate Committee did what leaders should do routinely. The committee removed the probable threat of reprisals by asking police senior officers to leave the hearing room and then asked the junior officers to candidly tell the committee how things were going with them. With their bosses gone and having extracted the promise from the Senate members not to reveal their names, the men opened up. "I've just joined the Nigeria Police Force", one of the constables said, "but I can say that I'm full of regrets. They accuse us of collecting bribe and I wonder why? We maintain the patrol vehicles attached to us to combat crime, we fuel them and if any of us is injured in an operation, we tax ourselves to treat that person". The above statement is eye-opening. If what the constable is saying is true, then Nigerians should better stop asking why the men engage in bribery or collude with criminals because that is partly the answer. Clearly, two wrongs do not make a right but if the leaders have failed to address the problems facing the police, then the blame for the crimes of the police must be placed squarely on the doorsteps of our leaders.

Not too long ago, the Obasanjo administration boasted about the "reforms" in the Nigerian police which included salary restructuring and compensating the families of those who fall in the line of duty. However, it seems that the government tells the public one thing and then does another behind the scenes. This is what a police constable said to the David Mark Senate committee on this issue, "They said there is N20, 000 for burial expenses and we read that the Inspector General of Police said there is another N500, 000. But in this state command, we have had at least eight cases of dead [deaths] in which the family has not received a penny. Since June last year, we have not received the said N20, 000 talkless of the N500, 000"

With all the above, one is apt to ask what the incentive is for the members of the police force to turn away from bribery and corruption? From what is coming out of the David Mark Senate committee, there is little reason for them to do the right thing. The reader should remember that this is the same police force that is usually outgunned by criminals because many of them still use old fashioned rifles that are no match for the AK 47 assault rifles that criminals use. A police officer who knows that his family would not be taken care of if he falls in the line of duty or gets injured would be less inclined to put himself in harm's way to keep the peace and save citizens.

The constable at the Senate hearing went further to state that the salary of a constable, before deductions, is N8,000. For a married policeman, especially with kids, this amount of money is pittance and would do no good. According to the same constable, before they joined the police force, they were told that the salary of a constable was 17,000 naira, but after joining, they were stuck with 8,000 naira, that is bad and the Inspector of Police needs to review this allegation and make necessary corrections.

The sad police story does not end here because at a similar session held in the Lagos state command, this is what one sergeant said to the senate committee: "Even the patrol vehicles they [police management] release to us, no matter how efficient on duty you may be, if you can't "maintain" the vehicle in your team, they would withdraw it from that team. In the Police today, they can issue 20 uniforms for 100 policemen and the distribution becomes the matter of whom you know and how preferential you are treated".

The above statement simply points to the fact that the culture of bribery is sometimes tacitly induced. Faced with the law of the jungle, eat or be eaten, they are forced to eat which in this case amounts to bribery and extortion.

One of the police sergeants explained to the senate committee that on graduation from the police college, they were simply given one set of uniforms. Anyone that wanted more usually would go to buy from the open market! With the salary these men and women are paid, where are they expected to get the money for second uniform?

One of the police sergeants put it right when he said, "This administration approved employment of 40, 000 policemen but if you must raise 40,000 goats or sheep, you must make provision for their manger and where they would graze" He added rather rhetorically, "How a Mopol transferred to Lagos from Maiduguri would survive is not their problem... He has no salary until he is posted to the roadblock" He then concluded, "If the Police is corrupt, then Nigeria is responsible" While this writer does not agree that the government is completely responsible for corruption in the force, one agrees that the government is providing an enabling environment for corruption to thrive by not providing adequate resources for the police force.

It is hoped that these revelations would trigger a reform in the police force. The federal government should now walk in the shoes of these men and women and come to their aid. In any country, the police is one of the most critical. A police that is forced by living conditions and government dereliction to choose evil over good, to embrace bribery over probity, to aid criminals instead of bringing them to book will remain ineffective.

PART 6

General Interest

Belief in Voodoo by Some Nigerians Hinder Holistic National Progress - November 11, 2008

I recently read a story about trafficking of young Nigerian girls across our borders to faraway places like Italy to work as sex slaves. The story is bad enough but what really caught my attention was the part that read, "another major factor oiling the wheel of trafficking in the country is voodoo. Insiders in the trafficking business say that once arrangements for victims' trips abroad are completed, traffickers seal the deal by taking the victims to shrines of voodoo priests for oath taking. There, victims are made to swear that they would never reveal the identities of their traffickers to anyone if arrested whether in the course of the journey or in the destination countries." The paper further reports, "when traffickers are arrested in Nigeria, victims have often failed to show up in court to testify against them for fear that they would die if they violate the oaths they took. In administering the oaths, traffickers usually collect the finger nails, menstrual blood and pubic hairs of the girls in preparing concoctions. NAPTIP's Deputy Director of Prosecution and Legal Services, Mr. Abdulrahim Shaibu, said his agency had had difficulty prosecuting traffickers because victims are afraid of juju and are hardly forthcoming." [Punch Online, Oct 24, 2008]

The above is indicative of the extent to which a segment of Nigerians allow their belief in voodoo to dictate what they do in life. Human trafficking is despicable; it endangers the lives of young Nigerian women, exposes them to deadly ailments like AIDS and embarrasses their families as well as the Nigerian nation. With all these negatives, it is mind-boggling that the women who are the victims believe so much in the retaliatory powers of voodoo that they are unwilling to cooperate with prosecutors to put away the men who orchestrate their plight in faraway countries. Their refusal to cooperate has made it difficult for the crime to be curbed. As a corollary, Nigeria's image continues to be tarnished internationally because the nation is seen as sending sex slaves to foreign nations.

The reader may pass off belief in voodoo as something prevalent only amongst people in the lower rung of the social and economic ladder or the less educated. The truth is that this belief permeates every facet of the society. Even many of the so-called educated elite hold very strongly to this belief. A friend of mine that works in one of the ministries in Nigeria once told me about his harrowing experience in the work place. The position he was occupying was highly sought after in the ministry. To make matters worse, his colleagues felt that they were bypassed for the job and so wanted to see him removed. He told gory tales of how he would come to work some mornings and find charms and amulets placed in strategic locations in his office. Sometimes, "they would sprinkle ash-like powdered substance on my table", he said. His secretary even started telling him stories of how office politics culminated in the use of voodoo to end the life of a man she knew. This went on for a period of time without effect but after a while, the man started experiencing panic attacks periodically. The sight of the charms and amulets began to basically paralyze his mind to the point that he could no longer concentrate on his work. He became less productive, always thinking of what to do. Whenever he felt sick, which became a frequent occurrence, he would wonder if the end was near for him because of the voodoo. This story attests to the fact that voodoo, in the workplace, actually reduces productivity. The victims of voodoo shenanigans become paralyzed with fear; they become afflicted with ailments that go with unsettled minds like hypertension and in the long run become less productive. The perpetrators, on the other hand, spend the time they should be using for work in plotting the next move. It is sickening! I have since talked to other people who note that this happens in more office settings than one would ever care to know.

During the administration of Governor Chris Ngige of Anambra state, the issue of voodoo reared its ugly head. The governor was forced to sign a resignation letter by godfathers who helped finance his campaign. The quagmire generated by this issue stalled governance in the state for a long time. As the issue played out, the godfathers of the governor began to reveal alarming details of how he was allegedly taken to Okija shrine to swear an oath in front of a deity. According to them, he had pledged to pay them their due if he became the governor. Trouble started when Ngige ascended power but refused to allow his godfathers the type of access they wanted. They went after him, reminding him of his pledge at the Okija shrine. Ngige later denied swearing at Okija but as far as this writer is concerned, tales of voodoo should not even be coming from the seat of power of a state government. Ngige is a medical doctor and many of the people that constituted his godfathers are also up there in education. Yet they have this belief in inanimate objects to the point that they allowed issues pertaining to it to paralyze government activities for a long time in Anambra State. What Nigerians learned from that saga was that belief in voodoo was having a profoundly negative effect in many government circles not just in Anambra state. We hear how highly placed government officials, in the western states, go to juju priests to get "fortified" so their "enemies" would not get them. Some even go to consult the juju priests to get some direction on how to run the affairs of government, setting the states and the nation backwards with their primitive beliefs.

And then there is the belief by some people that ailments could be sent by "evil people" via voodoo. The belief is that if an ailment is sent via voodoo, then trying to treat it with western medicine actually exacerbates it. As a result, people with all manners of ailments choose to go to the native doctors or juju priests instead of seeking western intervention. I once narrated the story of a childhood classmate of mine. The last time I saw this guy was in the early 80s before I left for the United States. About 15 years later, I was told by a mutual friend that he died. Obviously shocked, I asked what happened. The story was that he ventured into business and began to do well. As a result, his neighbor at the store became jealous of him and did something to him that made him sick. His ailment started with constant stomach pains; then he developed what felt like a solid lump in his stomach. This continued over many months and was diagnosed as "mbe afo" or "turtle in the stomach". It got its name because of the hardness of the lump and the ringing sound it made when someone tapped the guy's stomach with the back of the hand. They likened it to the sound that tapping the shell of a turtle makes. Because of the belief that the ailment was planted via voodoo, when the stomach pains first started, my classmate was taken to a native doctor who gave him some concoctions to ingest. Instead of improving, his condition continued to worsen. It was only after he died that they discovered that he actually had stomach cancer.

This type of story is not only peculiar to my former classmate. In Nigeria today, for some reason, there is diabetes everywhere. Of course, if not properly managed, diabetes comes with opportunistic ailments like eye problems and most notably, sore and gangrene. In a conversation with a medical doctor in Nigeria, he complained bitterly about how some diabetics at different stages of diabetic gangrene or sores, attribute it to the handiwork of "evil people". Instead of doing what doctors normally advice diabetics to do, which is control diet, exercise and take certain medications, patients go to native doctors or juju priests that tell them that the sickness is "enyi ule" or decay of the leg caused by "evil people". They then start ingesting massive doses of concoctions from native doctors that end up taking their lives.

A while ago, a contemporary told me the story of a conversation he once had with a friend of his. That was after he came back from Nigeria where he had gone to attend the funeral ceremony of his father. The friend called him up to commiserate with him on the loss of his father. They had a long conversation but just before the lady hung up, she asked one last question, "so have you guys determined who killed your father?". My contemporary was stunned by the question because no one told the lady or anyone that his father was killed by anyone and yet this lady was asking the question so self-assuredly. "He died of natural causes", my contemporary responded to the lady. She was not convinced. She went on to tell him how her own father died and it was determined that one of their very close relatives had sent the sickness that killed him via diabolism.

This type of silly belief is rampant all over Nigeria and Africa and is taking a devastating toll on many families where allegations and counter allegations of diabolism abound. In such discordant families, people are always suspicious of one another and when someone dies, the death must be attributed to someone somewhere. I once had to counsel someone by saying that if human beings truly possessed the power to send sickness to others through the air, then everyone would be dead because they would be exerting that power with alacrity. God was cognizant of the propensity of human beings to abuse power and so decided not to endow mortals with that type of extraordinary power.

It is a pity that these pathetic beliefs are partly responsible for the proliferation of false prophets and false churches in Nigeria. The "prophets" keep their churches afloat and maintain their congregation by giving false prophecies to vulnerable congregants against innocent people. They use such prophecies to hold on to their prey mindless of how much animosity and friction they create amongst families and friends.

The ramifications of rampant belief in voodoo can be found in every facet of life in Nigeria. In 1986, a notorious armed robber called Lawrence Aninih and his cohort, Monday Osunbor, took control of Benin City and environs. They terrorized citizens in every sense of the word. Their operations paralyzed commercial activities for a period of time as they waylaid and snatched trailer-loads of goods and summarily shot those who dared to stand in their way. Even the police was not spared by the bandits. At checkpoints, they shot at the police and in the end, took the lives of nine policemen. Most easterners that lived in Lagos at that time dreaded traveling back to the east for fear of running into Aninih and his group of bandits. You always planned your trip in such a way that you bypassed Benin City before 3:00PM.

It was during the Babangida regime. After months of sustained man hunt, it took the courage of a police constable to bring Aninih down. Aninih was in the house of one of his female friends when the police got a tip and the constable followed him there. The constable emptied a magazine of bullets into his legs, demobilizing and taking the elusive Aninih alive. The most intriguing thing about the whole saga was that while the nation huddled in fear of Aninih and began to alter their life styles to avoid falling into his net, the man operated openly in Benin City, sometimes acting as a modern day Robin Hood by distributing his stolen booties to the "poor" in the market place. He did not seem to be bothered by the fact that he was a wanted man neither did he seem to be worried about being caught. It was reported that when the police finally caught up with him, he had assorted charms and amulets around his neck. Some were littered all over the room where he was staying with his female companions. Inotherwords, his belief in voodoo provided him with the Dutch courage with which he operated. The charms prepared for him by some native doctor made him feel invincible. He believed that with the charms, he could never be caught and even if shot at by the police, the bullets were not going to hurt him.

His female friends also believed in his charms so much that they were not afraid to hang around a man that was on the news every night as being hunted by the police. It has become the norm that every time armed robbers are caught, proper search reveals charms on and around them. This is a clear indication that belief in voodoo is fueling armed robbery.

For the reader that may doubt how much these robbers and the native doctors believe in the efficacy of the charms, the following story should provide some answers. Sometime in the year 2000, one of the Nigerian dailies reported that in Northern Nigeria, an armed robber approached a native doctor to prepare charms for him that would prevent bullets from penetrating his body. After preparing the charm, the native doctor was so sure of what he had done and its potency that he invited the armed robber to put it to test. Wearing the charm around his neck, the native doctor positioned himself in front of the robber and asked him to fire his gun at him. The robber, who was sure that the native doctor knew what he was doing, obliged. The first and only shot shattered the native doctor's skull to smithereens. In alarm, the robber fled but the deed was already done and a man was dead!

No matter how we dice it, any attempt at holistic development of Nigeria must include a concerted campaign to debunk certain myths and primitive beliefs that make people do the wrong things or go in the wrong direction. As the police make efforts to bring armed robbery under control, they must not discount the idea of mass anti-voodoo education. That would help extricate, from the life of crime, young men and women that get into crime believing that charms would protect them. If the efficacy and potency of the charms are disputed and discounted, we may start seeing less and less incidents of armed robbery. It may seem laughable to start telling people not to believe in juju and voodoo, but if a plague as serious as armed robbery must be curbed, a multi-pronged counter measure needs to be instituted.

There are some Nigerians who see voodoo as a form of cultural heritage or tradition handed down by generations past. In their infinite wisdom, they want the "culture" to be preserved inspite of its negative effects on society. My response to this class of Nigerians is simple: Every culture or tradition has good and bad parts. As civilization continues its giant leap in the positive direction, traditions or beliefs injurious to the society must be expunged.

Many years ago, a tradition existed in Nigeria where newborn twins were thrown into the "evil" forest and left to die. It was believed that they portended bad omen for the society. The story was the same for people who suffered from stomach-bloating ailments. These inhumane acts were being carried out to supposedly appease inanimate objects in the form of deities. Thank heavens that the so-called traditions were later seen for what they were - cruelty and injustice of man toward fellow man. The deities lost their locus standi culminating in the abandonment of that sorry chapter for good. Today, we have twins, triplets and quadruplets all over the country. We have people who have suffered and recovered from stomach ailments. They lead productive lives and make tangible contributions to society. It is therefore a weak argument for anyone to cite culture or tradition as the reason why people should still believe in voodoo even as it continues to negatively affect the nation.

In part one of this treatise, I catalogued some of the negative effects that belief in voodoo is having on our society but the story does not end there because there are more. Belief in voodoo sometimes lead to wicked end results akin to discarding twins in the "evil" forest. To be more succinct, there are instances where people have made bold to take the lives of others because of belief in voodoo. For the avoidance of doubt, the reader should reflect on this story that was reported in the [Daily Sun of June 30, 2007], titled, "Fruit of Doom, Woman throws neighbor's child into the well". Adijat (last name withheld), a 25 year old woman, lived in Ibijoke street of Oregun, Ikeja, Lagos. Unfortunately, two years earlier, her baby had died. Obviously distraught, she was desperate to have another baby. In her own words, "I had tried everything humanly and spiritually possible", but was not successful in conceiving. The reader may be aware of the agony that childless women go through in the African environment. Some are blamed by the man's family and continually showered with unprintable invectives. In some families, it becomes a license for the man to look for another woman. Such reactions push some women into unbridled desperation.

Well, because of Adijat's belief in voodoo, she began to consider her options in the diabolic realm. First, she confided in a neighbor that shared the same belief with her, a man known as Manifa. Feeling empowered to act on her behalf, Manifa went to see a babalawo (native doctor). When Manifa returned, he told Adijat that, according to the babalawo, her sudden barrenness was caused by a neighbor simply called Iya Bashiru. Then came the shocker from Manifa: The only way Adijat could conceive again was to kill Iya Bashiru's child and take the corpse to the babalawo for a voodoo ritual.

It is unclear whether Adijat paused long enough to ponder the gravity of what she had been asked to do. What is crystal clear is that her unconditional belief in voodoo and desperation overshadowed any sense of reasoning or decency she may have had. She was ready to act.

On the fateful day, after Adijat had assured herself that all of her neighbors had left the compound, except for Iya Bashiru's 5-year old son, she called on the little boy and promised to buy him some biscuits if he ran an errand for her. When the boy came, she asked him to get the bucket with which they fetched water from the compound well. As the innocent boy headed to the well, she furtively trailed him. Once there, she overpowered and forced the boy into the bucket. Using the rope tied to the bucket, she let him down into the well hoping to pull up the bucket when the boy had drowned.

Unbeknownst to Adijat, there were still some neighbors in the building peering out their windows, in horror, wondering what she was doing. It was these neighbors that ran to the rescue of the little boy. But for the neighbors, an innocent child would have lost his life senselessly to a primitive belief that should have no place in a modern society. It is mind boggling that the babalawo had the temerity to request that someone commit murder. It is even more perplexing that the bearer of the sorcerer's request, Manifa, willingly delivered the death request without qualms.

This case became public knowledge because neighbors caught Adijat in the act. How about other cases that nobody may have seen? Many years ago, while I was growing up in Lagos, we were always warned to go out only in groups because of people who abducted children for diabolic rituals. Apparently, more than 40 years later, this ritual still persists. Primitive beliefs that should now be consigned to oblivion are still waxing strong and unconscionable acts are being committed as a corollary.

Our Forebears may have wallowed in the voodoo realm in their time because they did not know better. In this day and age, however, an age where in-vitro fertilization, a medico-technological advancement is giving succor to men and women seeking to bear children; where western medicine is improving quality of life and expectancy, the last thing that Nigeria needs are destructive beliefs engendered by voodoo. These beliefs are not known to add quality to life, increase life expectancy or do any good in society.

A story somewhat similar to the one above is unfolding somewhere in Akwa Ibom State. When part 1 of this commentary aired, a reader called my attention to a horrifying documentary that is making its way around the internet. It is the story of children, as young as 5 years of age, being abandoned by their parents in Akwa Ibom. The reason? The parents have been told by a so called man of God that the children were witches that brought misfortune to their families. Some of the children in the documentary had been beaten, tortured and disowned. One particular case sent a cold chill down my spine: A young girl had a three-inch nail driven into her skull by her family because she was said to be a witch. Another victim was made to sit on red hot fire and she was brutally burned. Another young boy showed the scars he sustained when his own brother poured kerosene on him and basically set him alight! It was sobering to see innocent children being victimized in the worst possible ways because a sadist who called himself a man of God branded them witches. The smile on the pastor's face was devilish yet he thrived by forecasting the worst for members of the community. He was even proud to say that he charged N400,000 for every case he worked on.

To this writer, the Akwa Ibom issue must not be treated with levity. It is evil, unacceptable and criminal. It requires that authorities get to the bottom of it. In a nation where many openly profess their belief in God, how can such cruelty be allowed to stand? The emotional injury that these children are suffering as a result of their inhumane treatment would take a long time to heal if ever. They will bear the scars for a long time.

Belief in voodoo has roots in almost every facet of the Nigerian society. Anyone that has ever taken a taxi in Lagos or commercial combi bus between Lagos and Ibadan would often see amulets dangling from the mirror visors of some of the vehicles. Many years ago, as a young youth corper living in Lagos, I confronted the driver of a Lagos taxi that I was riding in about his amulets. He said to me that the gross-looking objects protected him from accidents. He boasted that he had never been in an accident even though he had been driving his taxi every day for years. His belief in the potency of voodoo was so palpable that I decided not to waste my time trying to tell him otherwise.

The above sounds somewhat harmless until the reader pauses for a moment to reflect on the ramifications of it all. There is something wrong when the driver of a commercial vehicle that transports innocent people believes that inanimate objects, hung from the mirror visor, would protect him from accidents. As is clear to everyone, accidents occur frequently on Nigerian roads and for the most part, the causes can be traced to bad roads. However, incidents of over speeding and reckless maneuvers play a major part. Is it possible, therefore, that some of the drivers that over speed and get into accidents that end their lives or those of their passengers, engage in reckless driving or over speeding because of the faith they place in the voodoo on their mirror visor.? As I already noted, in several instances, innocent passengers become the victims of driver recklessness engendered by silly belief in inanimate objects. Since there is no study that has been done to gage the extent of the belief or how much accidents could be attributable to false courage that lead to speeding and reckless driving, it is still an issue. Nigerian police does have a safe driving campaign that encourages motorists to drive safely, eschew drinking and driving or driving recklessly. It will not hurt the nation to extend its safe driving campaign to education about charms and amulets and the false sense of security it provides in driving that could be exacerbating incidence of accidents.

Before I end this commentary, I would like to tell a story that was narrated to me by someone. Once upon a time in the village, a very influential man died and the date for the funeral ceremony was scheduled. A few days before the funeral ceremony, family members gathered to clean the compound and position the canopies. Friends and well-wishers were coming and going as is normal in the village. Before long, a man entered the compound. Most of the people inside the compound immediately recognized him and knew why he was there. He was the man, according to local beliefs, that could make rain go away or vice versa. Normally, he would go to the grieving family and strike a bargain with them that throughout the duration of the funeral obsequies, there would be no rain. In turn, the family would pay him handsomely. It had been a longstanding belief in that town and environs that men could make or stop rain.

The man went into one of the canopies where members of the family had gathered. After exchanging pleasantries with them, he spoke, "I have come to ascertain whether your family will need my services during the funeral ceremony? If so, I will ensure that there will be no droplet of rain for the 3-days that the event would last". After speaking, one of the family members, a geologist who fully understood why and how natural events like rain, earthquake and the likes happen, rose and addressed the rainmaker. "Bro", he said sarcastically, "as you can see, it has not rained in almost a week; the soil is dry and the weather is uncomfortable. Rather than chase the rain away, we will actually appreciate if it can rain sufficiently for the weather to cool off and for the dust to go away so that our visitors will be less inconvenienced". The startled rain-maker was speechless. The geologist had taken the wind out of his sails. The rainmaker later left the compound without the usual cola, money and wine. It is worth mentioning that throughout the 3-days that the funeral event lasted, there was no drop of rain on the ground inspite of the fact that the service of the rainmaker was not engaged! There is a moral to this story but it will be for the reader to figure out

In conclusion, let me say that I am aware that belief in voodoo did not start in Nigeria or Africa today. It was truly handed down from generation to generation and has been around for years. However, with the many negative effects that this belief carries, it is time to turn a new page and think differently. For how can Nigeria develop when some of her leaders go in front of inanimate objects to seek guidance on how to pilot the affairs of the states or nation? How can Nigeria make progress in the medical field and raise life expectancy when many believe that most ailments are caused by people and so must be treated with native concoctions? How can Nigeria develop a common sense of purpose, which is something that comes with a measure of peaceful coexistence, when inter-tribal conflicts are the norm, when families are at war with one another, when brother is against brother, when sister is fighting sister all because of false prophesies from voodoo priests and fake pastors that sow discord everywhere? How can Nigeria lay claim to moral high ground when parents are being made to brutalize their children, disown and tongue-lash them all because of the pronouncements of false prophets who brand their children witches? How can Nigeria truly curtail accidents from reckless driving when some of the commercial drivers believe that they can speed as they want and amulets will save them from accidents? The time has come for Nigeria and Nigerians to start on the right path so we can join other nations that are making progress in development because of their open mindedness and belief in the fact that there is such thing as coincidence in life.

Nigeria Needs a National Anthem as Inspiring as Onyeka Onwenu's Centenary Song - March 25, 2013

I opened my Facebook page yesterday and saw a posting that caught my attention. The caption was: *Centenary Anthem for Nigeria- This Land* by Onyeka Onwenu. I was not enamored by this but a comment placed under the post said it was an interesting song. I was curious to see what was interesting in the song so I reluctantly clicked on the link and put on my headphones to listen. The sonorous voice of one of Nigeria's musical icons, Onyeka Onwenu, heralded the beginning of the video which was ushered in with aerial shots of important places in Nigeria. I have always been a fan of Onyeka Onwenu.

In this video, clad in burgundy-colored Nigerian national attire and totting her signature silvery hair, Ms. Onwenu softly and characteristically belted out the very first line of the music with pictures of an organized orchestra showing in the background. I knew at this point that I was in for a treat so I literally adjusted my seat and made myself comfortable, ready to take it all in.

As the song wore on, varied footages of people, places and events that have made Nigeria proud at different stages of her existence were alternating with the pictures of Onwenu. My body became showered with goose pimples. As a lover of good music and one who also writes and plays music, I think I know a good one when I hear it and this is one heck of music. Along the line, other Nigerian singers, actors, actresses began to join in. I was taken to the biblical Beulah land! The captivatingly out-of-this–world lyrics extolling Nigeria's virtues, both in songs and picture, jolted me back to reality and reminded me of why the past 100 years of Nigeria's existence have not been entirely unproductive and hence must be celebrated. The song carries a powerful message that the centenary celebration should not be seen just as a ruse but that Nigeria has done great things, has great people and has a uniquely diverse population that plays up her strength or at least should. I was riveted. Each artist sang a part with a mellifluous voice that kept the goose pimples on me intact until the very last curtain call.

I could not help but remember a conversation I once had with a Nigerian contemporary of mine. It was during one of the summer Olympics. I noted that every time the United States national anthem was played, goose pimples usually covered my body. I commented that the feeling evoked in me was a combination of things – the music, the lyrics as well as the emotions that one could see on the faces of the athletes. I confessed that Nigeria's current national anthem did not quite do the same for me. The national anthem, which starts with an unusual and uninspiring beat, did not seem to have been well thought out. Every time it plays, I imagine a motley gathering of musicians with disparate goals, testing out their instruments and never quite getting it together until the anthem ends. And the words do not seem to inspire. A national anthem is supposed to inspire, provoke action and play up the strength of a nation.

In Onyeka Onwenu's centenary song dubbed "This Land", I think I found what is missing in Nigeria's national anthem. The music of the centenary anthem is well thought out; the melody is soothingly refreshing and it gives an indescribable out-of-body experience and the lyrics are inspiring. I instinctively closed my eyes as the music wore on and found myself dreaming dreams about Nigeria, imagining the great things Nigeria had done in the past and will still do. I imagined Aladdin's magic carpet sweeping Nigeria and Nigerians from the present rut and transporting her to a faraway land, a shining city on the hill with endless possibilities; a land where diversity is strength rather than a curse; a land where Boko Haram or kidnapping is non-existent; a land where the politicians will consistently ask what they can do for the nation rather than what they can extort from her.

The music which lasts just for 4.47 minutes is cast and choreographed in the manner of the famous "We are the world" music that the late Michael Jackson and Lionel Richie crafted in the early 80's. Just like "We Are the World" video rendition, Onyeka Onwenu's masterpiece is also peopled by an impressive cast of Nigerian performers. Each performer takes his or her turn to lend a powerful voice to a song that, in my opinion, will help in recasting a nation whose citizens have been forced to stop dreaming big because of a ruling elite that lacks the necessary sense of inspiration.

Ms. Onwenu may have inadvertently opened the door for a discussion about changing Nigeria's current national anthem and putting forth an anthem that will, whenever played, evoke, through its melody and lyrics, a sense of duty, a sense of greatness, a sense of unity in diversity and most of all, a sense of a shining city on the hill. Nigeria needs an anthem that, whenever played, will cast a shower of goose pimples on the bodies of Nigerians and spur them to greater heights. That is what Nigeria needs and there is no doubt in my mind, after hearing what Onyeka Onwenu and her group have done, that Nigeria is not lacking in talents that will develop a befitting national anthem.

As we celebrate Nigeria's 100th year of existence, let the discussion begin about how and when a new national anthem will be crafted and put forth as a part of the rebranding and repositioning of Nigeria for the next millennium. Let the discussions begin on how to right the wrongs that have bedeviled a once great nation. And let it be said that Ms. Onwenu and her group have set the ball rolling in the right direction. I leave the reader with an excerpt from the song as I heard it: "Here we are, standing tall, through adversity for 100 years… Together, we will make it strong and indivisible"

This House is not for Sale: How Scam Artists "Sell" Properties They Don't Own to Unsuspecting Nigerians – Feb 12, 2012

During my last visit to Nigeria, en-route to my hometown from Lagos, I went through Owerri airport. The flight into the airport, which was on a Sunday afternoon, was uneventful. However, once the driver of the car I was travelling in cleared the airport road and got into Owerri proper, all hell broke loose! Cars, motorcycles, "keke" or Indian-type tri-cycles and hawkers were all over the place. The roads were jammed just like they would on a busy weekday and business activities were as brisk too.

While the driver snaked his way through the huge Owerri traffic snarl, we got into Royce road. On both sides of the road, something caught my attention. Several of the buildings that lined both sides of the road had hand-painted signs that read, "This house is NOT for sale". I asked the driver why the signs were all over the buildings. "If you do not put the sign on your building", he said with a wry smile, "some real estate scammers will sell your building to unsuspecting buyers. They will take prospective buyers", he continued, "point out the building to them as theirs and even produce genuine-looking documents to back up their claims and then sell the house on paper". It dawned on me that a form of scam that has been around in Nigeria for many years, had now been taken to a more sophisticated level.

What the driver said reminded me of a story that someone once told me about this type of real estate scam in Lagos. The story goes that a man, hoping to settle in Lagos, had sought out and purchased a parcel of land in one of the suburbs. Then, block by block, naira by naira, he built the house of his dream and was very proud of himself having become a landlord in the city. To him, he had arrived, or so he thought.

Many months after he moved into his new house, an incident that completely changed his perspective about life in Nigeria occurred. He had just returned to his house from work one evening and was relaxing in his living room when two men knocked on the compound gate looking for him. They were let in and courteously greeted him. When he inquired what their mission was, one of them stepped forward:

"Sir", he said slowly, "we realize that this building is yours but the problem is that you built it on a parcel of land that belongs to us." The man was baffled by what he was hearing. "What we are asking", the stranger continued, "is that you find a way to move your building off our land and we would not bother you again". At first, the man thought that what he was hearing was a sick joke that could be wished away but the persistence of the men convinced him that he had some form of real estate crisis in his hands. How could someone expect that a house built on foundation as deep as 5 feet, would be uprooted from the land and taken away! The men must be crazy, he thought to himself. Invariably, though, the ill-fated visit by total strangers set the stage for a ding dong affair that culminated in his parting with a huge sum of money. It was akin to paying twice for the same parcel of land!

The above story is not just an isolated incident that one could refer to as out of the ordinary. Other stories abound where people have been known to settle three different groups after buying and paying for a parcel of land or the building on it. The perpetrators of the real estate scam have their schemes almost perfected to an exact science. They know the best time to strike. When a potential land owner pays for the land the first time, they pretend not to know. They lie fallow for a while, watching the now proud land owner start the building construction. Some are so patient that they will wait until the building was completed and occupied. They know that at that point the investment could no longer be abandoned considering that the owner would have poured in a lot of money in the building construction. At that point, like ravenous wolves, they strike, barring their fangs and unleashing pain and suffering on their prey.

Many reasons have been adduced as to why this type of scam has endured. In a place like Lagos, where many members of a family may jointly own a parcel or parcels of land, sometimes, without the consent of other members of the family, a few may proceed to sell their land to buyers without mentioning that it is jointly owned. Because they partially own the property or have a stake in it, they have access to or even possess important documents related to it. With such documents, they have no trouble selling the property in question. When the other members of the family that have obviously been blindsided become aware of the transaction, they seek to rescind the deal or get their own share of the money from the sale of the land. They therefore approach the new "owner" of the property and all types of demands begin. In other instances, it is just a clear case of scam, where people just forge documents of lands they do not own and proceed to sell them to unsuspecting persons. Anyone who has been to parts of Lagos where there are still vacant plots would observe that signs like, "This land is not for sale", are clearly emblazoned all over the perimeter fences.

The people that mostly seem to fall prey to this type of scam are Nigerians living outside the country but who wish to purchase parcels of land in the country and build. Because of their absence, they work through middlemen and never get to participate in the transaction except provide the funds when a deal is reached.

It must be emphasized that for every real estate scam, there are many successful transactions. The key is due diligence before engaging in any real estate undertaking. The first step in the purchase of any real estate property should be to engage in what this writer calls the verification phase. This is the phase when the potential buyer should investigate whether the property has documents like Certificate of Occupancy; whether the land is jointly owned by family members or just an individual. It will not even hurt to seek out those that have built on the parcels of land adjacent to the property to ascertain if they bought their own parcels from the same person or groups and what their experience had been. The verification part does not have to be done personally by the potential buyer. Attorneys who live and practice in the area, and hence know the area in question, could be retained for the investigation. Reputable real estate companies can also be retained, depending on the size of the transaction since they will also get their cut.

Just because someone displays a certificate of occupancy that looks genuine does not mean that it is. Real estate scammers can manufacture any document they want. It will take visiting the Local Government Area, where the land is situated, to verify the authenticity of any landed property documents.

As you scramble to get that land or building of your dream, take the necessary time to do the initial due diligence by way of investigation or you may later get that evening visit from strangers who would ask that you remove your building from their land.

In This Internet Age, Our Children Should Be Doing A Lot Better Than We Did -May 12, 2013

The secondary school I attended in Nigeria is a great school that has produced specialists in basically every discipline that exists under the face of the earth. These "old boys," as we call ex-students of the school, are scattered all over the globe, contributing their quota in their respective specialties towards the betterment of the world at large. The ex-students excelled in spite of short-comings in the school that included ill-equipped library and laboratory as well as the absence of many other academic necessities. In 1977, when I sat for the West African School Certificate Exam, because of space limitation in our physics lab, I took my physics practical exam sitting outside the sparsely equipped physics lab under the sun. One of the questions in the test was in optics (light). We were required to use a glass prism to demonstrate the deflection. I found myself conducting a light-sensitive experiment under the full glare of the sun. This anomaly threw a few curve balls at me but I managed to pull through.

During my fourth year in the school, the principal carved out a room that he designated as a library. A few books, not quite relevant to our studies, adorned the shelves inside the library. There were no true reference books or research materials in the library so the room just became a quiet room for students to go and study. What I am describing is not unique to just my school. Many schools in that era suffered the same fate of inadequate facilities but in spite of that, a majority of students excelled and went on to become great men and women in their chosen professions.

In my last two years in the secondary school, my subjects of choice were the sciences in addition to math and English. Those were the courses I sat for in the West African School Certificate Exam (WASCE), the mother of all exams in those days. We had specific text books for each subject and these texts were used by teachers for lectures.

I loved physics and needed it for my future because of my inclination towards Geology. However, there were particular sub-areas of physics in which I did not feel that I had as mature a grasp of as I should. Just like some of my classmates, I was yearning for more understanding of the subject and wanted more simplified reference materials to aid my understanding but not much aid came. I was not alone in this quagmire. Out of a class of about 147 students that sat for the WASCE in that year in my school, less than 15% took physics. The bulk of students that dropped the subject did so because of the difficulty in sometimes grasping the principles and the absence of more simplified reference materials to aid in more in-depth understanding.

What I described above was not just peculiar to physics, it cut across the many science subjects that were taught in our schools including mathematics. The general mathematics we studied excluded calculus. Calculus was a different course that was dubbed "additional mathematics" or "addico." It was basically reserved for the exceptionally gifted students. To underscore how tough the subject was made out to be, in my set, less than 6 students ended up taking add-math. The additional mathematics teacher did not make things easy. I attended the first three lessons of the class where he introduced the concepts of differentiation and integration. He made it sound like a subject from another planet that could only be understood by students with double heads on their shoulders. If you asked questions in class, you looked like you should not even have stepped into the classroom. Like many other students, not knowing that I would yet confront calculus in the university, I dropped the subject and just took general math.

One could go on and on about the difficult conditions under which people of my era and those before us had to tackle academics, but I think the reader gets the picture. These days, I tell my kids that if people of my era had the advantage they, of the internet era, have, we would have performed wonders. I will explain. In the last 20 years, the world has become a global village, interconnected through the information superhighway or internet. Today, a student in Nigeria could, via the internet, access sophisticated and well-stocked libraries anywhere around the world to research hitherto difficult subject areas and enrich their knowledge. You can conduct a research on any subject under the face of the earth right from your home, as long as you have a computer and internet access. When a teacher presents a subject and you feel like you do not have a good understanding of it, rather than drop the subject out of disgust, you can open up your computer and google that subject or connect to any of the sophisticated college libraries anywhere around the world for further research.

I earlier noted how difficult calculus seemed when I was in high school and how many students had to drop the course for lack of any additional help in understanding the principles. The internet age has changed all that. When my daughter was facing calculus and needed help, I tried to step in but discovered that, because I was not a trained teacher, I was not presenting the subject in an easy-to-understand way. I googled "how to teach calculus" and ended up in YouTube. I was shocked at the amount of information I came across. Tutorial videos abound on YouTube of people gifted with the art of teaching a subject in a way that anyone would understand. They take nothing for granted but simply take their audience through a step-by-step process, from the very basics to the more sophisticated. They present the course in such a way that it would be difficult for someone not to understand it. I believe that if we had that type of aide, several of my classmates that foreclosed their dreams of studying courses like engineering in the university, just because they could not cope with subjects like physics and math, would be scientists today.

I loved biology and wanted to understand every aspect of it because I was also eyeing medicine as a profession in 1977. But the closest I came to seeing how the interior of the human body looked was a single line diagram in our text book. For example, I understood the principle of peristalsis, as taught, but I wanted to visualize it more accurately if I were to become a doctor. Apart from what the teacher said in class, there was nothing more visual to illustrate to us what happens when food was placed in the mouth, masticated and mixed with saliva to begin its travel down the alimentary canal. These days, multiple software exist that show 3-D photorealistic animations of the interior of the human anatomy. The 3-D animations accurately show the movement of food down the alimentary canal. It shows how food is absorbed by the villi (villus) in the small intestine, after being broken down by enzymes. Watching the 3-D animations is like watching a movie. Everything you see is ingrained in the memory just like the details of a movie.

One of the challenges that many chemistry students faced in my time was understating the principles of organic chemistry and balancing chemical equations. Again, many dropped the subject as a result. Today, Google or YouTube anything you do not understand in chemistry and you will get help that takes you through it in a simplified manner. You can even save the material and watch it as many times as it takes to understand it. Google "balancing chemical equations" and you will see all types of easy-to-understand step-by-step methods that almost anyone will understand and follow. Students in those days that wanted to study pharmacy but could not go past chemistry in secondary school, would have been excelling today.

I tell my kids that they have no reason not to succeed in this internet age. They should not jettison their dreams because of subjects they perceive as difficult. I call their attention to the fact that there are so many mechanisms out there that they can use to supplement the knowledge they get in class. If a child is having problems in calculus as many do, rather than give up on their dream of becoming an engineer or scientist, parents should encourage the child to check out outlets like YouTube and Google where they can find tutorials posted by people who have found better and more effective ways to explain the subject.

Of course, there is always a caveat about everything. Internet as a source of knowledge is good but because internet materials are largely unregulated, one has to exercise prudence in what one imbibes as the gospel truth. The watchword is trust but verify.

Before I end this, let me state that I am not unaware of the fact that the education sector is still suffering in Nigeria. In spite of global advancement in technology, schools still lack necessary facilities. For example, many schools do not have constant electricity for students to fully make use of internet technology. Several lack internet connectivity and others still have ill-equipped libraries and laboratories. All these anomalies need to change. The change will start with holding elected officials accountable and booting out those that neglect the educational sector and refuse to embrace and imbibe new and emerging technology. Nigeria must join the rest of the world in making full use of the opportunities that advancement in technology and the internet age now presents.

Internet Scam Artists(419ers) Destroying Nigeria's Image In International Circles!- June 11, 2002

A few days ago, I walked into my office and when I turned on my computer, the first thing I saw was an email from a colleague (also a Nigerian) who was unhappy that Nigerians were still writing scam letters to the USA. He was particularly unhappy that their email administrator at work had written a fraud alert email and circulated it to thousands of employees warning them about Nigerian scam artists. My colleague's contention was that this type of approach painted every Nigerian as bad and that singling out Nigeria was somewhat unfair since other nationalities perpetrate this type of fraud. My colleague is right about the concerns about type-casting of Nigerians for the sins of a few but the problem is that by their actions, Nigerian scam artists have stripped their fellow citizens of any morale grounds to stand and speak up against being type-casted.

I later found out that the same fraud-alert email about Nigerians was also sent out by my own agency internet administrator! I felt embarrassed and ashamed at the fact that a few Nigerians who want to reap where they did not sow were now making the rest of us look terribly bad. I was mad that a few Nigerians who want to get rich quick but do not want to lift a finger to put in some honest work were damaging the good reputation that many Nigerians have built in the Diaspora. I was lost in thought as to how to respond to all these but it boiled down to the fact that the Nigerian government must begin a crackdown, like never before, on the people in Nigeria who perpetrate this evil.

The nature of the internet scam involved Nigerians writing emails to people in the western world, asking them to part with some money in exchange for depositing millions of dollars in Nigerian government money into their accounts for eventual sharing. Those that fell for the scam and wired money to these people, ended up getting nothing and losing the money they wired. There are other variations of the scam.

The extent of embarrassment that this scam artistry is causing Nigerians and her citizens in the Diaspora demands that plans be immediately put in place to identify and deal with the people who carry on this dastardly act. Undoubtedly, the activities of these scam artists keep foreign investors away from Nigeria while putting a cloud of suspicion over honest Nigerians here in the Diaspora. In anger, a Nigerian in the Diaspora told me that, "this is probably a good reason to elect General Buhari for president come 2003". He felt that if Buhari was elected, he would pass a new law against scam artistry retroactively and summarily deal with offenders!

I have heard about these scam artist stories in the past but the stories only sounded funny to me because I always felt that people would not fall for the scams. I felt that only a con artist would respond to an email, inviting him or her to come and reap where the person did not sow. It is equally a criminal mind that would agree to provide their bank account for the purpose of depositing phantom millions of dollars that belong to the Nigerian government. These days, however, these scam artists or 419ers, as they are aptly called, have changed their modus operandi: they have resorted to toying with people's emotions. Take this story for instance: a little while ago, the brother of a Nigerian contemporary of mine here passed away in Nigeria. He was not aware of his brother's demise because he had not been notified, but back in Nigeria, a scam artist had gotten wind of the news of the tragic event. Only God knows how the scam artist got my contemporary's phone number but he suddenly got a call from Nigeria. At the Nigerian end was a voice he neither recognized nor heard before. Without identifying himself, this strange voice said to him, "your brother just died, you need to send money, when are you going to send the money?" Can anyone imagine the type of emotional turbulence this type of thing would throw any human being into? He was not sure whether to believe the message being relayed to him, yet, the callous voice from the other end continued to ask, "when are you going to send money?" After this drama, the news of his brother's death was confirmed when he later called home. For such a tragic occurrence to be taken advantage of is a travesty. I relayed this story because often, we say that we would never fall for these con artists and that we would not take anything they say seriously. In this case, however, the news was correct only that the con artist probably wanted to know if my contemporary would send money through Western Union or any other source so he would be impersonated. You do not have to send money to them to be affected by this type of scam, the mere fact that they coldly toy with your emotions is enough damage. The way this news was broken, someone with a faint heart could easily pass out in shock.

I did not realize the magnitude and how widespread this crime had become until lately when I started talking to people about it. A friend told me what happened when a scam letter was sent to his office from Nigeria. The fax was not addressed to him but because it bore a Nigerian address, people in his office who knew he hailed from Nigeria furtively took the fax and placed it on his desk. How embarrassing can this be?

Incidentally, in church today, my ever-eloquent pastor said that the reason evil is multiplying in the society today is because people have become willing to live with certain evils as a way of life. This should not be, Nigerians here in the Diaspora and overseas must rise up collectively and condemn this evil. Those who know these fraudsters should turn them in and those internet kiosks in Nigeria that provide them with the email accounts they use for this mischief must start scrutinizing people a little more before giving out email accounts. Also, they must collect personal information from those seeking email accounts so in the event of a fraud, they could be traced. The Nigerian government should start setting up serious sting operations, working with people both within and outside Nigeria to expunge this malady. I believe that technology abounds for tracing these fraudulent emails to the originators when they commit crimes; that technology is what Nigeria must now employ. The United States and the British would be willing to assist.

Back to those Nigerians who say that they are not embarrassed by this evil because they "did not do it", I view this type of nonchalant approach as borne out of ignorance about the way life goes. They do not know that if this continues, sooner than later, their own uprightness will come into question, albeit tacitly, just because they are Nigerians. Take what is currently happening in the baseball league for instance: one retired baseball player said that some of the players use/used steroids. Even though we know that there are many good players that never used steroids in baseball, this singular allegation has put the rest of the exceptional baseball players under a cloud of suspicion. These days, people are discussing all those home runs we had been witnessing and wondering if it was steroids that actually powered them. I have even listened to TV commentators who went back to old tapes of players hitting home runs; they are looking closely at all the footages, trying to decipher which player had bulging biceps or thighs. This is an attempt to decipher who may have been taking steroids. Simply put, the whole thing has started taking away from the genuine achievements of good baseball players. In the same vein, if we let this Nigerian scam artists continue to have a field day without taking drastic action to stop them, very soon, clouds of suspicion will start hovering over the head of every Nigerian in the Diaspora. If you buy a nice car, people would wonder; if you wear good clothes, people would even wonder more. Against this backdrop therefore, I am urging Nigerians of good will and conscience to come together, put together a petition to the Nigerian president urging him to do more to stop this 419 scam artists. If you cannot sign this petition to stop the crime, do not hope to sign meaningless petitions to the United States government to protest that Nigeria is being typecast if signs start springing up in your work place reading "BEWARE OF NIGERIAN SCAM ARTISTS!!!". If that happens, I would still be on my soap box saying - I told you so. Time for action is NOW!

Some Nigerians Have a Penchant for Big Titles and Empty Displays -September 16, 2013

Nigeria has sadly morphed into a nation where the type of treatment or amount of respect someone gets from the populace is directly proportional to the number of titles attached to the person's name. Apart from a titled person being automatically perceived as a successful and financially-loaded person, one of the seeming benefits of being a titled person, which some crave to no end, is honorable mention when one arrives at public events - a form of praise-singing. Because they are automatically linked to wealth and general success in the society, titles such as Chief, Dr, Sir and others have become highly coveted in the society. There are some that feel unfulfilled if they have not acquired at least one title. They therefore give the pursuit and acquisition of a title an unbridled primacy. They are willing to get it at all costs – pay for it, bribe their way through, engage in corruption, make half-hearted donations to schools and churches or grease the palms of corrupt "royal fathers".

The latest craze is the idea of being conferred with honorary doctorate degrees by universities in Nigeria. This is not where the problem lies because universities all over the world confer honorary degrees on deserving citizens in their societies. The aberration in the Nigerian case is that while honorary PhD recipients in other climes do not add the letters, "Dr" to their names, aware that they did not earn it, the reverse is the case in Nigeria. The other day, I was watching a YouTube clip of a businessman-turned politician in Nigeria speaking extemporaneously on TV. He was having a great deal of trouble articulating his political manifesto. He could not demonstrate a sound grasp of current events in the country where he was hoping to be a major player in the political arena.

I was about to turn off the clip and declare him a political non-starter when his name scrolled past the bottom of the screen and started with the letters, "Dr". I later learned that he was awarded an honorary degree by one of the universities in Nigeria because he made a certain amount of donation to the school. Again, my issue was not with the fact that he was conferred with an honorary degree but the fact that a TV station that should know better added "Dr" to his name. I have since learned that it is a common practice in Nigeria. TV stations and others indulge them.

Because of these newly minted "PhD" holders, it is becoming very difficult in Nigeria to tell the difference between people who toiled for and genuinely earned their PhDs and the impostors in our midst. Suffice it to say that the impostors are not only cheapening the PhD degree, they make actual PhD holders look bad. It is unclear if the universities that dole out these honorary PhD degrees explain to their recipients that the degrees were merely honorary and hence not meant to be used as if earned. Although in a nation where titles have become the ticket to respect, honor, slavish adulation and even more wealth, telling them that the degree is honorary may not deter them from using them.

In the not-too-distant past, distinguished Nigerians that got these honors knew that they were honorary in nature and not meant to be used as if they had earned them. Hence you would not catch them adding the "Dr" letters before their names. Here in the United States, many leading and wealthy men and women have honorary degrees conferred on them by one university or the other for major contributions to the school and humanity, yet you will never see them attached to their names.

On one of my visits to Nigeria, several years ago, I was handed an invitation card for an upcoming event for the Christmas season. I sat down to read through the invitation. Two letters attached to the name of someone caught my attention. I knew the person in question and wondered when he went back to school to get some type of degree in jurisprudence. I turned around and asked my sister, who was sitting next to me: what type of degree "JP" stood for. After a hearty laughter, she said it stood for "Jerusalem Pilgrim". People that visited the Holy Land now have the letters attached to their names. It was not that way when I was growing up in Nigeria. I know a few Jerusalem pilgrims but never saw the letters JP added to their names. Times have indeed changed.

I crave the indulgence of the reader to tell a story of what happened during one of my visits to Nigeria. During a public event, the master of ceremonies failed to add the letters "JP" to the name of someone in attendance when he introduced him. During the interlude, I saw the man walk over to the MC and they had what seemed like a tense conversation before he went back to his seat. The next time he picked up the microphone to speak, the MC was full of apologies for omitting the letters "JP" from the name of the man when he introduced him. That is how serious this has become and one would not be surprised to hear soon that someone was sued for failing to recognize a JP during a public event.

The "all-hat-and-no-cattle" syndrome has engulfed the whole of Nigeria as a country as well as Nigerians in the Diaspora. If you ever attend a social event in major cities in the Diaspora, and you are a reasonable or modest individual, you will feel embarrassed and uncomfortable. About a year ago, I attended one social event outside Pennsylvania and could not believe what I was witnessing. Apart from the fact that the event started late, when it finally started, the MC spent more than a quarter of the time assigned for the event to, according to him, introduce the very important personalities in the hall. First, he introduced the "chiefs" and then "high chiefs". Yes, there is such thing as "high chiefs" in our midst. Someone joked that the concept of "high chiefs" began when some of the "chiefs" started feeling that some village royal fathers were cheapening the chieftaincy titles by conferring them on undeserving people. Their exclusive club of chiefs had been infiltrated and invaded so they got some willing "royal fathers" to help create the "high chief" category to literally separate the men from the boys. One would not be surprised if a new category of "super high chief" is created soon when the high chief category is once again invaded.

The most amusing part is how some of these people dress when they come to public events. Just to look traditional, some literally dress like it is Halloween. I saw someone dressed in what looked like a house robe and tied around his waist was a rope-like string that people restrain their curtains at home with. I had a hearty laugh but you could see how serious the man in question looked. He wanted to look extraordinarily different from everyone else and hence get their attention, respect and special treatment. All hat and no cattle!

During the event, I watched with amazement as the chiefs and high chiefs bantered back and forth to establish supremacy when kola nut was presented. The bone of contention was who would have the final say on how the kola nut would be broken - the high chiefs or the ordinary chiefs. As I watched this shameless display of silliness, I wondered what the children in the room would be thinking of this generation. The people in question believed they were upholding tradition, not knowing that they were actually trampling on it through their shameless public displays and struggle to be recognized. They did not seem to understand that what mattered most was the legacy they were leaving for those that were not chiefs to follow. I wondered if they understood that their legacy should be that of good public and private persona; a legacy of people who deliberate cerebrally before talking so as to make sense all the time. I wondered if they understood that their legacy should be marked by community service, advancement of education, encouragement of true democracy in Nigeria and most of all, leadership and foresightedness wherever they find themselves. Unfortunately, I have to believe that many of these people do not understand that to whom much is given, much is expected and that if you crave respect and recognition, you have to carry yourself with dignity and respect in all you do.

The reader should not take this as a condemnation of all chiefs and high chiefs in our midst because, just as I have come across the fake and empty ones, I have also come across many that truly earned the exalted pedestal upon which society placed them. You do not need to be shown what they have done that earned them the chieftaincy because their deeds speak for them. You engage them in conversation and foresightedness, wisdom, knowledge and community work ooze from them. You look back their path and you see a long trail of accomplishment and service to community that make you respect them even if they are not seeking respect. You can even tell that the ones that have not had the opportunity to make major accomplishments yet have huge potential. Many are making whatever leadership contribution they can wherever they live and one could see that given time and opportunity, they would do more.

The reader probably remembers remarkable Nigerians like Sir Adetokunbo Ademola, Sir Louis Mbanefo, Sir Louis P Ojukwu and more. Because of the contribution of these men to nation-building and commerce, they earned the title "Sirs", having been knighted. In those days, if you see "Sir" next to the name of anyone, you would not need to be told why because their achievements and contributions stood out. These days, the tide has turned. Every church, even if not reputable, now confers knighthood on people. Sometimes you see "Sir" next to the name of a shady character or someone with a questionable means of livelihood. As a result, the prestige that the connotation once carried has simply vanished. Churches knight members who are willing to pony up donations. They even knight potential donors in an attempt to get them to do something. The churches know that Nigerians crave titles and would pay any money they are asked to just to be bestowed or conferred with a title they believe would give them a leg up in the society, so they are making most of it. Our politicians seem to be the ones that hanker after these titles the most, especially the ones that have little to show in terms of personal achievement and contribution to society. To make up for that deficiency, they go after all types of titles, making donations and greasing palms sometimes with ill-gotten money. I get the impression that as soon as someone becomes a prospective politician in Nigeria, they go for what I call title indoctrination. This is where they seek out malleable "royal fathers" willing to confer chieftaincy titles on them with no questions asked. They seek out a church that will confer a knighthood on them so they can attach "Sir" to their names. They look for universities willing to grant them an honorary doctorate degree in return for donations or construction of hostels. Then they cap it all off with a visit to the holy land that adds "JP" to their names. Once this is done, they can now boast of answering Chief, Dr, Sir, JP. The table is set for them to start going around town seeking votes. At that point, because of all the titles attached to their names, the voters automatically see them as men and women of honor. No need to question their past or their manifesto. No need to question the source of their wealth, after all, the church validated their authenticity with knighthood.

This is what is going on in Anambra State as the gubernatorial election draws nigh. All manners of Tom, Dick and Harry want to become the governor of the state. Many of them are very lean on actual credential or track record but they garnish their names with high-sounding titles like Chief, Dr, Sir, JP and more. Some of them have been interviewed on television and one could hardly make out head or tail from what they say. Some find it difficult to even articulate what they hope to do for the state except that they should be accepted for being chiefs, Drs, Knights and JPs. In the end, they hoodwink the electorate and get by with minimum or no scrutiny.

This type of politics has been the bane of Nigeria. People are voted into office, not for what they have done before or track record, but because they present themselves as belonging to the elite group of multi-titled Nigerians that should be given whatever they ask for. It is time that Nigerians started ignoring high-sounding titles and started looking deeper into the people that come before them for votes. It is time that Nigerians stopped worshipping titles and started probing to unearth what those that want to lead us are truly made of. It is time that we started challenging those that hoodwink us with chieftaincy titles that truly amount to nothing and start by asking deeper questions about what they have done to merit the laurels and what they plan to do if they must be placed by the public on the special pedestal that they seek. Merely wearing a 5-gallon cowboy hat does not make a cowboy. You must have a healthy number of cattle to back up that name – cowboy, otherwise, you will merely be all hat and no cattle.

"Servants of God" That Deceive
Their Followers -June 23, 2014

This commentary was triggered by a YouTube video that was sent to me. The sender felt that, as a social commentator, after watching the video, I would be incensed enough to write something that would trigger a conversation on the issue. He was right, I was incensed!

The video in question showed the exploits of a pastor called Lesego Daniel of Rabboni Centre Ministries in South Africa. The video opened with a scene where several members of the church congregation seemed to have been hypnotized. They were sitting or lying seemingly lifelessly on the floor as the young pastor pranced around the stage like a tiger surveying its prey, barking out orders to the congregation. Soon, he announced that just like Jesus turned water into wine, stone into bread, and fed a huge congregation, he was going to feed the congregation with special food instead of bread.

He said the food would give them life and with that, he commanded them to go outside the building and eat grass. At first, it seemed like a joke or figure of speech until many members of his congregation, especially the young and energetic ones, rushed outside the church, as cameras followed, and actually started grabbing, stuffing into their mouths, masticating and swallowing grass like a sheep would. I could not believe my eyes. As they ate, he kept saying, "eat quickly" and the more he said that, the more diligently they obliged. One could tell from the way some of them were glancing around to see what the others were doing that a mild competition of sorts was going on as to who would eat the most grass.

Midstream into the chaos that had ensued, he asked the members of the congregation that remained inside the hall, "will those that are eating grass die?" "No-o-o-o", the group intoned in unison. He had this sadistic glee on his face showing that he was enjoying every bit of what was happening. He seemed to love the fact that he had power and dominion over vulnerable people. As he continued to prance around, he added, "if your husband is there or your wife, they are eating life for resurrection". At this point, the video of what was going on outside the church building, which was being shown on a big screen TV inside the building, zoomed into a little girl. She was crawling around on the ground and eating grass along with the adults. With a sickening glee that lent credence to his megalomaniac disposition, he muttered, "look at the little one". This ugly spectacle went on for a while until he felt he had made his point which was that he had power over his congregation. At that point he shouted, "Come back quickly".

Rising from the different locations to which they had scattered in search of grass to eat, the "grass eaters" started back towards the church. The enthusiasm with which some of them had dashed out of the auditorium when he initially commanded them to go and eat grass, was no longer there. They looked tired and less enthusiastic.

On the YouTube page, where the video of this dastardly act was posted one of the viewers wrote: "God will make an example of this wicked pastor. He will destroy his soul for all his ungodly works. People go to church to seek God and all they get is this wicked man standing in the way. God will cast him into outer darkness and all his demons with him". Many share this sentiment. Some of the people that profess to be servants of God end up meting out physical and emotional abuse on their flock. Another viewer of the video wrote, "This is a demon, be aware who preaches to you. God help those people in that congregation".

Of course, after eating grass, many of the people that indulged in the act got sick. One is almost certain that some of them will start doubting the so-called man of God and his teachings. He may have, by using the name of God to give instructions that never came from God, distanced some believers from the Christian faith. They will be wondering why the congregation got sick when they were obeying instructions from God.

This is not the first time that men and women who profess to be speaking with authority from God have caused physical discomfort or even death to their followers. These men are missing the point of the Christian faith – humility in the service of God and authenticity. They love power and tend to display their power over their flock by goading them into doing what people would not ordinarily do. Watching the video reminded me of a tragedy that occurred years ago because a pastor who preached in the name of God gave a command.

It was November 18, 1978, in Jonestown, Northwestern Guyana. More than 900 people, followers of Jim Jones, a self-styled pastor and minister of God, died from cyanide poison which they took at the behest of their pastor. The world was stunned as videos were released showing lifeless bodies of members littered under the makeshift pavilions in the jungle where the pastor had herded his followers.

Most of the followers of Jim Jones had left their families, loved ones and friends, back in the United States, and went along with him. They trusted him to help them seek and find the redeeming face of God. Many of them staunchly believed that, in forsaking their friends and families and going off with Jim Jones, they were following in the footsteps of the disciples that left their friends and families and went along with Jesus Christ. They did not realize that the man they were following was more of an egomaniacal lunatic than a pastor. Instead of helping them get salvation, Jim Jones gave them death. He was more interested in asserting his powers and maintaining dominion over the people. When he felt that his cover had been blown and that he was fast losing grip of the unbridled power he had, he went for the jugular and poisoned them all with cool aid laced with cyanide. He unleashed all that evil while prophesying the name of God just like pastor Lesego Daniels was doing when he asked his flock to go eat grass! But we thank heavens that God is a kind and forgiving God. Otherwise, for all the atrocities that mankind has been committing while prophesying His name, He would have unleashed on the world a level of destruction that will make the annihilation of Sodom and Gomorrah pale in comparison!

When the news of the atrocity in Jonestown first broke, after the initial shock, some saw the dastardly act as an aberration. Of course we know that, in different forms and magnitude the world has continued to witness various forms of atrocities either committed or perpetrated by men and women that doggedly profess the name of God. Did the world not learn a lesson from the Guyana tragedy? Otherwise, why would another "pastor" ask his flock to go and eat grass and they oblige? If Pastor Daniels is able to command his congregation to go out and eat grass, what would prevent him from pulling a Jonestown-style madness whenever he feels like?

There is obviously a proliferation of people that purport to speak with authority from God but are mere egomaniacs interested in asserting undeserved authority on others. The bible warned about false prophets, their proliferation and how to spot them. Avoiding falling prey to their machinations entails watching the words they utter, the deeds they do and examples they set. If their actions do not match what they say, then look before you leap. If what they say or preach runs contrary to the teachings of Christ, one has to be circumspect.

A few years ago, Huffington Post reported a story that will bring tears to the eyes of every one that has a heart. In Eket, Nigeria, a family was told by their pastor that their 9-year old boy was a witch! [Huffington Post, Oct 18, 2009]. The story goes that after the young boy was accused of "being a witch", as a form of exorcism, his father took acid and attempted to force it down the boy's throat. In the process, it spilled and portions of the boy's body, including his face and eyes were incinerated. In the ensuing weeks, the young boy's body could not withstand the physical trauma that the acid had subjected it to and so after a month in the hospital, he died!

Now, how ignorant or gullible can a father be to accept that type condemnation of a child given to him by God and whom he had nurtured for 9 years? Even more troubling is how perverted can someone who claims to be speaking with authority from God be to summarily condemn a boy barely old enough to give himself a bath? This excessive belief in witchcraft seems to be predominant in that part of the country but is a problem in many other parts of Nigeria and Africa. This issue is so pervasive that there are some church denominations that have pastors who actually purport to "specialize" in witch-hunting and exorcism! They claim to be able to pinpoint children and even adults that are witches. I saw a poster of a planned church gathering somewhere in Calabar Nigeria and the highlight of the event was titled, "Kill that witch!" That means it was a gathering where people take those in their families suspected of witchcraft for positive identification and exorcism.

We have read many stories of what exorcism entails. There is physical abuse, there is emotional abuse, there is excommunication, and there is alienation of the victims from family members. The stigma that goes with the people accused of being witches is so overpowering that some lose the will to live and hence try to end their lives.

It is instructive that the reasons for which some of the children are labeled witches are unbelievable. Sometimes a child is branded a witch just for being reclusive or non-conforming. In some instance a belligerent child is branded a witch. Even a child that has what would be diagnosed as Attention Deficit Disorder (ADD) in the Western world is branded a witch! A child that may be susceptible to hallucinations, "hearing voices" or "seeing imaginary things" all conditions that could be the result of medical abnormalities in the brain is branded a witch and condemned. The pastors that make these assertions always try to find a family misfortune that they can blame the "witch" child for. For example, if it is a family where a woman has been trying to conceive for years and could not, the pastor will say it is because of the "witch" child. If it is a family where someone has terminal ailment, the "witch" child is blamed. If it is a family where enough progress or development is not being made, the "witch" is blamed. Of course when a family believes that the source of their misfortune has been identified, the tendency is for them to go along with any suggestion to reverse their misfortune. Hence they agree to any steps suggested by the "man of God" for exorcism, no matter how harsh, unconscionable or ignoble.

I have been to three continents although I have lived in Africa and United States the most. But I cannot think of any place I have been, whether in the western countries or otherwise, where all the children are perfect. Here in the United States, I see children that are belligerent; I see children that are non-conformists; I see children that are reclusive and I see children that "hear voices", or have hallucinations. I see children that try to subvert their families in all ways possible. These children are not branded witches and ostracized or go on stomach-churning exorcism. Many are taken to medical doctors for proper diagnosis of the underlying medical problem that may be causing or exacerbating their condition. With diagnoses, medication follows. Hence people that are bipolar, hear voices or hallucinate are treated and many restored to normalcy. Why some so-called men of God have taken it upon themselves in Africa to be condemning God's children to untimely death and eternal damnation beats the imagination. Some try to justify what they do by the bible verse that says "suffer not a witch to live". If we literally follow all bible verses word for word, no one will exist on the face of the earth as we would all have been swallowed by the earth for our sins.

It should be mentioned that in the African environment, it is not only children that are sometimes branded witches. Sometimes these pastors also brand adults witches. These types of accusations trigger deep family feuds that last and linger for a long time. The scenario goes thus: someone becomes sick, instead of going to seek proper medical diagnosis, the person is taken to a church where the pastor prays and claims to have received word from above that the sickness was caused by a witch, usually a family member or someone close to the family. Bitter feuds develop between the families. The time that could have been used to take the patient to the hospital for true medical diagnosis and treatment is spent feuding with the accused family. Meanwhile, the ailment deepens and before long, things get to the point of no return.

A friend told me a while ago how, after his father's burial in Nigeria, when he came back, one of his friends called to commiserate with him. As they were chatting, his friend asked if they found out who killed his dad. My friend responded that his father died of natural causes as spelt out by the doctors but his friend was unconvinced and went on to tell stories of people who developed sicknesses all for men of God to tell them that it was caused by witches. Why can't someone die of natural causes? Why must every death be attributed to the handiwork of witches?

I understand that witch-hunting is banned in Nigeria but it does not seem as though people who engage in it are being prosecuted aggressively. The government has to take steps to stamp out this injustice.

Now, on a slightly different note here, the other day, I logged into my Facebook page and what greeted my eyes was a video of another pastor "ministering unto his congregation". He talked about power that comes from believing in God and then said he had the power to make even children in the womb of their mothers dance. Almost immediately, the camera zoomed into a seemingly pregnant lady sitting on a chair amongst the congregation. The woman appeared to be sleeping because her eyelids were closed. Just then, the pastor said something like "dance, baby dance" and the woman's tummy started making rhythmic motions as if the baby was actually moving in her womb in sync with the song that the pastor was singing. I was curious so as soon as the camera zoomed closer into her, I observed that the woman was the one subtly gyrating her hips and in resonance, her belly was following suit, creating the impression that the baby in her womb was moving or dancing.

This deceitful exercise continued for quite some time and sometimes to applause from the suspecting or unsuspecting congregation. After a while, I could no longer look at the shameful spectacle. I had concluded that here was another fake one bringing disrepute to Christianity and Christendom. What was the point of this exercise, I wondered. Let's just for a moment believe that this was real, what was the utility of a baby dancing in the mother's womb as a miracle? Christ's miracles were significant, valuable and did not need to be faked. If this pastor had any powers to effectuate miracles, rather than embark on useless, magic-like exercises, he should be healing the infirm or be doing something useful, not making a baby in the womb dance. He sought the easy path to create the impression that he had the power to effectuate miracles.

Over the years and the world over, countless number of young boys, genuinely drawn to the service of God as altar boys have been abused sexually by men they trusted, believed in and hoped would help them find the face and blessing of God. Some of them recount the abuse they endured and when asked why they did not refuse, would state how they were goaded into believing that refusing was tantamount to disobeying the wishes of God. It is painful to note that because of the traumatic experience they had, some of these altar boys have either completely fallen away from the service of God or have perpetually but inadvertently lost the ability to trust any man. Some flounder and have continued to search for identity all because of what people did to them in the name of God. How can the perpetrators of these heinous acts still call themselves fishers of men and try to liken what they do to what the disciples did thousands of years ago? The more painful part is that it is a handful of these bad apples in Christianity that try to soil the good work that others have been doing.

Then there are some "men and women of God" that engage in what has been debunked as fake healing miracles. This is not peculiar to any particular country or continent. It is happening the world over. Through sting operations, it has been established that some of these people plant fake sick people and then in the full glare of the congregation during church services, pretend to heal them just by laying hands on their foreheads. For the avoidance of doubt, as a Christian, I am a firm believer in biblical miracles and I believe that the power to heal still abounds in men and women even today. I recall when my mother used to visit us many years ago. On Sundays, whenever we were unable to go to church, we would turn to television ministry for that Sunday's service. Sometimes, the pastor would ask for people hoping for miracles to place their hands on the television, over his, and miracles would happen. I had no problems with these until we started reading expose that pointed to the fact that some of the people that purport to have been healed were actually planted in church and that sophisticated technologies were being used in church premises for communication between the cohorts that colluded in this and the main actors. It was a huge disappointment to know that all the deception was being done in the name of God. Vulnerable people rush to them to get healing but end up disappointed. They become alienated instead of strengthened in their belief in God. This makes it imperative that every Christian must be on the alert. If they start seeing things that seem too good to be true, they must look before they leap!

In spite of all these disappointments, I believe in miracles and have always believed. But miracles will only come from genuine men and women of God that live the word they preach. You shall know them by the type of lifestyles they lead, by what they say, by the deeds they do, by how they treat fellow human beings, by their disposition. Some call themselves servants of God but spew hate in the name of preaching and some are more political than the real politicians and their words and actions are guided by politics not true words of God.

March 27, 1997, police found the partially decomposed bodies of 39 people in a rented mansion in San Diego, California. They were members of a religious sect called Heaven's Gate. Their leader, Marshal Applewhite, had convinced members that the end of the world was imminent. He assured them that the only way to assure the safe passage of their souls to a better realm was via a spacecraft that he believed was tracking behind the Hale-Bopp comet. To get to the spacecraft, according to him, they would all have to commit suicide. Just like Jim Jones poisoned his followers in Guyana two decades earlier, at the behest of Applewhite, members of the Heaven's Gate ingested lethal doses of pre-mixed cocktails and wrapped plastic over their heads. This occasioned the quick death of all 39 members by asphyxiation. A leader who once claimed to be the direct brother of Jesus had cut short the lives of 38 people, in addition to his, while purporting to be speaking with authority from God.

Attempts by errant men and women of God to predict the end of time, are not new. Many have made predictions that failed to materialize. But they always seem to craftily justify the failure of their predictions and hence continue to maintain their followership. It is worth reiterating that Christ warned that even HE does not know "the day".

"End of time" predictions are not the only types of predictions that some of these people engage in. For example, every start of a new year, some come out with predictions of what "would happen in the year". While this is a world-wide phenomenon, it is very rampant in Africa's most populous nation. A Nigerian pastor once said, "Nigerians should pray hard because a prominent person will die this year". Of course in a nation of over 150 million more than one prominent person will die in the year! What is the unique prediction here?

Not long ago, I had a very funny but troubling exchange with someone from Nigeria on the issue of predictions. This was after the disappearance of flight 370 of Malaysia. He told me that a certain pastor in Nigeria predicted the location of the missing aircraft. He said it was in the bottom of the Ocean. When I said that telling us it was in the bottom of the Ocean does not reveal anything because the Ocean is vast, he became exasperated with me for daring to question the "holy" man's predictions.

If the bible is still the guide for these people, they should remember that when Jesus Christ was getting ready for his triumphal entry into Jerusalem, on what is now celebrated as Palm Sunday by Christians, he directed his disciples to go and get a colt from a certain location. He was specific in the description of the location and what they would find. The disciples found the colt exactly where Christ said and brought it to him. He mounted it and the triumphal journey to Jerusalem began. His instructions were not nebulous, ambiguous or open to interpretation.

Here in the United States, a pastor once told his congregation that he had been directed by God to raise a certain amount from his church or die! This is the God of Abraham, Isaac and Jacob we are talking about here! Did this type of atrocious demand really emanate from Him? Was it just hyperbole from the pastor to elicit action from faithful members? If it is hyperbole, why ascribe such an atrocious statement to God? These types of careless statements have made it difficult for people to truly discern who is telling the truth and who is not. The story is not much different in Nigeria where, for two consecutive election cycles, a certain pastor presented himself as a candidate for president. Before throwing his hat into the ring, he would tell his congregation that it was revealed to him that he was going to win. He failed both times. How does he explain to his congregation that an assurance he said came from God failed to materialize? These are clearly personal ambitions that should be seen and treated as such. This is not peculiar to Nigeria. Even here in the United States, some pastors have told us that the Lord asked them to run for president. When they did, they failed. Go figure!

Some years back, when a Nigerian pastor was arrested for fake currency printing, his laughable defense was that, "Judas was a true man of God but when Satan pushed him, he fell". Essentially, the pastor blamed Satan for pushing him into what he did. No one doubts the ability of Satan to goad mankind into transgressions. However, when one purports to be the face of Christianity; purports to speak with authority from God, there are certain codes of conduct that the person must strive, against all odds, to abide by. One cannot be doing the exact thing that one preaches against. On the YouTube page where this issue was reported, someone wrote, "If Satan is the culprit, then bring Satan and we will jail him. If you cannot produce Satan, then it will be obvious you are the Satan and we will jail you". That aptly summarizes how people feel about these aberrant pastors that continually taint Christianity.

I once attended a service where a visiting pastor was to give the sermon. Everything was going well until he stepped into the pulpit for what the congregation thought was to be the sermon. From his looks, it was clear that he spared no expense in taking care of himself, most probably at the expense of his congregation. From the suit he was wearing, to the gold watch he had on, the cuff links, his tie and the way his hair was groomed, he was flawless! He could have passed for a Hollywood model.

Unfortunately, when the sermon began, instead of being about God and the kingdom of heaven, it was about the pastor and his kingdom on earth. He talked about the helicopter that dropped him off that morning and how he took a limo to the church grounds. He talked about his house, how big and great it was and then added, "oh, by the way, it is all paid for". At this point, the audience began to exchange glances and raise eyebrows. This went on and on for a very long time. It was much later that he began to deliver the "real" sermon which at that point in time, at least for me, no longer had any effect or utility. He had presented himself as a material-oriented and attention-seeking man instead of a humble man of God. These types of preachers create the impression that they indulge in the personal use of the funds that the congregation contributes. They make things worse by flaunting their gains unabashedly. Instead of using the money to grow the church, do the type of ministry outreach that Christ engaged in, they use the money on themselves, buying expensive cars, expensive watches and suits and the likes.

I have become leery of this so-called prosperity preaching. This is where a pastor tells the congregation that if they tithe or make donations, they will be blessed with affluence, good health and more. Sometimes, I get the sense that they are saying that poverty and sickness are the direct results of not making donations or tithing! Yet, it is the poor and sick that offer their "widow's mite" and going by the bible, their types of gifts and offerings, may not be much, but they go straight to heaven much like the offering of biblical Abel. The size of one's donations or tithes should never be equated with the amount of grace that one gets from God. God is a generous God that bestows his grace and mercy on the rich, the poor, the sick, those that tithe and those that do not. Jesus spent most of his life ministering unto the poor, the infirm and the meek and even tells us, via the beatitudes, that, "theirs is the kingdom of God"

Sometime ago, there was a church service in Lagos, Nigeria, during which a pastor changed clothes three times before service ended. He started with a normal suit, then later changed into something of a zooksuit and then capped it off with another change. Meanwhile, he was pompously using jaw-breaking and highfalutin grammar in bamboozling the congregation. Two things bothered me about that scenario: Why is it important for a pastor to change clothes three times during a church service. Was he presenting the Grammy's? Second, a preacher's goal should be to effectively communicate his teachings (sermon), to his congregation. Effective communication is where the recipient fully understands the intended communication. During my research for this article, I observed that the same preacher stations armed guards around him, inside the church, in full view of the congregation, when he preaches! Granted, the security situation in Nigeria has degenerated to alarming levels but there are other unobtrusive ways to protect the church and its occupants during service. Naked display of armed guards around the pulpit during a sermon directly contradicts the preacher's message. On the one hand the preacher is telling congregants that if they believe in God, their problems will be taken care of but his actions show that he does not believe what he is preaching. How can he convincingly preach Psalm 127 biblical assurance that, "Unless the LORD guards the city, the watchman keeps awake in vain?"

The same pastor had the insensitivity and temerity to announce that he had ordered a Rolls-Royce that cost N120 million! This is about $718,000! How does one explain this type of profligacy to a widow or a poor family that contributes their widow's mite to him every Sunday? What would Jesus do if he had N120 million naira? Would he buy one of the costliest cars on the face of the earth or use it to provide hand-up to the less privileged? It must be emphasized, at this juncture, that there are many good and God-fearing preachers that ensure that funds raised in the church are used in the service of the poor, the hungry, the sick, the infirm. The great work they do must not be muddied or overshadowed by the profligacy of a few.

Some of these errant pastors call on the congregation to "sow seed" but when they do, the seed goes into their coffers instead of that of the church. They have made church a business venture to service their ostentatious lifestyles. The bible tells us about the reaction of Christ when he walked into the temple and people were buying and selling. He picked up his whip and lashed out at them, overturning their tables and chasing them out of the temple. He basically told them that the house of God was not for wheeling and dealing. I recall a Christmas service we attended in my home town many years ago with my brother Nnamdi. Just before the collection of the offerings, the pastor announced that he did not want to see offerings below a certain currency denomination in the offering plate. Nnamdi and I glanced at one another wondering what the church we grew up in had become. As everyone got up in procession to go and place their offerings in the offering plate, a former senator of the Federal Republic of Nigeria, apparently angered by the statement, rose and with both hands, displayed the exact currency denomination that the pastor had said he did not want to see in the plate. When he got to the location of the offering plate, he deliberately and dramatically placed his money in the plate. He wanted everyone to see what he did. The pastor did not consider that there were many in the congregation that could only afford the exact currency denomination he just banned. He was effectively telling them not to come and commune with their maker as they wished. It was a regretful spectacle. I felt sorry for what some "men and women of God" had become.

Someone once said that pastors that want money at all costs never take time to warn their congregation of the wages of sin. They are afraid to lose the people that fill their coffers. That is why in Nigeria, you see someone with questionable character in church with a special chair in the sanctuary area just because they have money. Those that do not have money but steadfastly follow the path of righteousness and give their widow's mite are not even recognized as part of the congregation. In Nigeria today, it is hard to hear pastors rebuking affluent people known to engage in certain crimes and corruption. They perceive them as the geese that lay the golden eggs and treat them like treasures. They give them places of honor in the church, special chairs in the sanctuary, bestow them with knighthood or the greatest church honors. But do they deserve such honors? Should they truly be held out as role models or exemplary characters for others to emulate? The message here seems to be that regardless of your income source or character, if you make it, the pastor should hold you up as distinguished in church. I have never come across a church where the poor has been knighted for their dedication and service to the church. When I was growing up, our church had a man we called the "sexton". He cleaned the church, kept the church grounds up to date, rang the bell, and did all the important things that made the church tick. But he was poor and would never be able to make huge donations. Yet, in my eyes, he qualified for all church honors. Jesus never shied away from calling out people for their wrong deeds regardless of their status in the society. He used very terse terms like "brood of vipers" and "hypocrites" to describe those that paraded wealth as if that was all that mattered.

The intent of this article is merely to caution people to look before they leap so they will not be disappointed. If a "pastor" tells you to take your life, just as Jim Jones and Marshal Applewhite convinced their groups to do, reject that and run because it is not of God. If a "pastor" says they know when the world would end, ignore them and move on because even Christ does not know when that would happen. If a "pastor" makes false predictions, know that they are not of God and run the other way. When a pastor pays excessive attention to those that "sow the most seeds" at the expense of other members of the church, the poor, the meek, it is time to reevaluate. If you get into a church where special places of honor are set aside for some, just because of their status or wealth, something is wrong because in God's eyes, everyone is on the same pedestal.

On the issue of donations to the church, I make bold to say that donations to church for church work are appropriate and legitimate! Donations for church ministry did not start today. Christ obtained the few loaves of bread and fish he multiplied to feed the masses from someone in the crowd gathered. That is a form of donation. In the same vein, the church has to be maintained and outreach ministries have to be performed with donations and offerings from generous members. Pastors and servants of God have to be paid because they, like other humans, have needs to fill. But if a pastor says that donation or tithing is a condition for good health or prosperity, then that teaching is not of God and must be rejected.

Before I conclude this article, I have to confess that as a Christian, brought up in a very religious household with a lay leader as a father, basically went to most Sunday school lessons in grade school, sang in the choir until my very last month in high school, I agonized immensely about writing this commentary. I did not want a broad brush to be used in painting all men and women of God. I am compelled, therefore, to aver unequivocally and unflinchingly, in VERY strong terms, that what I am saying here applies only to errant and aberrant pastors. They present themselves as the face of Christendom and taint everyone. My comments in this treatise have in no way shaken my belief in the Christian faith. I have seen the handiwork of God in my life, the lives of members of my family and extended family. I am a personal witness to the grace of God through pastors and the church body here. I have listened to people I know give truthful testimonies about the blessings of God showered on them through pastors and churches. I have seen people lifted from agony and misery by the actions of church bodies and men and women of God. Therefore, no reader of this article has my permission to use this article to broad brush all pastors.

I will end this piece by reiterating, at the risk of sounding like a preacher which I am not even remotely qualified to be, the biblical admonition that ALL, including this writer, have sinned and come short of the glory of God. All Christians must continually seek redemption and strive to abide by the biblical admonition of, "let your light so shine before men, that they may see your good works and glorify our father who is in heaven". It is a charge given to all and not just errant pastors. So while one hopes that pastors, as the face of Christianity, must continue to show the light by their words and deeds, all Christians have the same responsibility as well. My secondary school motto is "Lux et Veritas" meaning "Light and truth". It should be the watch word or mantra of all Christians under every circumstance and situation, no matter how dire. And for all ye men and women of goodwill, when in doubt about your thoughts, words and deeds, think, "WWJD"- What Would Jesus DO?

May God continue to shower his infinite blessings on us all.

A Tribute to Mothers on Mother's Day - May 2009

I wrote the original version of this piece in November of 2001. Although it was a tribute to all mothers for their unselfish deeds towards their children, I dedicated it to my mother who at the time was turning 79 years. Today she is 86 years young and is as mentally alert as ever. We are hoping for many more years for her.

From time to time, I get this nostalgic feeling that takes me down memory lane, to my boyhood days at the St. Mary's Cathedral Nnewi in Anambra State. One of the occasions I remember ever so vividly is the Mothers' day Sunday service.

On this Sunday, the service is dedicated to mothers. They read the bible lessons for the service. They sing very endearing songs about mothers and practically conduct the service. The highlight of the service is when one of the mothers rises to address the church. With the congregation listening attentively and clinging to every word uttered, she catalogs the selfless roles that mothers play in every family. She takes the congregation on a historical journey of how mothers struggle under thick and thin to fulfill their God-given roles in the lives of every human. Even though the memory of my boyhood days has inevitably faded far into the distant past, carrying with it sweet memories of those glorious days, I still remember and miss the Mothers' day celebration at St Mary's Church. It was full of importance, the most significant of which is that mothers are God's greatest gift to mankind.

During the service, a special time is set aside for mothers to go up the altar to offer their thanks and gifts to God while singing special songs that eulogize them. One of the songs: "Onwa itenani, ka osiso solu nnem, nnenne, nneoma." This translates to: "for nine months, my mother endured profuse perspiration, my mother, my mother, my sweet mother." This was a metaphorical depiction of the agony, suffering and pain mothers undergo for the entire nine months they carry babies in their womb. The suffering reaches its height, via labor pains, on the delivery day when the baby is actually born, but does not end there.

Another song goes this way: "Nathy Obienu, nne muluya, chukwukelu uwa, dalu, onye ebube". This means: "Nathy Obienu was

246

born by a woman, thanks be to God, the creator of the earth". Nathy Obienu was one of the pillars of the church at the time and a successful business man in my town. The song again was meant to shed light on the importance of mothers on earth. It says that in spite of the success of Nathy Obienu, he still came forth from the womb of a woman. This assertion could be extrapolated to include some famous people that have graced the face of the earth. They include the great Zik of Africa, Dr Kwame Nkrumah of Ghana, Nelson Mandela of South Africa, President Bill Clinton, Franklin Roosevelt, Prime Minister Golda Meir, Tony Blair, Ronald Reagan, Winston Churchill, Barack Obama, Napoleon Bonaparte and even our Lord Jesus Christ. As tough as all these people were and as much as they changed the face of the earth with their principles, their teachings, their actions and their deeds, towering over mankind like a colossus in their days, they came forth from the womb of women. That is instructive!

The women of St Mary's Church would sing other songs that showed that a mother's duty to a child did not end with labor and delivery. After delivery, then begins the long journey of cuddling, nurturing, caring for and molding the child. The task is obviously enormous, challenging and daunting but mothers live up to it. In fact, they fulfill the task with all pleasure.

So as Mothers' Day for the United States rolls in this Sunday, May 10, 2009, I dedicate this piece to my mother and all mothers for their patience, understanding, perseverance, kindness and most of all their unconditional love for their children. I have to openly thank my mother, Mrs. Lillian Uzoma Uzokwe, for all she did for me and my siblings; for allowing me to be me, for believing in me and for giving me the opportunity and encouragement to be the best I could. Most of all, I thank her or putting up with all my childish effusions and exuberance. With utmost humility, I thank the Almighty God for sparing the life of a woman I love, cherish and adore; the woman who endured twenty something hours of labor pains, forty nine years ago, for my sake. Mama, here is wishing you a pleasant Mothers' day and many more happy years. I am sure I can say the same for all mothers out there on behalf of their children, including my readers. Happy Mothers' day to all mothers.

Winston Churchill, in all his glory, said this about his own mother: "my mother shone for me like the evening star. I loved her dearly". President Barack Obama, the world's most powerful man today, noted in an interview that his mother, Ann Dunham Soetro, was the most dominant figure in his formative years. He further stated that the values she taught him continue to be the touchstone when it came to how he went about the world of politics. Of course we all know what those values fetched President Obama. Not bad! In the song, "I want a girl", William Dillon sings: "I want a girl just like the girl that married dear old dad". This is a very common sentiment amongst men regarding their mothers. In general, it is rare to find someone that does not have some form of glowing things to say about their mother. Even when people fall out with their mothers, the animosity is not always deep-seated. To those few who may not share in my upbeat feelings about mothers, for understandable reasons, I say hearken to the call by Naomi Judd and her daughter in the song entitled "love can build a bridge". Cling on to the greatest gift your mother has given you which is the gift of life and love. Build the bridge of relationship and love with her, for mothers are God's greatest gift to mankind and should be cherished and appreciated.

Ever seen those visitors that stand outside the studios of CNN, ABC, CBS, FOX and NBC during newscasts? Is it not intriguing that 85% of the placards they carry always read "Hi, Mom?" Ever wondered why every time athletes are interviewed during games, several end by saying, "Hi, Mom" or "I love you, Mom?"

I would like to borrow a few lines from Prince Nico Mbarga's African chart-bursting song of the 70s called "Sweet Mother". He sang, "Sweet mother, I no go forget you, for the suffer wey you suffer for me. If I no eat, my mother no go eat, if I no sleep, my mother no go sleep. She no dey tire -o, sweet mother, I no go forget the suffer wey you suffer for me yeah yeah". In the same song, Prince Mbarga crooned, "When I no well, my mother go cry, cry, cry, she go say instead make I go die, make she die-o, she go cover me cloth, beg God help me, God help me, my pikin-o-o". This song was very popular when it first burst into the musical scene in the 70s. It is still exceedingly popular amongst Africans today in spite of the fact that the artist has long passed on. To gauge the popularity of the song, all one needs to do is to play it during

Nigerian parties. The dancing floor would fill up quickly with most singing along. This is because the song echoes, in the minds of many, a sentiment they all share and believe in. It reminds us all why we love our mothers so dearly and so we sing along as if speaking directly to them.

Many years ago, I observed tears in the eyes of a young lady dancing next to me when this song was played. She was singing the song as loud as she could but still had tears rolling down her cheeks as she danced. I later found out that her own mother had passed on just a few years earlier and the song brought back memories to me.

Talking about the suffer wey mama suffer for me, I remember my childhood days in Lagos, Nigeria. As a domiciliary nurse, my mother would toil from house to house all over Lagos to perform her midwifery duties. By the time she got home at the end of the day, you could tell that she was very exhausted and deserved a long rest. But for her, rest was out of the question. She would instead begin immediately attending to other responsibilities at home, wash our clothes, cook, attend to every one's myriad of wants (while keeping her composure). That is vintage Mama and I can say that for all mothers. At the time, I never recognized the extent of sacrifice she was making. I felt that it was her job. I thought that as a mother, she was supposed to be superhuman. It never occurred to me, as I made my unending demands, that this woman may need some rest.

I see the same thing in my household today. As a nurse, my wife would work all night and come back to get some sleep at home. You would think that the kids would understand. No, whenever they need something, they would quickly run to the room, wake her up and make their demands, oblivious of the fact that they just deprived her of a well-deserved rest. The most intriguing thing is that she would calmly get up, attend to what they asked for without any tinge of bitterness.

Our first son is grown now and away in college but his mother is yet to relinquish her maternal oversight on him. From time to time, at her behest, we would buy school provisions, items the young man can easily procure out there, and drive some 108 miles to Philadelphia to drop them off for him. Every time that happens, I remember my own mother. Even as a middle aged man, my wife's maternal oversight towards our son has not diminished. Just this last December in Nigeria, on a visit with all my children, my mother was undeterred. In spite of her age, every morning, my mother would have me come to her room. She would pray for me and every one of my children and wife. She would be the first to ask if I had eaten; she would be the first to notice that I had lost some weight and needed to eat a little more even if the weight loss was deliberate. She would be the first to notice a new black head on my face and ask if I applied any medication on it.

Back in the United States, every time I call my mother on the phone, she would be the first to ask why my voice sounded a little hoarse and would wonder if I had a cold and advise that I take some medication for it. This is what mothers do and so even when I am tempted to say to my wife that our son is twenty and knows how to get himself provisions in college, I pull back remembering that I get the same attention from my own mother even at my age. Maternal love knows no age and that is how it was meant to be.

I sometimes have to drive my kids to extra -curricular activities like softball, chorus, drama and the like right after work and make the rounds again to pick them all up. Sometimes I have to stay for some of the activities. I get so exhausted after driving them around that sometimes once I step into the house, I fall asleep on the couch. But my wife does all that and yet comes back and starts on another chore. Mothers are just like the energizer bunny, "they keep going and going and going and..." We owe them a debt of gratitude.

In the past, I frequently had to travel out of town on assignment. In such situations, my wife would take care of the kids by herself. When I come back looking for any signs of exhaustion in her, it is never there, yet she accomplishes every single activity needed for the day-to-day upkeep of the children and attend to all their needs with equanimity. Only mothers can do all that without complaints. They work wonders and bring the needed balance to any family. God Bless mothers.

Mothers have been described in very many ways, all pointing to the fact that they nurture, care and guide. Phrases like "the love of a mother"; Mother Nature; motherly care; as gentle as a mother's love; Motherland and Mother tongue all point to the significance of the word "mother". Even the main circuit board in a computer is referred to as "motherboard!"- go figure.

During the Biafran war in Nigeria and in the face of the gradual annihilation of her relatives in Asaba, by the Federal troops, my mother had to deal with the agony of the concurrent loss of her father, uncles, brother and other relatives in the Asaba massacre. Through all these trials and tribulation, she summoned enough inner strength to continue to discharge her motherly duties to us all. She cried endlessly, grieved endlessly (something that broke my heart so much to behold as a child) but she never let up on the quality of care she rendered to us. In the course of the many uncertain days we awaited news of the fate of my two brothers that went to war to fight for Biafra, my mother never wavered in the discharge of her maternal duties towards me and my remaining siblings.

She attended to all our needs in the day and stayed up all night crying and by morning, we would wonder why mama's eyes were red and swollen but she would only offer reassuring words to insulate us from the agony she was enduring. Her main focus was to ensure we were not traumatized by that experience. That was motherly love at play. After that traumatic experience, she developed the resolve that since the war had deprived her of her father and many of her relatives, she was going to give her best to her kids and give her best she did.

Remember President George W. Bush during his presidential campaign. He never ceased to let anyone know how much influence his mother had in his life. He would often say "even though I have my father's eyes, I have my mother's mouth." So even with all the achievements of George Bush senior as the former president, the Bush children still credit their mother, Barbara Bush, as the glue that held them together and gave them the impetus to be the best they could. This is not to discount the role of fathers because fathers do have their own responsibilities towards their children and they play their role with grace. Mothers, however, are the galvanizing forces, the magnet (if you will) that hold families together.

Listen to Ruth Bader Ginsburg - United States Supreme Court Justice - in her nomination acceptance speech in 1994: "I have a last thank you. It is to my mother, Celia Amster Bader, the bravest and strongest person I have known". Justice Ginsburg echoed a sentiment that most of us have about our mothers. I certainly see my own mother as the bravest and boldest woman on earth. She never wavered nor flinched in her support for my other siblings and me in our times of need, in our times in trouble. She is always there to support us. Her love is unconditional.

Many years ago, when I was just a teenager, the authorities in my secondary school (high school) decided to reduce the number of black-eyed peas cake (akara) we were served for breakfast. They reduced it from the traditional four balls to three. The news was devastating for many of us that had healthy appetites for that delicacy which was almost all the students. I therefore joined in a minor protest in my school to protest that fact. I even made a public speech to other students urging them to refrain from eating the three akara balls we were served as a protest. Unbeknownst to us, the principal had a "mole" amongst our ranks. The "mole" subsequently sent the names of those he referred to as the "ring leaders" to the principal. Not long after that, we got news that the "ring leaders" would be suspended from school. The news hit me like a devastating punch on the solar plexus! I was unsure how to face my parents about the suspension. Suddenly moving from being a bright student with a bright future, to a suspended student was not my father's idea of progress. Knowing that if my father heard the news first, the roof of our house would probably come crashing down with his understandable anger, I decided to confide in my mother first. I walked into her office with tears in my eyes and once she saw me, she excused herself for a couple of minutes from the patients waiting to be attended to. She took me to a private room and then gently asked: "What is wrong, Obiora?" I took time and explained to her what had transpired.

When I finished my story, instead of immediate rebuke and expression of disappointment at how I had become a renegade, I got the most reassuring and soothing words. My mother was even concerned that going from four balls of akara to three was the wrong thing for the school to do. She believed that students should be properly fed. Placing her hand on my shoulder, she said, "You are not a bad boy, Obiora. I will talk to your father and he will go and see your principal about this". My mother's action, even when I was expecting a dress-down, was very instructive. That lesson still stays with me to this day. Often times parents judge children too harshly for "putting the family name in disrepute" rather than take time to understand the issue well and act accordingly. The lesson I learned is: DO NOT CONDEMN YOUR CHILD UNTIL YOU HAVE HEARD THE OTHER SIDE OF THE STORY. She could have chosen to pounce on me once she heard the word "suspension," but she calmly listened. She made true her promise and my father went to see the principal. This is the greatest role that mothers play in the house - the role of mediators that help avert over-reaction to the shenanigans of children. They put their children at ease; they listen to them and they don't rush to judgment.

I will end this piece with an observation. Part of my definition of motherhood is a person that brings forth life to earth. I find it coincidental, if not serendipitous, that the woman that I dedicated this piece to exceeded my definition of motherhood. She did not just bring forth my siblings and me to earth, but through her nursing and midwifery career that spanned more than 59 years and took her through Asaba, Ogwashiukwu, Jos, Lagos, Enugu and finally Uzoma Maternity, Nnewi, she took delivery of more than 30,000 babies. They are of different ages, of different professions and scattered all over the globe. Some of them are regular readers of my commentaries. From time to time, when my commentaries appear on Nigeriaworld, I get inquiries from some as to whether I was related to Lilian Uzoma Uzokwe. From my perspective, it is one of the greatest honors an unassuming mother could get and God bless her for that.

May God grant all mothers the inner strength to continue to do what they do best - being mothers. And to all those mothers near and dear to my heart - Anthonia, Ijeoma, Uche, Edith, Ijeoma Jr, Felicia, my mother and all mothers across the globe - I say Happy Mothers' Day.

Low Morale is Really The Issue In The Police Force Not Their Dress Uniform.– March 19, 2012

The Federal Government has approved a new camouflage uniform for the police. The new uniform was recently modeled by the acting Inspector General of Police, Mohammed Abubakar. The IGP explained that the advantage of the new police camouflage is that it will be cost effective to maintain, operationally durable and highly customized with security features to forestall impersonation. He added that the uniform will be environmentally friendly and is part of the government's transformation agenda to carve a new image for the police.

I always marvel at how unkempt some of the policemen can be in their uniforms. Some do not see the need in washing, starching and ironing their uniforms resulting in very dirty and rumpled uniforms. I have even seen some in bathroom slippers while dressed in their uniforms! If the IG is concerned about appearance, and he should be, the first step is to mandate a certain standard in personal hygiene and penalize those who flout it. Members of the police must always wash and iron their uniforms before wearing them for duty.

Physical fitness also falls under the realm of appearance. It is gratifying that for the first time, in the long history of the Nigerian police, we have an Inspector General that looks physically fit and hence smart in uniform. If anyone has to model the uniform, it is him. His physical appearance gives him the moral standing ground to go to police parade grounds and declaratively tell all the police chiefs that parading pot-bellies is no longer acceptable. They should all shape up or shape out. Physical fitness will not only improve appearance, it will enable our police men and women perform very well on duty. A physically fit policeman will take less time off from work as a result of illness. The other day, I read about two policemen that slumped where they were standing guard. If standing for a short period of time would make a policeman slump, how would that person react if he has to embark on a shootout with criminals that involve running and other forms of physical exertion?

Having said the above, it must be emphasized that there is more to a great police force than just uniform and physical fitness. Hence, the issue of replacing police uniform as a first step in police transformation agenda is a gross case of misguided priority. The IGP must do the needful first.

The greatest problem in the police force today, a problem that the IG should focus on if he wants real transformation, is the issue of poor morale. Low morale is the direct result of poor condition of service. We expect these men and women to perform miracles for us; catch criminals with their bare hands and take a bullet for the general population yet we fail to provide a condition of service that will boost their morale and make them give forth their best. We often forget that police men and women are human beings that have wives and husbands. We lose sight of the fact that they have children that go to school and hence need school fees. We feign ignorance of the fact that just like other Nigerians, they have relatives that they also have to help financially. Simply put, they are human and in accordance with Maslow's hierarchy of needs, they need good shelter over their heads and good food on their tables. Without these, Nigerians might as well kiss all expectations good bye. Maslow tells us that only after a human being has satisfied the basic needs of food and shelter will the person start seeking self-actualization. In the case of the police, self-actualization includes being patriotic, looking smart, dressing well and being willing to take a bullet for Nigerians.

Back in November, on a visit to Nigeria, we drove by several police barracks. I paid particular attention to one of the barracks. It had dilapidated buildings with crumbling walls all over. Water damage, evidenced by dark marks were all over the walls. Even though the dry season had already set in, one could see that plants were growing on parts of the walls that were exposed to the elements. Some had windows that seemed inoperable and some of the window openings were boarded up. These were residential quarters for our police force! They are expected to go home to these shanties after a hard day's work, get a good night's sleep and be hale and hearty the next day to step out again and put forth their best for Nigeria. Just the mold that would be accumulating inside the buildings because of warmth and moisture is enough to cause prolonged pulmonary discomfort and downright sickness. How could the government of Nigeria house the men and women responsible for the security of the citizens in an environment hardly conducive for living? Such an environment will always convey to the police force the fact that Nigeria does not care for them. That type of feeling is a morale killer. They will never be patriotic enough to want to take a bullet for the masses nor shun bribery and corruption.

Poor housing is not the only problem. We know that some of these men and women get salaries barely above the minimum wage yet they have children to feed and send to school. They have relatives to train and yes, they want to have their own cars and build homes in their villages. When they see that their salaries will never provide these necessary needs, they resort to bribery, corruption and extortion. We have read about several situations where policemen shoot citizens for not giving them "mandatory" N20 bribe at check points. For many, that N20 adds up and becomes their mainstay. One is not justifying corruption and extortion in the police force, but the IG must understand that as long as the condition of service for the police is poor, Nigeria will never get much out of many of them. He must address these issues head on before talking about new camouflage uniforms. Use the money to be spent on uniforms to embark on massive renovation of police housing units.

The other issue is benefits. A policeman in the United States does his job knowing that if he falls in the line of duty, his family will not suffer. They have good benefits. In this day and age of Boko Haram in Nigeria, many police men have fallen in the line of duty. Are their families being adequately taken care of? Probably not and that dampens morale.

The IG has said many times that the general attitude to work, of the police force is far below minimum standard. He is correct but he must now right the obvious wrongs that lead to substandard performance. After that has been done, we can step into the self-actualization realm and start talking about new camouflage uniforms. For now, a hungry man is not interested in new uniforms whether camouflage or plain.

September 11 2001 Bombings:
America's Indomitable Spirit Shines Through Even In Time Of Despair -September 17, 2001

O beautiful for spacious skies; for amber waves of grains…. Wait, there is much more for which this great country called America is beautiful, not just for spacious skies; not just for amber waves of grain, there is more.. America is beautiful for her people who, under the most trying times and in the face of one of the most heinous crimes ever committed against humanity, still stand tall and espouse the spirit of country. Yes, love of country and love for her people. Standing tall and in one indomitable spirit, America is condemning this horrendous crime against humanity.

I was in a training class when those planes crashed into the World Trade Center buildings. None of the participants in the training room knew what had happened until we went for break at about 10:00am. We found it odd that people would huddle around a TV in the work place at that time of the day. Right there and then we knew that something bad had happened but we never imagined the magnitude of the carnage! It was sickening and unbelievable.

Yet the unflinching spirit of survival that has so much characterized America was intact; the indomitable spirit that has led to so many heroic feats by Americans was riding high. It is the spirit that musters the last ounce of strength and courage in time of despair to overcome adversity. Even in tears, even in utmost disbelief, even in the midst of uncertainty, America was hopeful.

As we all wondered aloud why this calamity had befallen this nation, America did not lose hope. You would hear comments like: "the perpetrators of this evil will be brought to justice", "we would not allow terrorists to take away our freedom" That is the same spirit that America displayed after the NASA accident when Christa McAuliff and the rest of the Challenger crew died in the line of duty. America mourned them but stood tall; NASA mourned but regrouped and built a bigger and better program than they had before the accident. That is America, a nation always coming away from tragedies bigger and better.

That same unwavering spirit responded to John F. Kennedy's call and put Apollo crew on the moon; that spirit helped victims of Oklahoma city bombing rise from the ashes of despair; that same spirit lives on in this great country and out of this catastrophic setback, America will rebuild; she will become even stronger as a nation.

O beautiful for spacious skies.. wait, there is much more: America is beautiful for much more than spacious skies; She is beautiful for the willingness of Americans to bind together and speak with one unmistakable and resolute voice in times of tragedy. Without regard to political affiliation or religious beliefs; without distinction along racial lines, America has spoken again even as she mourns this devastating loss. She would rebuild; she would become better; she would become stronger and she would still prosper.

It was a beautiful sight to behold the Speaker of the House- Dennis Hastert (Republican) and House Minority Leader - Dick Gephart (Democrat) standing side by side and vowing to work together with the President to do what it takes to tackle this horror. The President asked for $20 million but in the most bipartisan spirit, they approved $40 million as down payment for cleanup and tackling the problem. That is America.

O beautiful for spacious skies.. wait, there is much more: America is beautiful for much more than spacious skies, She is beautiful for her compassionate spirit, the spirit that helps people through tragedy; the spirit to quickly rally around those in despair.

In the wake of this terrible tragedy of cataclysmic proportions, sympathizers traveled from states as far away as California to New York to lend a helping hand; to help clean up the rubble. Those who were not physically able to help clear the rubble just cheered the fire fighters and rescuers as they did their jobs. Others lent moral support by simply flying the American flag. But that is America; that is the same compassionate spirit that takes America to far-away nations to help starving women and children; to help end strife and pestilence. There is always a risk associated with that type of mission. American lives have been lost in the past but America goes anyway. That is compassion and that has been America.

People from all over the country are collecting what they could to aid the surviving victims and their families. This is not surprising to me as I have seen America do it many times before. It is America at her best. I should know because I have been a recipient of America's compassion in my time of personal tragedy. Most did not know me but they came anyway; they rallied around; they helped in any way they could. That is the America I know. GOD BLESS AMERICA.

I was moved to tears when I saw President Bush on TV discussing this tragedy. With tears in his eyes and humility in his demeanor, he spoke movingly about this horror but with resoluteness of purpose, he put everyone on notice that this would not go unpunished. His sincere display of sorrow, grief and sadness gave hope to grieving relatives of the victims and as one of the relatives put it: "we know the President is with us and it is reassuring". As he spoke in New York (mega phone in hand) while standing on top of one of the mounds of rubble scattered all over the grounds of the World Trade Center, his reassuring message sparked cheers of "USA, USA…" from the crowd gathered.

O beautiful for spacious skies.. America is beautiful for much more than spacious skies: America is beautiful for bravery. The fire fighters that died in the conflagration knew that the situation was bad; they knew that the risks were enormous; they knew that there was the possibility of collapse of the rest of the structure on them but duty had called so they responded; they wanted to save the lives of other Americans even if their own lives were put in harm's way. Many lost their lives in the process but this is America: the land of the brave; the land where people put their lives on the line to save the lives of others. That is the American spirit. GOD BLESS AMERICA.

Think about the New York Police Officer who was on patrol with his partner when this happened, he could have tried to do his job from a safe distance but he chose to tackle things head on. He went in to help a fire fighter take up his fire-fighting paraphernalia but never made it out. He lost his own life trying to save others; that is bravery. That is America.

O beautiful for spacious skies.. America is beautiful for much more than spacious skies: America is beautiful for her deep belief in the existence of a higher and more powerful and Supreme Being. When things that defy imagination happen, when the world seems to come to a standstill, when despair hangs on the horizons like rain clouds, America takes it to the hands of the higher Being. She knows when to surrender to the will of the higher Being. She has now done that.

The interdenominational services all over the nation on Friday in response to the call by the President were beautifully carried out. It exemplified the willing spirit of a people of faith, faith that tomorrow shall be better than today; faith that today's experience would make us better tomorrow; faith that you could actually turn deadly obstacles into stepping stones to a better future. That is America.

Even little children did not waver in their belief in a better tomorrow; they did not waver in their belief that this gloomy episode in the chapter of American history would pass. As I sat glued to my TV watching horror playing out before our very eyes, my son said: "Daddy, don't worry, the President says we would get those who did this terrible thing; we believe the President, we are America"

God Bless America and give her the fortitude to survive these trying times and come through bigger, better and stronger.

Now That Reuben Abati Is In The Corridors Of Power - July 20, 2011

I welcome the appointment of Dr. Reuben Abati as special adviser on Media matters to President Jonathan. Before his appointment, he was the chairman of the editorial board of Guardian Newspapers and wrote a regular column. His writings always evoked a deep sense of reflection. Many times, he wrote the very serious stuff where he usually chastised government officials for going down the wrong path or out rightly doing the wrong things. Sometimes he wrote the funny stuff where he depicted the plight of everyday Nigerian and how humor is used to cope in a world of hardship that Nigeria has become. I have read many of his pieces where he made very meaningful suggestions on how things could be made better in the country. He was very crafty too because when topics became too hot and sensitive for him to directly name names, he used two-person dialogues to make his point.

Many have come to see Dr. Abati as an accomplished writer in his own right. It is said that the pen is mightier than the sword and he wielded that pen very well. There are politicians who would think twice before doing things just because they wonder how Abati would characterize them in his next write up. He is that good. He has used the pen very well to help inform Nigerians, educate them, chastise them and crack up their ribs.

Last week or so, Dr. Abati was sworn in as a special adviser to the president of Nigeria on Media matters. Obviously, the appointment came because the president must have been reading his writings. He may have formulated the same opinion that many have that he is a critical thinker and always had a way of dissecting the issue at hand and proffering solutions. Put succinctly, the president must have assumed that the man of the pen will be able to help him on issues related to the media. Make no mistake about it, this is a feather on Abati's cap if he wears one.

The easy part of appointment and swearing in has passed; now Abati must face the difficult part. Although he is lucky that he is going into this position with an enormous goodwill, which he built over the years because of his writings, he must now deal with the mammoth expectations that Nigerians would have of him. Nigerians will judge him by the bar he set when he was just a writer. He was a great advocate of freedom of the press and access to the powers that be. He believed that people in public life, including the president, should be accessible and must always let Nigerians know what their intents are at every point in time. He has travelled to many democracies in the world and even lived for a while in the United States. He knows what true democracy is. He knows what press freedom is and also understands the concept of suppression of the populace. He has written extensively about all these. Now that he has stepped into the halls of power, now that he has the responsibility of advising the president and pointing him in the right direction on media matters, will he do his job even if the president's ox is gored? Will he fall into the category of those who talk the talk and then fall exceedingly short when time came to walk the walk?

How will Abati react when other writers, in line with freedom of press, seek important information from Aso Rock? Will he convince the president that the right thing to do is to open up the books and give the press what they want or will he wear a different hat and speak a different language? Will he suddenly start down the road of classifying every piece of information as sensitive and so not to be released to the public? Will Abati always encourage the president to be forthcoming and forthright to the nation even at a political disadvantage, something he has often advocated, or will he attempt to shield the man from the press and Nigerians when it becomes convenient? Inotherwords, will he let political advantage govern his actions or will he practice what he once preached?

How about profligacy, something that many Nigerian politicians enjoy? In Nigeria, it has become the norm that when you get a small political appointment or make a little money, even if by hook or crook, suddenly you become exceedingly important, traveling in 10-car convoys, blaring sirens and causing traffic hold up. Abati was at the forefront of criticizing politicians and Nigerians who flaunted this type of lifestyle. How would he react in Abuja if and when his car gets caught up in traffic? Will he ask his driver to turn on the siren and speed away or will he patiently sit in traffic like every other Nigerian until his turn? More importantly, will he be educating his colleagues in government on the need to ditch the convoy thing and live like normal Nigerians?

Abati has often written about ostentation and the silly display of wealth by politicians during parties and all manners of get together. Will he avoid such type of life and show example or will he quickly become immersed in the trappings of political profligacy? Will he advise the president to reduce his retinue of convoys and lead by example or will he suddenly start seeing such displays as essential in the lives of "successful and important" Nigerians?

I used to be protagonist of bringing back Nigerians who have lived abroad, seen and practiced democracy, to help show example and restore sanity to the nation. I stopped that advocacy when I saw that these Nigerians who have lived and practiced true democracy overseas and criticized the government to high heavens, end up when they return and join politics being the greatest culprits with respect to corruption and vices of that ilk. I can name several of them who came back and became governors, senators and legislators. Nigerians reposed confidence in them because of their sojourn outside the country. In the end, they let everyone down. They were in the forefront of corruption, nepotism and profligacy. This is the reason why I no longer get carried away by what someone says until they have had the opportunity to put what they say into practice. However, I, just like most Nigerians, will be willing to give Dr Reuben Abati the benefit of the doubt.

Abati must seize the moment and make a difference and show that all those writings mean something. He must show that his sojourn outside Nigeria means something even if others before him have disappointed Nigerians. Those before him who failed in the past adduced silly reasons like, "the president would not listen to what I say" for their failure. Honorable people who want to make a change must keep an option called "resignation" open. If you are hired to advise the president on media matters and he would not listen to your advice, then the honorable thing to do is resign. If you fail to do so, then you have become part and parcel of the system. I hope Dr Abati has that option open in his mind. It was good that during their swearing in ceremony, the president said he hired them to advise him not for him to tell them what to do. It was the right statement to make. Dr Abati must now seize the moment.

I wish him well in his new appointment

President Obasanjo Wants to Remake Nigeria's Foreign Image By Sweeping Her Problems Under The Rug

The shrill sound of the telephone woke him up from a very deep slumber. He lazily rolled over to the far end of the bed and fumbled for the light switch. Turning it on, he reached for the phone. "Hello", he answered. "Max"(not his real name), the excited voice on the other line crooned. "The wedding date has finally been fixed, I have sent out your invitation. Please do not disappoint me", the voice added. Maxwell Salami, a successful software engineer living in a suburb in the North Eastern United States, was very happy to hear that after many years of uncertainty, his cousin and best friend who still lived in Nigeria, had finally decided to tie the nut. It was going to be an occasion for him to see other relatives and friends that he last saw many years ago. After further exchange of pleasantries and catching up with current developments in their lives, they hung up.

For the next several days, after the telephone conversation, Max weighed the pros and cons of traveling to Nigeria for the wedding with all members of his family. Eventually, financial reality check forced him to settle with going alone. Once the decision was made, it was time to attend to first things first. He had to make his flight reservation.

He hopped onto his computer and began to surf the net, looking for a good price deal on flights emanating from JFK to Lagos. After about 25 minutes of Internet search, he zeroed in on a flight that would take off from New York, land briefly in London Heathrow Airport the next day. He would then change planes, but would fly with the same airline to Lagos Nigeria. He was very pleased that the total amount of layover time in Heathrow Airport before proceeding to Nigeria would be one hour and twenty minutes. "Honey, I found a great deal on the internet", he called out to his wife who was getting ready to take the kids to an evening activity. "What was it", she responded excitedly. Max explained and then showed her the price on the computer screen. She was very happy that they were not going to shell out the exorbitant amount that people had been telling her for the flight ticket. "Now I am going to consummate the deal by booking the flight with my credit card", he told her. "Go on", she said happily before leaving.

Maxwell put a check mark in the box that indicated acceptance of the terms of the on-line flight-booking contract. This was a routine he had become used to. Being a frequent flyer within the United States, he had made countless airline reservations through the Internet and paid with his credit card. After checking the box, a message came up on his computer screen, telling him that he would now be directed to another screen where payment would be required so that his flight would be confirmed. The statement further stated that if payment was not made, the reservation would not be complete and the flight of course could not be confirmed. As Maxwell waited to be redirected to the said screen, he whipped out his credit card, ready to enter the number and expiration date. After a few seconds, a new screen appeared but instead of asking for his credit card number, in bold letters, a message read, "your booking is not yet confirmed". It further read that because of his destination, Lagos Nigeria, he had to call an 800 number to complete his transaction. He was given a reference number to supply the attendant when he called the 800 number. Maxwell was baffled by this but decided to do what was being asked because he really felt that he had a very good price deal.

He quickly picked up his cell phone and dialed the 800 number. In a few seconds, an attendant answered. After identifying her name and that of the airline, the lady pleasantly asked, "What can I do for you today?" "I just made a reservation with your airline but was given a reference number to call and complete the booking", he told her. "What is your reference number sir?" the lady asked. He supplied her with the number and for a few seconds he could hear her typing it in. "Okay, I just pulled up your itinerary and reservation", the lady said. "You will now have to take this reference number and go to a ticket counter in any of the major airports like JFK or Newark. They would be able to issue your ticket when you get there" Stunned by all this, Maxwell notified the lady that he had made countless flight reservations on the internet and paid with his credit card from the comfort and safety of his house. "Why are my being given all this runaround this time?" "Because people from the part of the world where you are traveling to have perpetrated a lot of credit card fraud. To purchase with credit card, you will need to be identified in person. This process is an attempt to stem the tide of credit fraud in those areas" As if she had not rattled Maxwell's cage enough, she added nonchalantly, "Please note that you will have 48 hours to complete the transaction otherwise the reservation would be erased by the system. You may also go to any major travel agency and please be sure to go along with the reservation reference number and a photo identification". Seeing that there was no use protesting, Max ended the conversation and slowly put the phone down.

Why is this commentator recounting the above story, the reader might ask? One is recounting it because of the so-called "Image and National Economies" project that was launched in Abuja, on July 14, by President Olusegun Obasanjo. The president stated that the project was an attempt to "tackle the negative publicity and impressions that harm the nation's good name"[The Guardian, July 15, 2004]. The incident described above, which is real and which happened to a real Nigerian living and earning an honest living in the United States, buttresses General Obasanjo's argument that Nigeria's image has been battered abroad and was in need of repairs. It is also a testament to the fact that a few bad Nigerian apples have succeeded in soiling the whole bunch. The credit card machinations of a few is costing those Nigerians that live honest and honorable lives in the United States.

This writer is aware of a business concern here in Pennsylvania who would not even entertain the idea of going to invest in Nigeria even though he sees Nigeria as having a lot of potential. His reasons? He reminds me of how foreign businessmen have been swindled after being lured into Nigeria by Nigerians for business investments and cited a particular case where a businessman lost his life in Nigeria in pursuit of money owed to him by some Nigerian business "associates". He talks about the seemingly unchecked crime rate in the country and points to the frequent incidents where passenger buses are waylaid and business people murdered in cold blood by armed robbers. It is sad that this is happening in a country that needs the help of foreign businesses to thrive.

In his speech during the launching of the Nigerian image reform project in Abuja, the president stated, "it has become imperative to inform the whole world that Nigeria and a majority of its citizens contribute positively in various areas of human endeavor". Again, the president is right. It would take concerted campaigns to bring the world to see that for every bad egg in Nigeria, there are thousands of good ones.

The disagreement I have with General Obasanjo on this "image project" is when he said, "it is time for us to collectively take definite steps towards shaping and articulating the kind of image we want our nation to have. We have to showcase the best of Nigeria at the local and international" By that statement, he seems to be insinuating that we have to sweep the bad under the rug and trumpet (showcase) the good. That would be a double life as far as this writer is concerned. The truth is that Nigeria and Nigerians are not completely innocent of the crimes or problems that they are being branded for. The only problem is that the crimes are being perpetrated by a few. Some Nigerians have been involved in all sorts of crimes abroad; they have been convicted of drug trafficking, advance fee fraud, credit card fraud and the like. It is important therefore for us not to pretend that we are unaware that such problems exist.

The image project should have a two-pronged approach. While we tell the world that corruption, fraud and other crimes are not the norm in Nigeria, we should simultaneously be cleaning out the skeletons in our collective cupboards by dealing summarily with the people who bring disrepute to her image both in Nigeria and abroad.

If Nigeria is seen by other countries to be policing herself and her citizens with stiff penalties for crimes committed outside and inside Nigeria, they may no longer see the need to be punishing all of Nigeria for crimes committed by a few. For example, on the issue of robbers waylaying and killing passengers traveling from one part of the country to the other, there is no amount of image making that would change the mind of a foreign investor who is afraid that he may lose his life if he travels to Nigeria. Therefore, rather than try to cover up such crimes with image making, the president should first develop a plan that goes after the hoodlums that embark on such acts. Stiff penalties cannot be ruled out. If we start registering strings of successes in apprehending or eliminating such hoodlums, we may not even need image-making anymore because the results would speak volumes.

During the image making project launch in Abuja, General Obasanjo said, "I know of a country which has a very high incidence of HIV/AIDS...and decided that they are not going to talk about HIV/AIDS because they want to present a cleaner, a more favorable image of themselves to the world" Frankly this type of image-making borders on deception if not outright fraud. It is unconscionable that a nation would hide its AIDS statistics while people die from the disease. If the nation hides the statistics, how would they get help in handling the epidemic from other countries? It would be more prudent to take massive action like AIDS education, establish more diagnostic and treatment centers and work against poverty that encourages prostitution. If a country has a high incidence of AIDS and takes the right actions to combat it, the image making part would be to let the world know what actions are being taken to combat rather than hide it.

We have been told that there are 1 million AIDS victims in Lagos state alone. Should we hide that statistic and tell the world that we do not have AIDS in Nigeria when infact hundreds are dying? Emphatic no. The right thing to start taking good steps to combat it and then tell the world what we are doing. Every country on the face of the earth, including the United States, has AIDS victims. The difference lies in how it is being handled.

Mr. President, while your intention on this image-making project is good and you should be commended, you must do it right for it to work. The 600 million being allotted to the project could be used for both image making and image repair through corrective actions.

University Of Nigeria Alumni Gather In Atlanta To "Restore The Dignity Of Man"- Oct 19, 2010

I graduated from the University of Nigeria 27 years ago. Armed with a first professional degree in architecture, I felt well-equipped and enormously confident to face the professional challenges that life was bound to throw at me. My indebtedness to the University, for giving me the best education was the reason why I joined my fellow lions and lionesses, last weekend, in Atlanta Georgia. The occasion was the celebration of the 50th anniversary of the founding of the institution by Nigeria's former president, Rt Honorable, Dr Nnamdi Azikiwe. UNN alumni in the United States used the occasion to raise funds in support of programs aimed at reawakening the one-time roaring lion.

The wide-bodied aircraft that my wife and I boarded in Philadelphia landed uneventfully in Atlanta just after 8:00PM on Friday, October 15. We quickly took a shuttle that ferried us to the Hilton Garden Inn, Atlanta, the venue of the two-day convention. While in the hotel lobby checking in, it was a delight for me as we found ourselves in the midst of alumni of University of Nigeria. They came from all corners of the United States as well as directly from Nigeria. Exchanges of pleasantries and loud laughter permeated the air as those that graduated from the University earlier found light-hearted delight in referring to newer graduates as cubs rather than lions. Before we retired for the night, I had a taste of Southern Hospitality as one of my townsmen, resident in Atlanta, Joe Aralu, took my wife and I and another UNN alumni couple, out for a very scrumptious dinner. That short drive gave us a glimpse of Atlanta - a very lively city. The hospitality did not end there as it was followed up the next day by Chuka Uzokwe and Mike Okeke.

The next morning, as we had breakfast in the dining hall, the tempo of the event began to build as some alumni started filtering into the dining room. One of my greatest delights came when the former vice chancellor of the University of Nigeria from 1980 to1985, Professor Frank Ndili, walked into the dining room with his wife and some family members. My mind went back to my days in the institution and the academic excellence that his name always conjured because of his work in the school and his personal achievements in academia. He was not only a respected vice chancellor but a distinguished scholar, being the very first Nigerian nuclear physicists after bagging a PHD in nuclear physics from Cambridge University, UK, in 1965. As if that was not enough, he continued to distinguish himself in many areas by his membership in high profile organizations like European Organization for Nuclear research, Geneva, the Polish Institute of Nuclear research Warsaw, the British Nuclear Physics lab Daresbury and more. Incidentally, Professor Frank Ndili was going to be the keynote speaker at the UNN alumni convention that very night and I longed to hear what he would say about the declining academic standards that the school has experienced in recent years.

Before long, the plenary session started with the president of UNN Alumni - USA, Dr Michael Okoroafor, delivering his keynote address. In his address, Dr Okoroafor noted that it was at the behest of the former vice chancellor of the University of Nigeria, Professor Chinedu Nebo, that the UNN Alumni -USA was born. The goal of the organization, which had her very first convention in 2007 in Atlanta, he added, was to literally "revitalize the wounded lion" that is the University of Nigeria, "to roar again". He catalogued some of the help that the alumni has already provided to the University like donating computer systems and color printers, container shipment of textbooks and journals, institution of an annual distinguished lecture series, establishment of a one million endowment and development fund and partnership with Nigerian Higher Education Foundation in New York to train faculty and staff of the university in principles of good governance and academic leadership.

Dr Okoroafor highlighted some of the maladies that have plagued the university in recent times like "poor academic rankings, incidents of sexual harassments, pay for grade, requiring students to purchase lecture notes, lack of community outreach and stated that this is a major reason for the alumni to work with the administration of the current vice chancellor, Professor Bartho Okolo, to "drive a restoration agenda for the university".

In his address, the current vice chancellor, Professor Bartho Okolo, declared that the incidence of cultism had been laid to rest. He took the attendees on a photo tour of the progress, so far, in the institution. They include the construction of a new entrance structure to the university, the construction of a southern access road, the development of a water tank to ensure permanent water supply to the school, the construction of a new administration block and the largest library building in Africa, new university book shop and a new undergraduate teaching laboratory. He added that a new university stadium was under construction. Professor Okolo stated that, in spite of the difficulties of the present time, graduates of the University of Nigeria were still sought after by employees and noted that a graduate of the institution broke "a century old academic record of the Imperial College of London"

From left to right: Alfred, Prof Ndili and wife, Prof Bartho Okolo

Professor Okolo went on to say that he was not unaware of the problems that the university was facing but stated that his administration was taking several measures to reverse the trend. Some of the steps include attracting and retaining quality staff, producing knowledgeable graduates, employing new forms of technology in teaching, creating an environment conducive for learning, providing constant power and water. He emphasized that his administration has sent more young staff for overseas training than any other administration and has embarked on the establishment of the widest wireless network owned by any university in Africa. He revealed that the university has an MOU with Hitachi to install smart boards for students to interface with the internet and that all lectures would be delivered via PowerPoint presentations. To the delight of attendees, he said that a data and network center building was just commissioned by Nigeria's president, Dr Goodluck Jonathan and that his administration was on track to modernize all hostels that were built 50 years ago.

In his keynote address, during the evening banquet, former vice chancellor, Professor Ndili, opined that if the quality of education was declining, then "we must find out why and fix it". He stated that when the University of Nigeria was founded by Dr Azikiwe, 50 years ago, it was only the University College of Ibadan that was in existence. He however noted that the university college was seen as elitist and was not addressing all the academic needs of Nigerians since it did not have a full curriculum. As a result, the University of Nigeria was founded, offering courses of study that included Engineering, Law, Estate Management, Pharmacy and the like. In a short time, professor Ndili said, University of Nigeria produced her first graduates, who, for many years, performed excellently in the civil service exams administered to new graduates entering the workforce in Nigeria. The excellent performance of these graduates was part of what contributed to the legendary excellent academic status ascribed to UNN graduates.

Professor Ndili admitted that University of Nigeria has been through hard times before. "During the civil war", he recounted, "most of its infrastructure were destroyed and the university was saddled with the responsibility of rebuilding". This was compounded when the school was declared a federal institution but the federal government did not provide enough support to sustain it. The school was hurt by inadequate funding and poor infrastructure but it was undaunted in the march towards excellence. Hence, in 1975, the university awarded the first PHD in physics. About the same time, the University of Nigeria teaching hospital, under professor Udekwu, performed the first open heart surgery in Nigeria while professor Martin Aghaji, of UNTH, performed the very first cardio thoracic surgery in Nigeria. He noted that some of the issues that led to the decline in quality have been endemic crisis, limited exposure to the wider world of academia, leadership and followership issues, inadequate funding and poor infrastructure. He expressed the opinion that for the school to get back where it was before, all these issues must be addressed.

Before the banquet ended, a fundraising session netted some money for the alumni to pursue the programs it lined up to get the one-time roaring lion of Nigeria to wake up from its slumber and roar with more tenacity and ferocity. Dr Michael Okoroafor, the President of UNN Alumni -USA, also passed the mantle of leadership to the newly elected president.

posing for a photo at the university alumni convention in Atlanta

As our air craft made its way through the windy skies from Atlanta to Philadelphia, on Sunday morning, I was lost in thought. Education is the mainstay of every nation, I thought to myself. The tertiary institutions, like the University of Nigeria, that have produced pillars of the society in the days past, must not be allowed to languish or exist in name only. If Nigeria must join other nations in the technology race, then our tertiary institutions must be equipped to prepare our young men and women. As stated by the various speakers at the convention, whether it is Harvard, Yale, Cornell or Emory University, the alumni plays a very strong and supporting role in ensuring the upkeep of their schools. The UNN Alumni - USA, has an ambitious goal of helping to reawaken and restore the dignity of the institution we once loved dearly and were proud of. It is a worthy cause that all and sundry should support because a quality education will produce better leaders that will make Nigeria what we all long for it to be. I hope that all alumni of the institution will find a chapter close to them to join and ask what they can do to lend a helping hand to the institution that gave them so much.

Using Humor To Play Down Hardship
In Nigeria - December 23, 2010

Nigerians were once branded the happiest people on earth. That sounded crazy at the time but it was just an affirmation of the song penned many years ago by the indefatigable Fela Kuti. He called it "Suffering and Smiling." Fela was depicting a nation where there was too much hardship and yet the people bore it with a certain inexplicable equanimity. In the midst of suffering, they would be smiling. A man pulling many times his own weight in goods, with a wooden truck or wheel barrow, under a 95 degree baking sun, with sweat pouring down his face and cascading down his body, would be expected to be looking tense with a sad disposition on his face. That is not Naija. Inspite of the back-breaking work that pays little, the man will be smiling while making jokes with anyone that comes close to him as he makes his way through the busy streets.

People will be in a house without electricity and hence unable to run the fans that ward off giant mosquitoes. You would expect them to be mad at a government that continues to fail her people in the power-delivery sector or PHCN that has failed to get its act together. They will hardly show any anger instead they will be making light of the situation by describing the sizes of the mosquitoes that play harmonious music around them in the night and laughing heartily. So, inspite of the suffering occasioned by mosquito bites, with attendant burgeoning of malaria parasites and sickness, you still find Nigerians smiling the next morning, ready to go out and face the task at hand. Inspite of the suffering of the previous night, as soon as power is restored, even for the slightest minute, you find them jubilating, "Up NEPA" or in this case, "Up PHCN". It is amazing!

Nigeria is a nation where people always find a way to cut through the everyday misery that confront people in traffic, in banks, on dilapidated and pothole-ridden roads and the like and be happy. Not quite a few days ago, I watched an Okada rider carrying three "passengers". One person between him and the motorcycle handles and two people in the back. The lady in the back also had a child tied behind her back! Effectively, the man was ferrying 4-people, with an assumed combined weight of 700 pounds on a motorcycle that was designed for a probable maximum load of 400 pounds. The danger is obvious because the load on the tires will always put them in jeopardy. Also, the fact that he was carrying someone between himself and the motorcycle handles, made it difficult, if not impossible, for the okada man to be able to react properly in the event of an emergency that requires maneuvering the bike. One would think that the danger that these people were being subjected to would show on their faces as sadness. That was not the case. They were instead immersed in a conversation that was cracking them up in laughter as the okada "driver "meandered through the bad road, periodically extending one hand to wave at people along the dusty road. The only explanation is that people in Nigeria easily adapt to the situation they find themselves and make the best of it.

I visited the bank a few days ago and saw a long line of people being attended to by only one teller. It meant that one could spend as much as 90 minutes just to make a simple withdrawal. Again, the people in the long queue were busy watching a TV behind the teller that showed some kind of European soccer and heartily discussing the game while the line snailed along. Essentially, Nigerian people have developed very powerful coping mechanisms to deal with the many twists and turns that they have come to expect from and in Nigeria. These days, I get jokes through my email that are specifically tailored to Nigeria as a nation and Nigerians as a people. Apparently, there are Nigerians who have taken it upon themselves to develop, write and circulate these satirical jokes or humor to make light of tough situations in the country. I would like to share a couple of the jokes in the article. I am not sure who to give credit for the jokes to but whoever are the originators, credit goes to them.

One of the jokes goes thus: A casket-maker was on his way to deliver one of his caskets when the vehicle he was riding in broke down in a traffic hold up. Sensing that he would be late for the timed delivery, he balanced the coffin on his head and started walking down the highway, towards his destination. Before long, he got to a traffic checkpoint manned by men of the Nigerian police force. "Where you dey carry that thing go?", one of the policemen thundered at him, hoping to extort some money from him. The man replied, "I no like the place where them bury me, so I dey try relocate". On hearing that, all the policemen at the check point took to their heels!

Of course the above joke tries to make light of the situation Nigerians find themselves in on a daily basis. If you live in Nigeria, there can be no escape from the harassment and extortion from the police whether you are in a vehicle or on foot. If you are in a vehicle, they will stop the vehicle and demand money even if you have not contravened any law. Drivers of commercial vehicle are the ones that they extort most. They stop them at traffic checkpoints and brazenly ask for money ranging from twenty naira to fifty. As we drove from Owerri to Ozubulu, just a few days ago, I witnessed several instances, at road blocks, where police took money from commercial vehicle drivers in front of us. As I tried to complain at the brazen nature of the whole activity, a nephew of mine in the car retorted that I had not seen anything yet. He stated that the policemen at checkpoints now carry lots of change with them. So if a commercial vehicle driver gives them say a two hundred naira bill at the check point, knowing that their standard collection is twenty naira, they would reach into their pockets and give change to them! This is amazing! Practicing illegality in broad daylight as if it is legal. The problem here is clear: If the police who are supposed to apprehend bad people just take money from drivers and let them go unsearched, the criminals they are supposedly looking for will continue to elude them because the criminals will be glad to part with even larger sums of money and the police will heartily wave them off.

In this era of kidnapping in the south east, where suspected hoodlums sometimes travel on foot or on okada bikes, people on foot have even become fair game for the police. My understanding is that the police can now stop an individual and conduct a body search to make sure that the person is not a kidnapper before letting the person go. While I am not criticizing them for searching pedestrians on the streets, because desperate times call for desperate measures, the problem is that the Nigerian police will always try to make a buck off it. A pedestrian stopped for search could part with a few bucks and be let go pronto, defeating the purpose of the exercise.

Another joke goes thus: A pastor was praying in a church and after the prayer, he said that the Lord told him that the church should sow seed of fifty thousand naira for the next Bishop's ordination coming up in twenty years. Well, one of the church members wondered aloud, "so this man no believe say Jesus is coming soon" Well, this joke again tries to highlight, in a subtle way, the discrepancy that has now permeated the gospel ministry in Nigeria. The pastors say one thing but do another. Their goal has become simply to make money. Everywhere you go in Nigeria today there are gospel or evangelical churches preaching just one thing, "sow seed". They use up the time that is for sermon to basically solicit money all the way. Most simply use the money for things that do not necessarily enrich the spiritual being and welfare of the members. They solicit money to build huge, state of the art churches, dress themselves in Hollywood style, ride the best cars, even buy jets, fly around the world. When I was growing up, sermons were always dedicated to the spiritual uplifting and wellbeing of church members. The Ten Commandments always took center-stage because even if one was not a Christian and followed those, one would live a great life while making the world a better place.

Yet, another joke goes thus: A man died and went to heaven. There, he found that there were different hells for each country of the world. He then decided to pick the least-painful hell to spend eternity. The man went to the German hell and asked, "What do they do here?" Someone responded to him, "First they put you into an electric chair for an hour; then they lay you on the bed of nails for another hour. Then the German devil will come in and whip you for the rest of the day. The man did not like what he was hearing so he decided to move to the next hell station. He then checked the USA hell, Russian hell and others and the story seemed to be the same for all of them. He chanced onto the Nigerian hell and finds, to his surprise, that there was a long queue there. Amazed at the fact that there was a long queue in front of the Nigerian hell, he asks, "What do they do here?" The attendant replied, "First they put you an electric chair for an hour and then they lay you on a bed of nails for another hour. The Nigerians devil then comes in and whips you for the rest of the day". Bewildered, the man retorted, "But that is the same type of hell that other nations have but they do not have long queue in front of them". At that point, one of the men on the queue pulled him aside and said, "People are rushing to the Nigerian hell because there is never electricity so the electric chair does not work. The nails were paid for but were never supplied by the contractor so the bed is very comfortable to sleep on and the Nigerian devil used to be a civil servant so he comes in, signs in and goes back home for other business."

Account of My Visit to Nigeria September 2004

I stood with my son on the lone open space in the grounds of the bus stop, waiting to be checked in for travel to Nnewi in eastern Nigeria, I suddenly smelt the strong odor of sulfur or burning rubber in the morning air. It was somewhat sickening. The sun had appeared in the sky for the day but was casting an unusually mud-colored haze over the horizon. Surveying the crowded landscape, my eyes came to rest on a stretch of land in the median dividing the busy expressway. A thick plume of black smoke was emanating from there, ferociously wafting upwards into the morning sky. All across that stretch of the median, heaps of burning thrash that included a motley mix of plastic, rubber and tires littered everywhere. I was beginning to get angry with Nigerians for their disdain for the environment but a wiser instinct took over my sense of judgment. I reminded myself that I was back to Nigeria! In this land, people have become self-destructive, engaging in acts that pose daily threats to their health without qualms.

"Welcome back to Nigeria", I muttered to myself under my breath. It was all I could do to maintain my sanity while a serious pollution hazard raged on across the street from Izuchukwu bus stop where we were standing.

I had just arrived Nigeria two days earlier from the Netherlands. It was an uneventful flight that took my son and I into Lagos on a Friday evening sometime after 6:00PM. The only complaint I had so far was that we had to wait for almost two hours to pick up our baggage after arrival. When all the wait was finally over, I still had one missing baggage. I was told that it was a routine occurrence and that I should check back the next day at the airport for the missing baggage. This changed my schedule because I had planned to leave for the East first thing the next morning. After we cleared customs, we walked out of Murtala Muhammed airport building, into the waiting hands of my relative. As we exchanged pleasantries, I noticed that some people had gathered around us. I peered into their faces to see if I could recognize any of them but all I saw was a sea of strange but expectant faces. My relative discreetly cautioned that they were touts. They followed us as we began to walk to his car and when we got there and started to place our bags in the car, one of the touts told us that he had been taking care of my relative's vehicle. Another plainly wanted us to just "dash" him something. I maintained a straight face but could tell that my son was exasperated by what he saw as invasion of privacy. Just before we drove off, a heavy downpour ensued and before long, the road to the airport was flooded and water was barreling down everywhere. The drainage system along the road was in shambles otherwise why would a few minutes' worth of rain start flooding the road leading to the international airport of a country like Nigeria? I quickly suppressed my civil engineering instincts and continued to survey the landscape. It was now getting dark and as the driver continued into the Lagos night, pedestrians were suddenly dashing out of the roadside and crossing the street, prompting him to suddenly slam on his brakes many times. The absence of street lights in most locations made matters worse because it was difficult to see the pedestrians ahead of time. "Driving in Lagos is risky business", I said. "That is what we deal with daily", my relative intoned.

Right after we arrived at my relative's house, NEPA struck; everywhere turned pitch black. "Welcome to Nigeria", I again said to myself. Then, just as though a philharmonic orchestra conductor had given a starting signal to an ensemble, generators began to come alive. Every apartment around seemed to have a generator. Before long, the night was filled with the sound of generators laboring to sustain air conditioners, refrigerators, fans and the likes. The noise was dizzying. Some of the generators were humming gracefully while others sounded like the zoom clang of war machines. Momentarily, my relative went out to the balcony and before long, the sound of his own generator was added to the motley mix. I looked out the window and discovered that the generator was right there on his balcony, belching out as much noise and smoke as it could. Instantly, my mind went to the many news reports that told stories of entire families dying overnight due to carbon monoxide inhalation. They were running generators too close to where they slept.

It is a pity that the government is incapable of supplying steady electricity to the masses and so the government should be partly held responsible for the carbon monoxide poisoning of people who run generators too close to their sleeping quarters. People place the generators close to their apartments so that they would not be stolen since robbery was the order of the day in an economy that is in shambles with soaring unemployment.

We stayed in Lagos for two days so I could pick up my missing baggage. I had the option of flying down to Enugu and then being picked up by family for the less than two hour drive to Nnewi. I rejected that option because I wanted to see firsthand the current condition of the Lagos Onitsha road. Very early on our second day in Nigeria therefore, we drove down to the Izuchukwu bus stop in Yaba to board an Nnewi-bound bus. It was while we waited for our baggage to be loaded onto the bus that I beheld the sordid sight of burning thrash. While the trash burned, saturating everyone's lungs with unhealthy chemicals, hawkers were all over the place doing brisk business. They were selling all manners of items ranging from food to newspapers and water. As if not to be outdone by the hawkers, beggars were everywhere also. Some were without their eyesight and others had various forms of physical deformities that would genuinely preclude someone from making a living. For the 45 minutes that we stood there, more than 12 mendicants came our way, asking for money. Each time they came, I was genuinely moved to hand out whatever I could but a terrible story I had been told on arrival precluded me from giving my widow's mite. The story was that a man was approached for alms in one of the public places in Lagos. Out of compassion, he brought out his wallet and handed out some money to the seemingly incapacitated man. Much later, hoodlums who had earlier seen him bring out his wallet and noticed that he had some money attacked him. I continued to agonize about the fact that I could not do anything for them but I was determined not to cut my nose to spite my face.

Lagos has become a haven for all manners of luxury cars especially Mercedes Benz. As I watched the luxury cars zoom by, I almost started developing the mindset of people who feel that there is no suffering in Nigeria because of the ubiquitous presence of luxury cars and cell phones. Nigeria is a land of contrast though because for every luxury car that zoomed by, there was an equally rickety car following it. Sometimes one wondered how those run-down cars and buses managed to navigate the many bad roads in Lagos. They did not seem road worthy at all and the common thread that tied them together was that their exhaust pipes emitted black plumes of smelly and obviously dangerous smoke. That was a source of environmental concern for me. In my judgment, if there is any place that car emissions tests should be mandatory, it should be Nigeria. It may not be feasible, but for the sake of the health of the citizens, something needs to be done desperately. Pollution hazard is real in Nigeria! Cases of respiratory ailments like asthma are on the rise in the country. Infact, just a few weeks before I got to Nigeria, I lost a very dear relation of ours, Caro, to asthma. One can then understand my concern about environmental pollution and its attendant effects. Also, stomach ailments of every type are present. Add that to the fact that the average life span in Nigeria has now dipped into the late forties and then one would understand the urgency of tackling environmental pollution. For this reason, I tend to agree with Obasanjo's ban on the importation of ageing vehicles because no one knows what they belch out into the atmosphere through their exhaust pipes. The health of the masses should be paramount here.

One must not fail to comment on the conditions of the food items that street hawkers sell. Sometimes they cook the food items very close to open and stagnant drains with flies of all kinds perching on the food after traversing the drains. Some cook the food under the scorching heat of the sun with sweat pouring down their bodies right into what they are cooking. My mother, who had arrived Lagos from Boston just a week before I did, narrated how she witnessed a woman pounding what seemed like yam on the side of one of the busy roads in Lagos. For some reason, the woman's pestle fell off her hands and rolled towards an open drain near her. She simply picked up the pestle and continued pounding away. Of course in the end, she would sell the food to the public. My mother was of the opinion that people would not eat the food if they knew what happened. I have a different opinion however. Perpetual and incessant suffering seem to have hardened Nigerians to the point where they no longer worry about their health and welfare. They knowingly buy food cooked near open sewers; they stand around without raising alarm while unscrupulous elements burn tires, filling their lungs with dangerous chemicals that could hasten their demise. Fela was right, Nigerians suffer and smile at the same time. They live for today and never worry about what could happen the next day.

After we boarded the Nnewi-bound bus, I was seated strategically behind the bus driver because I wanted to see everything along the way for myself. On perimeter walls along Ikorodu road, hundreds of posters announcing upcoming events were plastered. It was an eyesore! In an attempt to stop people from sticking posters on their walls, some landlords equally wrote signs all over their walls that read - "post no posters on this wall". What they may not realize was that they were equally defacing the walls, inadvertently replacing posters with graffiti.

As the bus started towards the East, a quick jolt from a pothole on the road reminded me of the hazard ahead - the hazard of bad roads, potholes and the ubiquitous presence of members of the Nigerian police force. Passengers in the bus had all settled into their seats when a man suddenly rose from his seat and with a bag in hand, scurried towards the driver in front. He was shouting "driver wait-o-o make I go down" The driver slowed down and asked what was amiss. "I entered the wrong bus", the man said. "I wan go down here", he added. In a very sarcastic but firm tone, the conductor asked, "You sure say the bag you carry be your own?" He said an emphatic yes so the driver let him out. As soon as the journey continued, the conductor stood up and told the passengers that the reason why he asked the man if the bag was his was that a new type of trick by hoodlums had started. "Criminals sometimes board the bus empty handed but half way, they pretend to have entered the wrong bus and ask to be let off. When allowed to disembark, they would call down the conductor and tell him that one or two bags in the luggage compartment belonged to them. The conductor would then open the compartment and hand them the bags they identify as theirs only to find out later that the bags belonged to someone else. He then pleaded with all passengers to be vigilant. "Any time the bus stops for someone to disembark, please look out the window to ensure that the person is not taking your bag or box with him". I was alarmed! I had my laptop and the only manuscript of my upcoming book in one of my boxes stowed away in the luggage compartment. I had forgotten to make a backup copy of the manuscript of the book. My relative however assured me that he would be looking out for my bags anytime the bus stopped to discharge passengers. It was at that point that I saw a sign on the panel behind the driver's seat that read, "your luggage at your own risk". There was another sign next to it that read, "Turn off all cell phones". I began to wonder whether the bus had become so sophisticated that it had navigational instruments that the cell phone could disrupt. I leaned towards my relative and asked, "what's that sign for?" He began to explain, "Armed bandits started using cell phones to intimate their cohorts of bus locations along Lagos Onitsha road. In response to the threat, bus drivers prohibited the use of cell phones during travel. "Fair enough", I thought and the bus rolled on.

I kept looking out the window as the bus slowly departed Lagos. The condition of the road had not changed much. It was still in the same sorry state that I saw it last. Lagos- Onitsha road, a network that connects many important cities in Nigeria, was neglected that much. Where potholes were not taking center stage in the middle of the road, men of the Nigerian police force recklessly placed roadblocks or cordoned off some lanes. As a result, there was nothing like a smooth ride for any substantial stretch of the highway. Every time the bus driver picked up speed, we would encounter a pothole or roadblock that would compel him to slow down again. It seemed like the roadblocks were placed every 5-miles. In some areas, the police stationed them right beside giant craters. In a somewhat sick way, they had fallen in love with the potholes, I felt. That was understandable though. The potholes combined with the roadblocks helped them bring even the most obstinate driver to a stop with attendant extortion. Our bus driver continued to meander through the obstacle-ridden road. It was a very dangerous venture but the driver seemed oblivious of the fact that the center of gravity of the bus was high and that it was susceptible to tipping over.

It struck me that buses were not flagged down by the police. They concentrated on cars and vans, especially the flashy ones. I asked why the buses were not stopped and was told that the drivers recently protested the constant extortion they were suffering at the hands of the police. The protest yielded some dividend because since then, buses were no longer harassed along the road by the cops. "Way to go", I said excitedly. It showed what could happen if Nigerians stood up for their rights. However, it was different for private vehicles. When stopped, the cops usually asked to see the particulars of the cars. Those who "did the right thing" were allowed to go. Those who failed to cooperate were delayed for the flimsiest of reasons that include dents on headlights!

Still concerned about the condition of the road, during one of our stops along the way, I alighted from the bus and walked towards a pothole on the road. I simply wanted to get a better sense of how thick the asphalt and aggregate layers used to construct the road were. In roadway design, the more the number of vehicles that use a road (called average daily traffic), the thicker the asphalt and aggregate (stone) layers should be. My preliminary observation, without the benefit of any major analysis, was that the thickness of asphalt and stone used to construct the road did not seem to be adequate for the amount of daily traffic that the Lagos - Onitsha road sustains. For those who wonder why Nigerian roads disintegrate prematurely, the above partly explains it.

I could not keep my eyes off of the highway. After a while, I began to feel that the engineers responsible for it needed to have their credentials examined. Along most of the stretches of the highway, it was difficult to find clear-cut shoulders for vehicles to safely pull into in the event of emergencies. Where shoulders existed at all, they were so small that they did not do much good. No wonder why we frequently hear about motorists being killed by passing vehicles as they stop by the wayside to change flat tires or jumpstart ailing vehicles.

My train of thought was suddenly interrupted when a well-dressed man in our bus suddenly stood up. With bible in hand, he called on the name of the Lord and there was a faint "Amen" from the passengers. As if disappointed by the response, he raised his voice a notch and repeated the same line. This time, and to my surprise, there was an enthusiastic "Amen" from the passengers. At this point, some who were already half asleep came alive. He started preaching and every time I looked back, I saw very attentive faces listening to him. Clearly, Nigeria was a nation of God and frankly that pleased me. However, the more I listened to the man, the more I remembered the multitude of posters that we saw throughout Lagos. Every major road had banners and posters hanging above it, displaying the schedule for an upcoming religious event. Some of the posters made some wild claims like "casting away demons" and the whole nine yards. I could not help but observe that the pictures of the pastors on the posters showed very healthy-looking men in custom-tailored suits. In cases where their hands were shown on the posters, one saw expensive-looking rings and watches. I kept wishing that everyone I saw in Nigeria looked as healthy as the pastors but that was not the case.

In Ikeja, it seemed like every 4th house was a church. They had names like "Evangelical this", "Redeeming that", "Holy Ghost that". We even saw a church that had the name, "Computerized Holy Ghost …". I was stunned! Did that mean that you could now type your request into a computer and it would instantly become heaven-bound? Or is it that computers now perform miracles or aid in the "casting away of demons"? That was hard for me to decipher but as a Christian, my intent here is not to question the authenticity of or denigrate any church. I doubt that I am even worthy to do so. I just feel that the envelop of commercialization is being pushed beyond limitless bounds and the gullibility of a nation in distress is being exploited maximally. That should not be.

After listening to the preacher in the bus for a little while, I forced my attention back to the condition of the Lagos - Onitsha road. This time, I zeroed in on the drainage situation. If drainage is not properly incorporated into a road network, after rainfall, water will percolate in low spots along the road. Gradually, the water would start seeping into and weakening the soil around and beneath the tarred road. Inexorably, this leads to premature road failure. I saw a few roadside ditches that were supposed to serve as drainage but because they were open, sand and mud had already collected in and covered them halfway. I kept wondering who approved the payment of the designers and constructors of the road. In my opinion, Nigeria does need a minister for works that has the principles that Dr. Dora Akunyili of NAFDAC has espoused. The nation needs a minister that would not shy away from terminating contracts awarded to inept contractors and designers. We need a minister that would not hesitate to fire inept and corrupt government engineers that are supposed to be inspecting the work done by contractors and making recommendation for their payment.

As the bus continued to roll, sometimes swerving suddenly to let another vehicle pass, it became clear that the absence of pavement markings on the road was causing confusion to motorists. Pavement markings, the yellow and white lines that separate one lane from another, play a vital role on roads. It delineates the path of travel for motorists and assigns right of way in a sequential manner. Because of the absence of pavement markings on the Lagos-Onitsha road, drivers zig zag along the way as they see fit. There is no respect for the right of way of other vehicles. I recall that as we continued along the road, another bus labored to overtake our bus on an uphill climb. After a while, our bus was neck and neck with it. When I looked out the window, I felt as though I could put out my hand and shake the hand of the people in that bus! The distance felt that close and it was both dangerous and unnerving. A little down the road, I saw vehicles that had careened off the roadway. Others were lying on their sides suggesting that they may have tipped over. While I cannot definitively say that the absence of pavement markers caused the accidents, I cannot discount it either.

Very soon, we were in the outskirts of Benin City and after bypassing a kombi bus, the driver's cell phone rang. He talked for a while and then told his conductor that suspicious-looking men were driving around the vicinity. "The Lord would guide the bus", he muttered and then accelerated. But then, we started hearing a flapping sound in the rear of the bus. The conductor said that it was coming from a van that was trying to overtake our bus. Before long, the van zoomed past but the flapping sound continued. The driver slowly came to a stop and the conductor quickly got down. A few seconds later, he came back into the bus and announced that the right rear tire was flat. What a coincidence, I thought. Our tire had gone flat just after we heard that suspicious-looking people were in the neighborhood.

The bus driver then announced that passengers seated on the right side of the bus should disembark. I was seated on the left side but decided to disembark. The job of fixing the flat tire fell on the conductor while the rest of the passengers anxiously crowded around him. My mind was still fixated on the warning about men that looked suspicious so instead of joining the passengers that crowded around the conductor, I kept a distance from them. From there, I had a panoramic view of the area around the bus. In my mind, it would give me a chance to see any suspicious activity and forewarn the rest of the passengers. In hindsight though, I wonder what I would have been able to do had any untoward thing happened. About ten minutes later, we resumed the journey and a little while later, I fell asleep. I had lost my will to stay awake and continue to assess the condition of the road.

"Bla-a-a-a-h" the shrill sound of the horn woke me up. I looked out but could not tell why the driver was honking the horn but noticed a man in the distance ahead of the bus. He was standing alone and was flagging down the bus. He had what looked like a gun in his hand. I wiped my eyes and looked closely, he was dressed in civilian attire and indeed had a gun in his hand! Before I could collect my thoughts, the driver was beginning to slow down for him. I could not understand the driver's reaction. I felt that he should be speeding up to get out of the way of a gun-totting man in civilian attire. Instead, he was stopping for him. Very soon, the bus came to a halt in front of the man. "We are finally face to face with an armed robber", I thought, but to my surprise, the conductor dutifully opened the door and the man came in. "Ogbuefi", the driver hailed him. The man responded cheerfully, smiling broadly. "Did they show you the armed robber?" the driver asked him. "No", he said smiling and then the bus set out again. They began to discuss the activities of men of the underworld along that route. I could not handle the suspense anymore so I leaned over to my relative. "Who is this man and what does he want?" I asked. "He is an armed escort for the bus company", he eagerly responded. "Because of the prevalence of men of the underworld along Benin - Asaba road, the bus company now has armed escorts that guard the buses once they get into Benin." He further said.

My subsequent discussions with other people revealed that they felt safer with the armed escort in the bus. I had a different take on the issue though. The escort would have been more effective if he concealed his weapon and sat normally on one of the chairs without revealing his identity. The way he had himself exposed, he could actually be the first target of men of the underworld in the event of a raid. Also, while it is true that the physical stature of a man does not equal the amount of courage the person possesses, I was disappointed at his somewhat diminutive stature. It was simply not reassuring to me but I quickly pushed that out of my mind and the ride continued.

The issue of armed escorts in Nigeria is assuming an alarming proportion. Everyone with money these days has armed escorts. My question is simple: Who regulates their activities? Who controls who should carry weapons or not? Who does one complain to in the event of an assault by escorts? If Nigeria does not act fast to check this, in the near future, the nation would turn into the Wild West. At that time, if you disagreed with your neighbor, the next thing you know would be the barrel of a gun stirring down your face. If Nigeria must turn to private security, then all applicable laws must be put in place and enforced.

Something funny happened when we got to Umunede in Delta state. The bus had stopped and the conductor announced that passengers could go down to relieve themselves. My son enthusiastically stepped down with the rest of the people. A few minutes later, he quickly re-entered the bus looking startled. "Did you ease yourself?" I asked. "No, I do not want to anymore". I did not understand what the problem was as he sat straight-faced on his chair. Later, I found out that he followed the other passengers out, expecting a rest room but soon saw them all lined up in an open area "doing their thing". Not far away from the men were the women also "doing their thing" in their own way. When he saw that, he hurried back to the bus. I did not know whether to be amused by that or what but I told him that we were almost home. Soon, the bus took off again and the journey continued.

The drive from Umunede towards Onitsha was uneventful because of the relatively smooth road network. Very soon, my eyes caught the glistening metal trusses and lattice structures that was the Niger Bridge; I was elated that we were almost home after more than six hours on the bus. As we drove onto the bridge, I focused my attention on the left side of the Niger River, the spot that was supposed to be dredged and used as a Port to ease the importation headaches of businesses in Onitsha and environs. Currently, these businesses have to send their shipments to places like Port Harcourt and Lagos. They would then transport them into Onitsha area through bad roads and the harassment of "waitin' you carry" policemen. Of course, just like any wise business person would do, they pass on the added cost of transporting their goods to consumers. The result is more inflation in the country. As I looked at the abandoned project, I kept wondering why the Federal government of Nigeria lacks the wisdom and vision to move the nation forward through projects like that. The eastern senators in Abuja, who should be pushing a project like that, are more interested in being the president's lackeys, jumping when he says jump and rubberstamping whatever he asks for. The last time I checked, senators and congressmen in any good democracy work hard to push for the interest of the areas they represent. It is a pity that the political system in Nigeria is nonsensical; otherwise, citizens would have been able to vote out or recall these selfish men that call themselves our representatives.

I have heard people say that the Onitsha port project would cost too much money.. Regardless of how much it costs, it would pay for itself within a few years. Also, some have opined that the technology to do the dredging is not there. Again, that is nonsense. Tell that to Japan. No one should be fooled by the naysayers that only talk about impossibilities. It is a pity that the Nigerian government has not found that project a worthy one to embark on. Simple economics dictates that if the businessmen in the eastern states are able to bring in their goods through the sea directly into Onitsha, the added cost of trucking it into Onitsha from other locations, which is currently passed on to consumers, would be spared. This is common sense although common sense does not seem to be common amongst the so-called leaders in Nigeria.

Just as I was trying to push the issue of the Onitsha port from my mind, the bus entered the Onitsha side of the bridge and all hell broke loose. We had gone from driving on a smooth stretch of road into a 'hell hole'. The truck began to meander through deep gulleys and craters along the road and I started wondering if another Biafran war occurred there while I was away. It was that bad. Broken down vehicles were all over the place. This bumping and grinding continued all the way. It even became worse when we entered the Onitsha-Owerri road that was supposed to be under construction by the Greek company CCC. Some parts of the road that had already been constructed were being swept away by erosion and would obviously need to be redone at the expense of the Nigerian tax-payer. All the stabilization measures, which any first year civil engineer student knows, which a contractor must put in place during the initial stages of road construction, were lacking. The Federal government awarded a road contract of that magnitude in the east to an inexperienced contractor and yet in the northern states, they award such contracts to seasoned contractors like Julius Berger. Is there a message here? This bumping and grinding only ended when we got to Oba junction, some 90-minutes later. A distance that should take no more than ten minutes to cover took us 90-minutes!

After we pulled into Oba, the bus driver accelerated because the road was half decent. Before long, what was left of the proposed Oba airport was stirring at me, deserted and desolate. This time, even though I knew that the project was basically abandoned, just the sight of it infuriated me. I thought about the myriad of accidents that occur along Lagos -Onitsha road, including the ones we saw coming in. I thought about the hundreds that have lost their lives along that road. I wondered how many of those lives would have been saved had the Oba airport been put to reality. I began to count off my fingers the number of airstrips in the northern part of Nigeria. It was clear to me at that juncture that Nigeria needed to have a national conference where all stakeholders would sit down and discuss the modality for existence. This neglect of certain parts of the country had to end. This continued case of "monkey dey work but baboon dey chop" should not continue or be tolerated anymore. Regardless of what I was thinking though, the bus rolled on but the sense of elation I had when I first sighted the Niger Bridge from Asaba had now given way to profound sadness as we steadily approached Nnewi.

Something else was on my mind as my hometown came into sight. Eight months before I traveled to Nigeria, I had called Nnewi to chat with a friend of mine but it turned out that I caught up with him at a very bad time. The local time there was about 12:00 midnight and they were hearing the sound of gunshot without knowing where it was coming from. The next day, in the afternoon, I called Nnewi again and spoke to a relative of mine. She confirmed the fact that they could not sleep the previous night because of the sound of gunshot. She however added that there was no report of any robbery incident, in the town, the next morning. Her conclusion was therefore that it must have been the new neighborhood watch group demonstrating their presence - a tactical maneuver to discourage would-be robbers. "Since their inception, security has improved", she told me. While I was happy to hear about improvement in security, being woken up by the sound of gunshots at night was hardly my idea of normalcy. This issue was therefore on my mind as our bus came to a stop at the closest bus stop to my home and we alighted.

I am happy to confirm the existence of the neighborhood watch groups. They have iron gates installed at strategic locations on certain roads and the gates are locked at specific times of the night. Once the gates were locked, vehicles were no longer allowed egress or ingress unless the occupants were known and properly identified. As soon as darkness fell, any person still outside must carry a constant source of light like a lantern. Not doing so would subject the person to being detained till morning. Suspicious characters were handed over to the police. Overall, my impression after my stay is that some peace has once again returned to a town that was almost overrun by robbers a year or two ago.

I have to hand it to my hometown folks, they are very resourceful and exceedingly enterprising. I say this because of the extent of development that has occurred in Nnewi in a very short time. All manners of industries, factories, hotels and banks abound everywhere in the town. These enterprises are privately owned without any dime of support from state or federal government. I checked out some of the items manufactured in Nnewi, like automobile spare parts, bottled water and food items and most were of first-rate quality. The edible ones carried the appropriate NAFDAC seal of fitness for consumption and I was very impressed. Also, from what I could gather from the users of the automobile spare parts, the products perform as well as imported ones. I even visited one of the newest hotels in town called Beverly Hills hotel. Just the landscaping alone made one feel like one was actually in Beverly Hills California. It had an Olympic size outdoor pool and well maintained tennis courts. On the day that I visited the hotel, a certain musician was shooting a music video inside the grounds, a testament to its splendor.

I have mainly used this medium to point out the ills that plague the Nigerian nation, but I would also like to use it to commend those men and women, in Nnewi and Nigeria as a whole, who are pushing the envelope of personal initiative. In spite of the odds stacked against them like absence of pipe borne water, constant electricity and good roads, they are performing beyond one's wildest imagination. They not only provide industries and businesses that have helped sustain the economy of the East and Nigeria, thereby uplifting the name of the country in industrial circles around the world, but they also provide the much needed employment to thousands of young men and women who would otherwise be jobless with its attendant implications. Most of the factories in Nnewi now export some of their products to neighboring countries and conduct high scale business transactions with powerhouse Asian countries, the United Kingdom and of course United States. It is indeed very commendable.

Having said the above, I must caution that the development in Nnewi has come at a very huge price! Rapid development has led to uncontrolled urbanization. The town is now bursting at the seams population-wise. As I write, the boundary that formerly delineated living areas from commercial areas has been blurred completely. Some factories are actually located right inside crowded living areas so people live and sleep next to factories that belch out industrial fumes and discard effluent waste on farmlands. Also, almost every house now seems to have a store for the sale of provisions and other items in it. Sometimes, music would be blaring from the stores to the obvious discomfort of neighbors. Of course some churches begin their services in the dead of the night, using bullhorns and microphones to sing, to the obvious peril of sleeping neighbors.

Overcrowding has led to the proliferation of Okada (motorcycle) riders. Okada is used to chauffeur passengers back and forth and seems to have practically overrun the town. While I agree that it is an invaluable and cheap means of transportation, inability of the government to regulate their speed or get them to stay on the right side of the road is causing a lot of havoc. This madness is compounded by the fact that the roads are in very bad shape. It rained on the very night that I arrived Nnewi and the next morning, the roads were practically impassable, replete with what looked like retention ponds but were actually potholes. It became more convenient for pedestrians to walk on the fringes of the road to avoid being splashed with muddy water by Okada riders. The most surprising thing is that people have become so used to all these mammoth inconveniences that they no longer bother them. At one of the "bus stops" next to my family house, I watched one morning as a well-dressed man with what looked like "Ghana must go" bag in hand flagged down an Okada bike and hopped on. As the Okada man took off abruptly, the sudden forward motion of the bike thrust the passenger backwards and he fell back and into a pothole filled with muddy water. I was incensed at what government insensitivity was doing to the citizenry. If the road were maintained, there would be no pothole for the man to fall into, I fumed.

However, something funny happened. Right before my very eyes, the man that fell off the Okada bike quickly got up, picked up his now soggy bag and started laughing hysterically. He was still standing inside the puddle while water dripped down his pants! I was stunned. It was a clear case of "suffering and smiling" as Fela once sang. The Okada driver had already moved a few feet before he realized that his passenger had fallen off. At first, he had a remorseful look on his face but when he saw that the victim was laughing, he burst into laughter himself. Well, their "happy-go-lucky" attitude was contagious because I burst into laughter as well and so did others that noticed what had happened. While I applaud this type of resilient spirit in Nigerians, I fear that it also leads to complacency. Is it possible that not "getting mad" enough to call the government to the carpet for ineptitude and dereliction of duty is tacitly stoking the fire of incompetence? Is it possible that the attitude of "suffering and smiling" is a tacit acceptance of government relegation of its responsibility to the background? Is it possible that if the man who fell into the water-laden pothole felt angry sufficiently, his mindset and those of the people around him would lead to speaking up against a government that has failed to rehabilitate roads in Nnewi? I realize that government does not have to do everything but it needs to listen to the yearnings and aspirations of the people. Leaving them with roads replete with potholes is not a good way to govern.

One peculiar thing bothers me immensely about my hometown. Business moguls and industrialists expend inordinate amounts of money on factories, hotels, blocks of flats, banks and the likes but the roads leading to those structures are neglected. I realize that they do not owe the town anything but would it not make sense to pull resources together, call the bluff of the Anambra state government and rebuild the roads? They have built first-rate industries, banks and hotels and must now build first-rate access roads to the structures. It was disappointing that even banks did not find it necessary to "mend" the roads that lead to their offices. This is not peculiar to Nnewi alone, it seems to be prevalent all over Southern Nigeria.

On one of my trips to the Nnewi market, my eyes caught a poster with the American flag and statue of liberty colorfully splashed on it. I went closer. The heading of the poster read something like, "Helping people get US visa lottery". It had pictures of several people with testimonials on how the company helped them obtain the US VISA lottery. The poster promised that for a fee, someone could also be helped. I turned towards the young man standing beside me. "This is scam", I said. I explained to him that no one from here or anywhere could influence the outcome of the visa lottery. "The only thing anyone could do for you is to file for you through the Internet. That's all they can do" I said and walked away.

Having berated the government in this treatise for dereliction of duty, there is an area I must give it a passing mark for. It is the area of liberalizing communications. Everyone seemed to have a functional cell phone in Nnewi and Nigeria these days. Even market women in Nkwo Nnewi have their cell phones. Without warning, they would whip it out from places you least anticipate and start making or answering calls. It was hilarious. The height of my surprise was when a bricklayer, dutifully mixing cement on site, suddenly stood upright, reached into the pocket of his khaki shorts and whipped out his cell phone. ""A-l-l-o-o-o", he screamed into the mouth piece. One of his kinsmen had just called to remind him about an upcoming meeting. After his conversation, he looked at his phone, "a-a-a-h, I need to recharge this phone, my credit is down", he said. Apparently, he was referring to his "pay as you go" phone card. I must say that those phone cards cost a fortune. For a 20 to 30 minute call, an Econet or MTN card cost one thousand and five hundred naira! To put the cost in perspective, a police new recruit in Nigeria is paid eight thousand naira a month. It means that if he ever makes a 20 to 30 minute call, he would have used almost a quarter of his monthly salary. The cost needs to come down but that does not take away from the fact that it is indeed one of the tangible successes of the Obasanjo administration.

Being of an "inquiry" mind, I tried to see if there was any tangible way of measuring the benefits of the liberalized telecommunication system. We all know that one of the benefits of the phone system is that private or business discussions that would normally be done face to face and require driving or flying from one place to the other, could be done over the phone. This eliminates the need to drive or fly and reduces traffic congestion. "Is Nigeria getting that benefit?" I asked one of the business moguls. "No", he said emphatically. "Since the cell phone boom, whenever I call the people who owe me money, once they see my name on their caller ID, they do not answer the phone. As a result, I still pay them surprise visits in their offices or their houses", he said laughing. "I still drive and fly as much as I did before the cell phone boom and I think it is the same for many other Nigerians", he added

In Anambra state, Governor Chris Ngige seems to be winning the public relations war against his one-time political godfather, Chris Uba. Even as I endlessly complained about the poor condition of the roads and the absence of pipe borne water, people insisted that Ngige was doing his best but was being handicapped by Chris Uba and the federal government. I brought up the issue of Chris Uba's reported admission that PDP did not win the state during the 2003 elections. Most of the people admitted being aware of that fact but would rather retain Dr. Ngige because he was doing a "good" job. One area that this writer would like to give credit unequivocally to the governor is the area of payment of salaries to government workers. Most of the workers I talked to reported that they now get their salaries regularly. Even those on pension had no complaints. Hopefully, this trend would not be reversed any time soon.

Before I traveled to Nigeria, I had heard about the credits that the governor had been taking in the area of road construction. To see things for myself, I visited some of the road projects. While I applaud the man for doing a lot better than his predecessors, it needs to be said that some of the road networks may not stand the test of time. They were not constructed on the proverbial solid foundation neither were the basic tenets and guiding principles in roadway design and construction followed in their execution. It may be politically expedient to hastily build a series of road networks to temporarily satisfy the yearnings and aspirations of Anambra citizens. However, in this writer's opinion as a civil engineer, it would serve the citizens better to have durable roads even if the government builds just a few of them at a time. I also visited the site of a culvert construction along Nnewi-Ozubulu road. Again, it was well intentioned but no one seemed to have told the workers who were laboring under a slight drizzle, that soil could never achieve optimal compaction when wet. As we left the site of the culvert, I made an instant decision to visit my alma mater.

We pulled into the school compound some minutes after 12:00 noon. The students were on recess and the sea of white shirts milling around the school compound made me nostalgic. The kids in the classrooms were as raucous and rambunctious as we were during my own time. After showing my son around, we headed towards Ojukwu house, the hostel where I lived for 5-years. Suddenly, I could feel the presence of someone coming behind me. I quickly turned around. "Sir, are you looking for someone?" a boy dressed in immaculate white shirt and pants asked. "Not really", I answered. "I am just taking a look around". Seeing that he was not sure what else to ask me, I stretched my hand towards him, "My name is Alfred Uzokwe and this is my son, Alfred Jr." I said. "I was a student in this school from 1973 to 1977." I noticed his eyes widen when I said 1973. He introduced himself as the senior prefect and so I asked for his permission to carry on. It struck me that the senior prefect looked so young. During my first year in that school, that was three years after the Biafran war ended, we had bearded and older men as senior students. Some of them were said to be veterans of the Biafran war and you could tell by the way they barked orders at younger students they called "nwa awo" or toads. Here I was standing in front of a soft-spoken senior prefect with jaw smoother than a bottle. Times change, I thought and we walked on.

As we approached Ojukwu house, the school field came into view. I had told my son, back in the United States about our 1976/77 inter-house sports and how I won the 100-meter dash and anchored the 100-meter relay to a winning finish for Ojukwu house. I felt that he would want to see the school field so we temporarily changed course. The closer we got to the field, the more I felt that something was not right. Then it hit me, the field had shrunk to almost half the size it used to be! Erosion, which was seriously threatening the school grounds had claimed a sizeable portion of the school field. It had shrunk so badly that for one to complete a 100-meter race, one would almost have to run around it one and half times! I looked back and noticed that my son was giggling. "Is this where you performed all those track and field wonders?" He asked light heartedly. "Believe me, the field was a lot larger than this then", I said ruefully. I pointed out the original field boundary to him and could sense that the devastation suddenly dawned on him. "Why are they not doing anything about it?" he asked. "Well, beats me", I said and sorrowfully started back on the path towards my former hostel and he followed silently.

The hostel doors and windows were wide open when we got there so we marched right inside. I instantly faced another shocker! The asbestos ceiling was covered with graffiti made with soot from candlelight. The walls had all manners of drawings and obscene writings in black markers. I was exasperated. "Who is the house prefect?" I asked. A young man standing at the other end of the dormitory raised his hand and instantly started towards me. By this time, other students started gravitating towards us. Before long, about 15 young men were gathered around my son and I. "My name is Alfred Uzokwe and I lived in this house for 5 years." I said again. "When I lived here 25 years ago, this hostel used to be immaculate. The walls were devoid of graffiti and the lawns were well kept. I see now that you guys have desecrated it and turned it into something else". I could tell by the looks in their eyes that some wondered what gave me the temerity to come in there to address them. Nonetheless, they all listened and none uttered a word.

When I noticed that they had become interested in what I was saying, I switched gears. I began to advise them on the need to ensure that they did not throw away their chances of being the best they could be in life. "A big chunk of the academic and behavioral foundation I have to this day, which I am exceedingly proud of, was developed and nurtured in this school", I said. By the time I was done, I noticed that those who initially stood there with clenched teeth, rolling their eyes at every word I uttered, had mellowed. They thanked me in muted tones when I asked to take my leave. As my son and I walked away, I kept wondering why the teachers would allow students to deface a dormitory to that extent. In our days, one could not get away with such wanton destruction and disregard for school rules. Clearly, the teachers had lost control. If they cannot control how the students behaved, how could they guide and motivate them to be good students academically? No wonder why the standard of education continues to plummet in Nigeria. These days, letters written by some final year students in the secondary school, leave much to be desired grammatically.

"That dormitory was…" I did not allow my son to finish what he wanted to say about Ojukwu house before I interjected. "I know" as we headed towards the car. "Are you youth corpers?" A woman's voice said from behind me. I turned around and sure enough a lady was standing there. "No, we are just taking a look around. I used to be a student here" I said and then introduced my son and myself. She was very happy to see us. She took us around other parts of the compound to show us the devastation that erosion was exerting on the school. She complained that old boys of the school had not come through with promises they made. She showed me a building they started and abandoned after setting up the foundation. She said she would have wanted me to speak to the students had I come earlier. I assured her that I would do so next time and then promised to help rally the old boys in the Diaspora. We took our leave and headed home.

Back home, I was still discussing the experience I had in my alma mater when my nephew walked in. "Our school certificate examination result is out", he said excitedly. "I am going to check my result at the Internet café", he added. Not long after, he came back and jubilantly announced that he passed all his subjects. "How did your friend do?" I asked. "His result did not come out", he said sadly. "How come your result is out and his own is not?" I followed up. "Well, he actually took the exam at a special center in Benue state" he told me. "What is a special center?" I asked. He explained that special centers are privately owned test-taking centers. They use private invigilators and as long as a

300

student is able to pay the exam fee, which runs into thousands of naira, the student could take the exam.

I was later told that several students now leave their schools and go to special centers to take the school certificate exam because of liberal invigilation and lax identification process. Many opined that liberal invigilation may be fostering examination malpractices. No wonder why my nephew's friend had to travel from Nnewi to Benue state, live in an apartment near the special center for two weeks while taking the school certificate exam at the special center. After listening to all these, I became convinced that the concept of special centers for the school certificate exam was a bad one and needed to be re-examined. Nigerians are too money minded to be trusted to put probity and excellence ahead of financial gains. I was going to send a letter to the school certificate registrar about the special center issue but time was no longer on my side then. We had started gearing up for departure to Lagos en route to the Netherlands and United States.

On the day of our departure, we again went to the motor park in Nnewi to board a bus. After placing our belongings in the luggage compartment, the conductor announced that passengers could now start boarding. As I entered the bus, I noticed that another man was inside, patting people down for concealed weapons. When it came to my turn, I was patted down and then the man said, "you are not taking that bag into the bus, you need to check it into the luggage compartment". I dutifully complied and handed my bag to the conductor and my relative watched outside as he placed it in the luggage compartment. Obviously, the reason why they require that all hand baggage be placed in the luggage compartment was to reduce the chances of criminals bringing concealed weapons aboard the bus. While it made me feel a little safer, it was nonetheless unnerving that a one-time pristine environment was fast turning into the Wild Wild West. "What was the world coming to?" I wondered. When you board a simple bus in the village, you have to worry about armed robbers and accidents occasioned by bad roads. And when one travel out of the country by air, one had to worry about terrorism. It was now a dog eat dog world.

The journey back to Lagos was more bearable, probably because I slept most of the time. We came down at the Ojota bus stop where my relative was to be waiting to pick us up. After bringing down our boxes, I looked around and he was nowhere to be found. Clearly, it was perilous to be standing in a place like that with four suitcases and two hand baggage. We seemed to be arousing the curiosity of many of the cab drivers and touts. "Oga, where you dey go?" they would ask. "We are waiting for someone", I would respond. Then the person would walk away and another would come with the same question. It became very overwhelming. In a space of about 20 minutes, we had more than 20 inquiries. The more time passed, the more it became clear that standing there with the suitcases was like dangling meat in front of a hyena. What the touts may not have known was that the suitcases did not have anything of real value. They merely had a few clothes and foodstuff like ogbono, egusi and onugbu. Impulsively, I flagged down a taxi and asked the driver to take us to Sheraton hotel, which was close by. "Eight hundred naira", he bellowed. "Which one you dey now? That is too much", I said. "You go pay fuel for me at 52 naira per liter?" he asked sarcastically. As soon as he mentioned fuel, I said "Ok, I go pay 500" He agreed and we started loading our effects. "Everything here is priced in the hundreds and thousands", my son retorted. "I know", I said. "The first time I visited the United States in 1978 or so, the exchange rate was one naira to 65 American cents. Today, it is 138 naira to the dollar!" I explained further. He was shocked by the leap in inflation. "Most of it is man-made", I added.

It was coincidental that at that very period, General Obasanjo had just raised the cost of fuel to 52 naira per liter and the Nigerian Labor Congress was threatening a strike. It is a pity that the government raised the fuel price without taking any steps to cushion the effects on the masses. Clearly, the cab drivers were jerking up their costs to make up for the high fuel cost. The government did not seem to care about the effects of the hike on the ordinary government worker, who would still need to ride cabs and buses at higher rates, even though their salary would remain the same. That price hike was unconscionable on the part of this government. I am glad that a principled man like Chinua Achebe has made a powerful statement against government intransigence. He rejected the national award that was to be bestowed on him by Nigeria's president. Nigerians are closely watching to see if others would follow in his footsteps.

"How much is it for one hour?" I asked the proprietor at one of the Internet cafés in Lagos. We were to depart Lagos for the States that evening and I had gone there to catch up on my emails. "Eighty naira and you go pay in advance-o-o", he responded. I was not sure if the emphasis on paying in advance had anything to do with me but I simply handed him my money and began to browse through my emails. The system was very organized. The cost was reasonable because at the prevalent exchange rate, 80 naira translated to less than 60 cents per hour to use the Internet. From my perspective, that was another good revolution in Nigeria - affordable access to the Internet.

After reviewing my emails, we went to the airport at the behest of my relative. He wanted to ensure that our names were on the flight manifest for that day. Our flight was to depart that evening after 10:00PM. We got to the airport around 11:00AM and went into the KLM office. A man coming out of one of the offices told us that the main office would open by 2:00PM and that boarding for our flight would start around 4:00PM. I told him that our return tickets were confirmed back in the USA and that our seats had even been assigned. I then asked if he could look through their manifest to see if we were good to go. Without looking at the tickets, he said, "we have a new computer system now and it works fine, you do not need to be reconfirmed, just come back after 4:00PM and board". I was still skeptical. "Could you check your new computer system then?" "No need" he said, "you are fine".

We later left and came back by 6:30PM after a grueling traffic jam at Ikeja. We queued up in line and by the time it was our turn for check in, it was about 7:10PM. Then I saw a sign that said that check in would end 8:00PM. In my mind, we were in good shape. One of the counters opened so I stepped forward and presented our tickets to the lady sitting behind the counter. This lady was the epitome of everything that is wrong with customer service in Nigeria. She looked like she had just had a dose of quinine- a very bitter medicine. She did not even look up as she snatched the tickets from my hands and immediately started punching the computer keyboards furiously as though a fight had been declared between her fingers and the keyboard. After a while, she sighed and then began to gather our ticket, which she had spread out in front of her. "Your tickets are not confirmed", she said and then shoved them into my hand. I was dumbfounded. "It is confirmed and I have seat numbers already assigned all the way from the US", I said. "It is confirmed from Lagos to Amsterdam but not from Amsterdam to the United States", she thundered back. When I saw that she could care less about customer service, I stepped even closer and gently asked what she wanted me to do then. "Go up to the KLM office and have them confirm your ticket and then come back".

I looked at my watch and it was almost 7:30PM. Realizing that check in would end in thirty minutes, I hurried upstairs to the KLM office where I encountered yet another line. It then dawned on me that the problem was not just peculiar to me, all the people in line had the same problem. Just as it got to my turn, a phone rang and as we glanced around to see where the sound was coming from, the man that was supposed to be taking care of us reached into his pocket and whipped out his cell phone and started discussing private matters while we waited and time ticked away. So much for customer service, I thought. I kept resisting the urge to ask him to get off the phone because I knew what the consequence would be for me. Finally, he attended to me and I hurried back downstairs. By then, it was just a few minutes to eight and the people at the check in counter were just rounding up. Luckily, we got in. I looked at our boarding passes and discovered that the seat numbers they assigned to us were the same we were assigned when the flight was originally booked in the United States. What was then all that hassle about reconfirming our Amsterdam to Detroit leg of the flight for? Why was I sent on a wild goose chase? Is it possible that the wicked witch at the KLM counter derived some pleasure from seeing people sweat? May be.

As the A330 airbus lifted off the tarmac into the Lagos sky about two hours later, I found myself feeling somewhat reluctant to leave. Inspite of all the madness, all the confusion, all my complaints about bad roads, epileptic electricity, the trials and tribulations from the wicked witch of KLM, the annoying antics of Okada riders, it dawned on me that I had a swell time in Nigeria, especially in my beloved hometown Nnewi. "I will be back", I muttered to myself under my breath. I then turned towards my son and asked, "When you get back to the States, where would you tell your friends you went to?" "I will tell them that I went home", he said with a smile. I was pleased with that response. We indeed went home. East, West, North or South, home is the best. I closed my eyes and dozed off as the wide-bodied aircraft thundered into the night sky.

Account of My Visit To Nigeria
December 2102 - February 4, 2013

As has become customary for me, I was in Nigeria during the Christmas period of 2012. I entered Nigeria through Lagos airport and then headed for my home town Nnewi. Whenever I visit Nnewi, I love being out and about, seeing friends, family members and even strangers as well as just looking around the village I grew up in but left decades ago. This particular morning on the 23rd of December, we drove from my house, and headed into town.

As we approached one of the banks along the road, I decided to stop by and get some information from their customer service people. Our car was just a distance of less than 60 feet from the bank but traffic was jammed and cars were moving at a snail speed. Rather than just sit in the car and be twiddling my fingers, I decided to disembark and walk the rest of the way to the bank. The driver was to meet me there. I leisurely walked down, looking around to catch a glimpse or two of the environment for inspite of the traffic jam and all, people were making brisk businesses and the mood was festive. A series of motorcycles (okada) were parked in front of the bank when I got there. I imagined that a lot of people must be inside the bank building making last-minute withdrawals for the Christmas festivities. There was no space for me to walk through from the side except for a small sliver of opening between two motorcycles. Instead of walking back out to the bank road, which was teeming with people, and then going in frontally, I decided to chance slipping through the two okada bikes. Just at that time, the huge bank perimeter fence gate swung open and a car began to pull out of it under the guidance of two security men. Just as I tried to squeeze myself through the two bikes, my right leg brushed against the exhaust pipe of the one on the right and all hell broke loose! A stinging pain shot through my leg and I leapt into the air! Apparently, the bike on the right had just been parked and the exhaust pipe was still flaming hot. To add salt to injury, I was wearing shorts so my bare skin was what came in contact with the hot exhaust pipe.

I hobbled towards the entrance gate and made my entrance, unaware that one of the bank security guys saw what happened. The man ran towards another bike parked inside the bank premises, probably his own, all the while saying, "I am getting fuel to put on it". He kept an eye on me as I stood still by the small security gate, writhing in pain and trying to collect myself. "What did you say you were getting?" I queried. "I want to douse fuel on the burn so that it will dry out and not develop into a major wound". "I will pass on that", I said. "Can you find Vaseline, instead?" I managed to say. "Unless someone goes into the market", he said in a very concerned tone. At this point, I could see the outline of the burn slowly developing where my right leg made contact with the exhaust pipe. "Can you get engine oil?" I said, feeling that it would be a better palliative than nothing. He reached into the bike, scooped a small bit of oil and came and doused that on my leg. Meanwhile, other customers were coming and going. "Thank you", I said to the young man. I could still feel the pain but was moved by the manner in which he tried to help someone he did not know. I reluctantly went into the bank, exiting after I had made the inquiry that brought me there in the first place. Meanwhile, the burn mark had become very clear and periodically gave a stinging feeling that shot through my leg at intervals. I walked back out to the car since the drive had arrived

When I entered the market, I had the chance to talk to a few people hawking their wares. One of them complained that something was missing this Christmas. To him, business was not as brisk as it used to be at that time of the year and he attributed it to the problem of insecurity that was presently sweeping through the South Eastern states. People were being kidnapped and released only after their families had paid huge sums of money that ran into millions of naira. He said that many people that used to return and come to the market, making tons of purchases for the Christmas celebration, food items, assorted drinks, did not seem to have returned. "Even some of those that live here", he complained, "went to spend their holiday outside the town just to be safe" This caused a sober reflection in my mind.

This same insecurity issue has caused people from my town to start doing something that was hitherto unheard of. Some now hold the traditional marriage ceremonies of their offspring in places like

Lagos and other big cities instead of the village. I even understand that if you hold such events in the village and invite important men and women from the town, many will not show up. The same insecurity issue was now taking tangible toll on commerce, not just in the Nnewi, but everywhere in the South East. I was sad about this development. However, I cannot emphasize strongly enough the need for the government and everyone concerned, as part of trying to tame the insecurity situation, to provide jobs for our teeming youth. I saw many of them during this Christmas season that had no jobs to go to even though they are university graduates. They attend universities, graduate and then come out to face unemployment. Some have been unemployed for more than three years. While nothing will ever justify the crime of kidnapping, a wise English adage says that the idle mind is the devil's work shop. No matter the type of development going on in Nigeria, if we continue to have youth unemployment of the magnitude we have today, that development will never be complete.

One of the things I observed in Nigeria is the reckless use of electricity, even this writer is culpable! People seem to believe that because they pay for electricity, they have the right to turn on all the lights and appliances they have in their homes every time. I saw many homes, including mine, where in broad daylight, all the outside and inside bulbs in the house are all on. The fans are circling and air conditioners are humming even in rooms that no one is using. Why would someone turn on exterior lights in broad daylight even if the person is the one paying electric bill? It clearly seems that in Nigeria, we have not started thinking sensible energy use and what it can do for us. If people only used the energy they need in houses, offices and so on in Nigeria, the so called energy need threshold that PHCN is trying to reach can be reduced. If you do not need a light bulb outside your house in the afternoon, turn it off. If 400 houses turn off just 5 bulbs of 60 watts each that they are not using, that is 120,000 watts or 120 kilowatts saved right there. It will save energy that someone else can use or help extend the number of people that will have light, increase the strength of the current and even extend the amount of time you get light. If an air conditioner is not needed, it is prudent to turn it off. I am sure that many will wonder if this writer is trying to control how they use the light they pay for. Far from it but as one who has been involved in Leadership in Energy and Environmental Design here in the United States, I fully understand the advantage of energy savings and believe that it is time that Nigerians adopted the principles of energy savings.

I saw many buildings that are so poorly designed that natural lighting and ventilation did not seem to have been considered during the design phases of the buildings. For such buildings, it seemed like people always needed to turn on the lights every time of the day. A good architect should design residential buildings with ample and well-placed windows in such a way that there would be no need for artificial lighting or constant air conditioning during the day. The windows should be placed so strategically that the rooms are fully lighted in the day with cross ventilation. People should start thinking along that line and demanding that from their designers. The sun's energy could be harvested via roof-mounted solar arrays or photovoltaic cells. The solar energy, thus harnessed, could be used to power small appliances, light bulbs, fans and the like. Such measures could drastically reduce the amount of energy needed from PHCN with corresponding decrease in electric bills.

One very sunny afternoon in Nnewi, a contemporary of ours came to our house and after exchange of pleasantries, he began to talk about a "comprehensive" medical test he was going to undergo the next day. He said it was going to cost him N38, 000(Thirty eight thousand naira). I asked what the N38, 000 test would include. "It will analyze all the organs in my body and tell me the condition of my health", he said excitedly. He added that he had undergone the same type of test before and the doctor said that his kidneys and liver were working very well. "Can you describe how this test is done?" I asked. "When you get into the doctor's office", he started, "he will give you something to hold in one hand for a few seconds, then soon, pictures and information about the condition of all the organs in your body will start showing on a computer screen. It will show your kidneys, your liver, everything", he elaborated with unbridled enthusiasm. I was stunned that such a "wonder" machine was available in the world talk less of in Nnewi but wondered how something one holds in the hand can show pictures of the organs in the body and their performance. I wondered if the test included invasive insertion of a laparoscope in the body. "Does the thing you hold in your hand penetrate into your body?" I continued to probe, careful not to come across as a pessimist. "No, you just have to hold it in your hand for a few minutes", he replied. I became suspicious!

"Do you have the result of your last test?" I said casually. "Yes", he quipped and brought it out. It was a computer printout. First, I glanced at the top of the page and saw that the test result was dated 2004 and his age was quoted as 49. I know him very well and know that he was not 49 years in 2004. I then said, "I thought you had this test in 2011?" He nodded in the affirmative. "Why does it say you had it in 2004 at age 49?" I asked, becoming even more suspicious of the test. When I got no answer, I started reading through the report and was amazed. It basically listed all the organs in the body. For each organ listed, there was a column that stated what the normal reading or range should be and an adjacent column listed what his actual readings were. Under the column for kidneys, it had a "normal range" of around 100 to 220 but stated that her actual reading was 67 and yet did not flag it as a problem. This was the same for practically half of the results shown. If one had to go by the test results in comparison with the normal ranges quoted, the man was in a serious medical problem! I do not remember what the units of the numbers were but I turned to him and queried, "Do you realize that based on your kidney reading alone, you are a dead person walking?" I elaborated that the result states that the reading range for a normal kidney was 100 to 220 but that his kidney reading said 67. I also looked under the column for the heart and it had all kinds of readings for ejection fraction and impedance. I am not a biotechnologist, but there is no way that an object held for a few minutes in the hand would detect the ejection fraction of the heart or read and interpret renal function. At best, it will read the pulse rate and probably the systolic and diastolic measurements.

I knew now that our friend was being scammed and I was really hurt. I gently told him that I believed he had been scammed and explained why something held on the hand could not possibly diagnose the condition of the organs in the body. I could tell how disappointed and dejected he became but for some reason, he seemed to trust that what I was saying made sense. I came close to asking to be led to the doctor's office but on a second thought, I ditched the idea. I later convinced him to use some of the N38, 000 to go for a true and comprehensive lab test in a reputable lab. It would entail drawing his blood to test for liver and kidney functions, cholesterol, sugar, white and red blood cells, and more. He would then take the results to his real doctor for reading and analysis as well as determination of any required course of action. I later learnt that many people were being sent to go through this so called comprehensive test and that the owner just acquired the "computer machine" from one of the Asian countries. The owner must be making a killing off of people that believe that he had brought a life-saver. When money-making entails endangering lives this way, we all owe it to humanity to point these things out. In my almost 12 years of writing commentaries, I have gotten hundreds of feedback from people about what happens in the health sector in Nigeria and how people have died because of wrong diagnoses, misleading interpretation of ailments and outright scams. It is true that there is nothing I can do per se but whenever I become aware of a seeming medical scam, I will pass it on to the public to be on guard and that is the reason I put this out there.

This brings me to an issue that has bugged me for years every time I visited Nigeria. I saw it at Balogun market in Lagos; I saw it at Owerri in Imo state and also saw it in my home town Nnewi. Simply put, it is prevalent all over Nigeria. It is the issue of unsheltered stands for display of food items and drinks in open market places. Items on display usually include assorted drinks like fruit juices, canned beers of all sorts, grape juice like Ribena, canned soda (mineral), spirits like Hennessey and all manners of wine. These items are displayed on tables or elevated platforms where customers would easily catch glimpse of them. The problem is that sometime after noon, especially during the Christmas season, the sun's intensity is at its highest. It is not uncommon to get to temperatures in the mid 90 degrees Fahrenheit. If I still recall my chemistry class right, one remembers that heat induces chemical reaction and changes things from one state or chemical condition to another. Take the fruit juices for example: some are packaged in a paper-like container coated with a thin film of plastic. I understand that the inside of the package is coated with a certain chemical to preclude the juice from adhering to it. This juice is part of what is displayed perpetually under extreme temperatures, for more than 8 hours a day every day on tables or platforms. I do believe that the perpetual heat which these drinks are exposed to would invariably be inducing some form of chemical reaction, even if a mild one, between the chemically coated container and the juice. Infact, the heat could be altering the chemical composition of the juice making it less potent or unfit for consumption.

Makers of some of these drinks, especially the juice-based ones, encourage keeping them cool as a way to prevent them from going bad and here we are doing the opposite. The same applies to the alcoholic drinks. Take the canned Heineken, canned Star beer, canned stout and more. How can one tell if these drinks have not been chemically altered after sitting in the baking sun, eight hours a day and many days in a row? I was at an event in Nnewi where a can of Heineken was opened and no single foam came out of it. The person that was to drink it simply said, "this one is not good", threw it away and picked up another can which incidentally did the same thing. I wonder if that had to do with over exposure to the baking sun. In the quest to make some money, we must also strive to be our brothers' keepers. You even encounter situations where some pharmacies display medications in the same manner. Now everyone knows that certain medications become less potent or even toxic if exposed to heat. Some even carry labels that say expose only to room temperature yet people discount that. Capsulized medications, for example, should not be placed under intense heat. This issue needs to be explored by NAFDAC.

When I got back to Lagos in preparation for my flight back to the United States, we visited Balogun market to get some souvenirs for travel back. One thing bothered me immensely at Balogun market. I had read in one of the dailies the very day we were going to the market, how multiple family members died in their home overnight and it was suspected that they died from inhalation of carbon monoxide poisoning. They had their generator too close to their sleeping quarters. When we got to Balogun, I saw that people were doing the same thing that just killed a family of five. Small generators littered everywhere very close to stalls, humming constantly and belching out fumes. In most cases, the generators were kept so close to store owners that there was no way they would not be taking in the fumes. Some of the market stall spaces are so confined and covered in all three corners, as well as the top, that the fumes would have no escape route. Because of the absence of electricity, people are forced to buy portable generators and since they would not want them stolen, they place them very close to their stalls while the generators are running.

PART 7
Echoes of the Civil War

Ojukwu's Biafra Memoir - Things I'd Still Like To Know - December 31, 2010

I was saddened, the other day, to read that Dim Chukwuemeka Ojukwu had taken ill and was flown out of the country for medical treatment. His condition was described as Cerebral Vascular Accident, another word for stroke. We wish him a speedy recovery and all the best because he remains an enigma that will always be remembered whenever the history of Nigeria and particularly Eastern Nigeria, is chronicled in print or orally.

When I first read about his illness, a statement he made in 2003 during an interview with Paul Odili of Vanguard Newspapers came to mind. He stated, "I am the final Biafran Truth". Ojukwu is right. He probably occupied the most vantage position during the war and that stands him in the greatest stead to provide one of the most encompassing accounts of the war.

In 2006, I wrote an article titled "Ojukwu's Biafra Memoir- Things I'd like to know" In that article, which will be reproduced below, I emphasized the need for Ojukwu to write his memoir and have it in circulation as soon as possible to set straight some of the assertions that have been made about Biafra and the war. As I read about his ailment, the need for his memoir became even more critical and important. There are still things one would love to know about the Biafra war. Below is the article.

In support of Ojukwu's assertion, one could state, without fear of contradiction, that as the man who made the far-reaching declaration in May of 1967 proclaiming the birth of a new nation called Biafra, he stands the most vantage stead to tell what transpired on a broader spectrum. Indeed, as the man who made the day to day decisions on how the war was prosecuted, General Ojukwu remains the final and most comprehensive source of the history of events that unfolded in those tumultuous years. For the sake of posterity, therefore, the story needs to be told and the sooner, the better. Hear Molara Woods on her internet blog page, "… there's no point being the final truth if that truth is not told" [Molara Woods, August 29, 2005]. Her statement underscores the fact that most people are yearning for Ojukwu's perspective on the events that led to the Biafran conflict as well as a blow by blow account of what transpired during that war.

For the avoidance of doubt, I wish to state that one is not discounting the accounts of the war as rendered by other principal actors like General Madiebo, General Effiong, Col. JOG Achuzia and the likes. However, each one of these brave men chronicled their accounts from the vantage points of the war theaters or sectors they commanded. As credible as their accounts might be, they did not comprehensively cover the gamut of activities that took place during that war. Also, not being at the helm, they may not have been privy to certain decisions that were made and why those decisions were made. Essentially, no account will be as comprehensive, authoritative and as broad-based as the one that emanates from the desk of the man they all reported to, the man called Ikemba Nnewi.

This writer has presented a civilian account of the war in the book titled: Surviving in Biafra- the Story of the Nigerian Civil War. The book renders account of the war from the perspective of a six-year old boy growing up in a war-torn nation, where air raids, hunger and privation were the order of the day. Those who have read the book, though, will agree that it brought up some innocent but genuine questions about how and why certain events took place during that war. It will therefore be an understatement for me to say that I was exceedingly delighted when I read parts of the interview granted to the Sun News by Chief Odumegwu Ojukwu in which he confirmed that his memoir would be out soon. This is what Ojukwu said, "I don't want to give out what rightfully should be in my book. But you know, what I will tell you about this book is that I think it will come out in due course. If not this year, next year. It couldn't be later than that. I'm working at it [Sun News, April 30, 2006]

In that interview, Ojukwu gives some momentary but riveting glimpses into what Nigerians might expect to find in his long-awaited memoir. For instance, this is what he said about the propaganda coming from the Federal side during the war: "Throughout the war, it was difficult, but one thing that always worried me, mainly because of the Nigerian propaganda, is that they [Nigerian troops] would suddenly burst into my house wherever I was and I would be arrested, perhaps, in pajamas. I don't know any General that looked dashing in his pajamas (laughter). So, to avoid such humiliation, I would never, ever, throughout the years of the war, go to bed in pajamas". That statement is very insightful, at least to this writer. It was heartening to know that General Ojukwu also worried, as we all did during that war, about the massive propaganda that was coming from the Federal side on how they intended to run over Biafra in a short while, obliterating everything in sight. Infact, Brigadier Adekunle was once quoted as saying that they would shoot every living thing on sight and when they exhausted that, they would shoot inanimate objects! That was frightening.

Ojukwu also touched on the issue of Col Victor Banjo and the Mid-West incursion during his interview and here is how he put it: "Of course, I was betrayed by Banjo. I spent days writing out the project that will take him to Lagos, specifically mapping out where he could go. I was betrayed by his decision to take over Benin. No! He was to circumscribe Benin. That cost us a lot of men, days, weeks. I felt betrayed, of course, when he thought the only way out of the difficulty he had put us into was to make a coup in Biafra. It was a betrayal that cost them their lives. It's unfortunate".

The Midwest incursion still remains a subject of intense discussion, till this day, at least amongst the Igbo people. Many believe that if the Midwest incursion, led by Col Victor Banjo, had not failed or was not "sabotaged", perhaps, the outcome of the war may have been different. Some question the wisdom of putting Banjo in command when his loyalty to the Biafran cause could not be categorically ascertained. I still remember the euphoria that greeted Biafra as the event unfolded. Suddenly, we heard that Biafran troops had made it through the Midwest, perhaps seized Ore and were marching towards Lagos! There was jubilation in Biafra. Momentarily, what we had heard about the dexterity and courage of Biafran commanders and the infantry turned into an instant reality. Considering the fact that this was happening during the beginning months of the war, we started believing that the war was possibly ending very soon and in favor of the young nation. The euphoria generated by this apparent success of the Biafran soldiers was still hanging palpably over the horizon like a rainbow when a devastatingly painful news tumbled in: Biafran troops had retreated back into Biafra with the same lightning speed that they entered Ore. Instantly, jubilation turned into sorrow. Hope turned into despair. The disappointment did not end with the retreat of Biafran soldiers. After the debacle, rumor began to make its round that the retreat was orchestrated by saboteurs. Not long after, Col Victor Banjo, Major Ifeajuna and Col Alale were fingered as the culprits. The young nation was inexorably plunged into the pool of self-doubt. Biafrans could rationalize why Victor Banjo, a non-Igbo, would betray Biafra, but it was difficult to explain the treachery ascribed to Major Ifeajuna, Major Alale and one Mr. Agbam. It was the very first time, as I noted in the book, Surviving in Biafra, that the word "saboteur" was introduced into the Biafran lexicon. From then on, this "saboteur" phenomenon continued to sweep through Biafra like an ill-wind and never abated until the last shots were fired. Some would argue that it hastened the demise of the young nation.

Many years after that war, many are still writing about and discussing the Midwest incursion. Some try to explain, rationalize or justify the penalty meted out to Banjo and his group in September of 1967, while others maintain that the men were mere victims of circumstance. Ojukwu's categorical statement, in the Sun News interview, that he was betrayed by Banjo, seems to lend credence to the school of thought that put forth sabotage as the reason why the incursion failed. One would hope, fervently, that the Biafran leader will treat this matter exhaustively in his memoir as soon as possible.

Anyone in Biafra, during that war, would agree with this writer, that the days, weeks, months and years were filled with all manners of highs and lows. Certain major events heightened the mercuric morale and enthusiasm of Biafran masses while others, like the Midwest incursion, dampened morale across the board. Suffice it to say that in many instances, it was difficult to tell the whys and hows of what happened. Infact, sometimes, it was difficult to separate facts from fiction. A Biafra war memoir written by Ojukwu would go a long way in laying to rest the many conjectures that have been put forth. Furthermore, there are certain events that still stand out in this writer's mind but some of the whys and hows are still unclear. I would highlight some of them below and hope that Ojukwu's upcoming memoir will treat them exhaustively.

Defection of Dr. Nnamdi Azikiwe

The defection of Dr Nnamdi Azikiwe to the Nigerian side was one of the most demoralizing moments during the days of Biafra. I narrated in the book, Surviving in Biafra, how the news brought tears to my father's eyes, a man used to keeping his emotions under check. My father's reaction mirror's the feeling of most Biafrans to the news.

When the war started, the presence of heavy weights like Dr Azikiwe, M.I Okpara, Dr Akanu Ibiam, and others, provided a certain amount of moral satisfaction for Biafrans that the right thing had been done. But when Dr Azikiwe suddenly left Biafra for Nigeria, the last bastion of Biafra's locus standi was crushed to smithereens. Again, the dreaded word, "saboteur", came up, further fuelling the distrust that had taken a dangerous stranglehold on Biafra and Biafrans. As a little boy, what was etched in my mind was that Dr Nnamdi Azikiwe had joined the ranks of those that betrayed Biafra. I recall that when he came to Nnewi, in 1979, to campaign under the aegis of NPP, the defection was still on my mind. I was torn between shedding an impression that I developed during the war, as a little boy, and accepting that the Dr Nnamdi Azikiwe still had the interest of the Igbos at heart.

Dr Azikiwe has been quoted as saying that he went to Nigeria to help end the war because the suffering had gotten out of hand. Whether that was the motive and if he achieved his aim remains a subject of intense discussion till date. One is therefore interested in reading an exhaustive account, from Ojukwu, on what happened, his take on it and the probable effect, both salutary and deleterious to Biafra.

On Kaduna Nzeogwu

When the Biafra war first started, there was this talk about the invincibility of Major Kaduna Nzeogwu. He garnered that from his role during the 1966 coup. The fact that he was on the Biafran side was always touted as a potent reason why Biafra would prevail. Biafrans sang many songs in his honor. It was therefore a huge shock when he was reportedly killed, in the war front, during the early stages of the war. Again, this was one of those events that crushed the morale of Biafrans. The surprising thing though, is that inspite of the devastating effect of his death, no one has so far written an authoritative account of how and where he died.

Many years later, because of my unabated curiosity about Nzeogwu's death, I bought a copy of Col Achuzia's Requiem Biafra and tried to see what I could find. Surprisingly, he did not talk about it. I also read General Madiebo's book and never got anything out of it about this issue. However, when I read Obasanjo's book about Nzeogwu, I was surprised by the letters he presented as having been written to him by Major Nzeogwu, even as the war was going on. One of the letters seemed to be asking him for logistics and support to end the Biafran war. Obasanjo later stated that after Nzeogwu was killed, it was the Federal troops that found "his partially decomposed body" and gave him a burial with military rites. I am hopeful that the upcoming memoir of General Odumegwu Ojukwu would shed a lot of light on this all important issue so that it will be laid to rest once and for all.

General Ojukwu and the war fronts

Certainly, there were many stories about Ojukwu's invincibility during the war. As children, we used to compare him with General Gowon and end up asserting that he was superior to General Gowon. Ojukwu was frequently referred to as the General that routinely led troops in the war front. Well, Ojukwu was quoted, in the Sun News interview as confirming that he personally led the battle to retake Oguta from Nigerian forces. He further stated that when he got to Oguta and saw the Nigerian troops raising the Nigerian flag, after the capture of Oguta, he cried! He then added that he personally led the troops that retook Oguta. Just to satisfy my curiosity, one would love to read more about the battle to retake Oguta, the actual role that Ojukwu played and what was going on in his mind as he put his life on the line.

Biafra's Ingenuity

My father used to talk about this all the time. He believed that if Biafra had survived, with all the brains that were concentrated in it, she would have had a straight ticket to technological superstardom. This includes the manufacture of the dreaded Ogbunigwe, refining of crude oil without any sophisticated technological gadgets and more. One would love to read more about this in Ojukwu's memoir.

Finally, the subject of the Biafran war remains a passion that would probably never abate in me and many others. Even though I was very young when it started and ended, I still vividly recall the events that probably altered the course of my life and that of many. Sometimes, I still catch myself playing some "what-if" scenarios in my mind. What if the war never took place and I grew up in Lagos, how different would my life have been? What if all those people, near and dear to my heart, were not killed, what would they have become today? The thoughts that led me to write the book, Surviving in Biafra, still linger some. The difference, this time, is that I feel fulfilled from the perspective of the fact that I was able to put forth my thoughts for the world to read. Every time someone sends me a copy of the numerous references to the book worldwide, that sense of fulfillment continues to rise. However, there are still gnawing questions that need some answers to provide eventual closure to the Biafran war. Those questions, in my humble opinion, can only be provided by the man who was at the helm on the Biafran side. That man had the most panoramic view of all during that war. All reported to him and he made many of the decisions. His memoir, I believe, would answer a lot of these questions and hopefully close a very sad chapter in the history of Africa.

Ojukwu's Death Gives Revisionists The Opportunity to Distort History

I was still in Nigeria, for the burial rites of my own mother when the death of Dim Emeka Odumegwu Ojukwu was announced and confirmed. Although his lengthy stay in the London hospital, without much positive news about his health condition, had given away the fact that the end was probably near. Ojukwu was one of those enigmatic personalities that one never imagines would one day succumb to the frigid hands of death.

Ojukwu was different things to different people. Some simply saw him as the bright and well-spoken oxford university graduate that exuded an immense amount of confidence at every turn. To others, especially those from the other side of the divide, during the Biafran war, he was a villain for his role in the Biafra-Nigeria war. To yet others, including this writer, inspite of his political missteps when he came back from exile in 1982, he was the epitome of courage, having mostly sacrificed his father's wealth as well as his own comfort, to attempt to beat back the north that was bent on total extermination of Ndigbo, through genocide, in 1966. This singular act, by Ojukwu, made him a hero to me from the time I was seven years till I turned ten. I still see him, even in death, as the man that helped prevent the total annihilation of the Igbos; the man that stepped up to the plate even when many would have turned tail and run, and offered up his service to Biafra. He will be missed and may his soul rest in peace.

I have always been concerned that should Ojukwu pass away without putting forth his memoir, a lot of history about Biafra will go with him. I was also concerned that many opportunists would seize the opportunity to attempt to revise history in their favor. Well, what I feared most has started happening! Revisionists and opportunists are springing up from the woodworks and making unsubstantiated statements about Ojukwu and Biafra. Just this last Saturday, on my way back to Ikeja Lagos, to ready myself for my homeward journey back to the Unites States, I picked up copies of several newspapers and started reading. First I read a statement attributed to General Domkat Bali that stated that when Ojukwu joined the Nigerian army, with an Oxford University degree, he was suspicious of his motives. He, Bali, was not convinced that Ojukwu, whom he believed could have been able to get any job he wanted in Nigeria when he graduated and came back, joined the Nigerian army out of patriotism. To him, Ojukwu already had, inside his mind, a secession proclivity! To think that Domkat Bali, the man that almost gleefully announced the execution of Maman Vatsa, during Babangida's regime, has the temerity to make such a statement was surprising. His role during Babangida's regime made him one of the army chiefs with question marks against their names at the time he retired. Now he sees an opportunity to portray himself as the good cop and Ojukwu the bad cop. He tried to cast himself as the man that joined the army because of patriotism while Ojukwu joined the army because he already had in his mind the intent to secede from Nigeria with the Igbos. His assertion is so absurd that it is not funny. Any one that has followed or at least read about the history of Nigeria would know that Ojukwu, at various times, before the civil war broke out, believed in nothing more than one Nigeria. Infact, during the genocide that claimed the lives of thousands of Ndigbo in the north, Ojukwu was still pleading with Igbos not to return en mass to the east, fearing the move would disintegrate Nigeria. When the pogrom continued unabated, Ojukwu had no other choice than to start calling back home the Igbos. He did that to put an end to the butchering of his people. He declared Biafra because the easterners could no longer find respite or succor in the entity called Nigeria. If one reasoned and talked like Domkat Bali, then one may be inclined to assert that Bali joined the army for the purpose of ensuring the demise of his one-time army comrade- Mamman Vatsa. How would he like that analogy? It is ridiculous but then it is as ridiculous as the outlandish statement he made about Ojukwu.

I also read a very long article in the Punch newspaper where Professor Sam Aluko made several statements purporting that Ojukwu basically did not make any decision about Biafra without consulting him. He said that Ojukwu took to him as his right hand man because he was a great economist. I found his entire claim suspect. If what attracted Ojukwu to him, as he claimed, was because he was a renowned economist, why was Ojukwu not just seeking economic advise from him? Why would he be seeking military advice from a man without military training or experience? He even said that when he went back to the Nigerian side, he was still in contact with Ojukwu and Ojukwu was telling him about all his war plans. Why would Ojukwu, the leader of Biafra, be divulging his military plans to a man that was certainly going to be revealing them to the enemy, the Nigerian side? This does not ring right. If Aluko believed that what he was saying in the punch was right, why wait for Ojukwu to die, when he could no longer speak for himself, to make the statements? The reason is simple: He could have been challenged by Ojukwu and in a flurry of exchanges that would have ensued, Nigerians would have distilled what really happened. Something tells me that Sam Aluko is not telling the truth.

In the coming days, weeks and months, many more outlandish statements, about Ojukwu, who can no longer speak for or defend himself, will be made. One is inclined to say that had Ojukwu released his memoir before his death, all these outlandish statements would have been manageable but unfortunately, the hand of the clock cannot be turned. To this writer, it was a mistake; an opportunity to set the records straight was missed. Some say that the memoir would now be released posthumously. While that would still be valuable, it will never be the same as when he was alive. There is speculation that any memoir released now would be sanitized in an attempt to burnish Ojukwu's image and so will not necessarily be the "final Biafra truth" as Ojukwu once stated. In any case, Nigerians are forewarned that opportunists and revisionists would be having a field day for many months and years to come. The watchword should be, "Caveat emptor- Buyer beware.

PART 8
Keynote Speeches

Improving the Quality of Education in Nigerian Schools Through Infrastructure Maintenance and Upgrade: A Case for Active Participation by Diaspora Nigerians. *A keynote speech to Members of Mbaise Association of Maryland USA.*

The President, Mbaise Association of Maryland (MAM), the chairman, distinguished guests, ladies and gentlemen. I am honored to stand before you tonight to deliver the keynote address on the occasion of Mbaise Educational and Cultural Night. I thank your president, Mr. Ken Amanze, for inviting me and I thank you all for having me.

Any cause that is geared towards the betterment of education, especially for Nigeria always gets my attention, hence my presence here today. My father, bless his soul, used to pontificate: "Education will make you dine with kings and queens". As a young man with youthful exuberance and all, I did not understand the significance of what he was trying to convey. To me, it was merely a mantra he used whenever he felt that I was not working to my academic potential. Today, I doubt that there is anyone in this hall that would dispute the veracity of that statement. Let's face it, for many of you in this hall tonight, education is the reason why you occupy important and financially very rewarding positions in your various places of work. The intellect and attendant confidence garnered from education is the reason why you can always stand toe to toe with your counterparts in various fields of endeavor, from all over the world, matching their performances inch for inch and in several cases, outclassing them.

My friends, having said the above, I have a story to tell you. It is an unfortunate story of what is happening several thousand miles away from here, in the land of our birth. In September of 2004, I was in Nigeria with my son. That was his very first time of visiting. While there, I took him to my former secondary school, my alma mater, if you will. Obviously, before then, I had told him about the wonderful education that I got from the school. I had discussed with him the confidence and sense of independence that I imbibed from the school. I had also told him how our school lab prepared my contemporaries and me very well in the areas of physics, chemistry and biology.

When my son and I stepped into the school compound on that September afternoon, I was not only alarmed at what greeted our eyes. I was embarrassed. The school compound had become a shadow of its old self. Erosion had created gullies in every conceivable part of the landscape, making it difficult to drive around the school. The lab that I talked so much about was exceedingly deficient. The interior of the dormitory where I spent 5 significant years of my life, was infested with graffiti. The field where I ran some of the 100-meter races that I told my son about had shrunk down to half the former size because of the denudating effects of erosion. I was unable to get into the library but guessed that, like other infrastructures in the school, it was also deficient.

The first thought that went through my mind was: How could students study under these types of deplorable conditions and succeed academically? How could the nation, in good conscience, condemn her future leaders to such difficult academic environments and expect them to be the best they can? My son had his own question, "Daddy, is this the field where you performed all those wonderful feats in track and field that you always talked about?"

What I just described here is the same in many other public secondary and university institutions in Nigeria. Be aware that students produced under these difficult academic environments are expected to someday, just like you and me, compete internationally.

Now the questions that urgently beg for answers are thus: What consequence(s) is Nigeria facing as a result of the decay of infrastructure in our public schools? What are the ill effects of classrooms that are not conducive for studies or dormitories that are no longer fit for human habitation? Well, everything in life has a cause and effect. The cause here is the absence of needed or suitable infrastructure to create enabling environment for academic success. Of course the effect is clear: We now have graduates from secondary and tertiary institutions, who are academically deficient even in their supposed areas of specialization! Put succinctly, the standard of education has fallen precipitously in black Africa's most populous nation! This should be a source of concern to all of us. That is precisely why Mbaise Association of Maryland has carved out today as Education Night MAM hopes to raise funds that would help improve and sustain the quality of education in Nigerian schools through infrastructure maintenance and upgrade.

With an ill-equipped lab, how can a student learn how to conduct a chemical test as simple as titration? Yet, this type of knowledge is a prerequisite in the fields of chemistry, biochemistry, pharmacy and the like. With an ill-equipped or dilapidated lab, how can a student learn how to conduct tests on heat, light, sound and mechanics? Yet, these are prerequisites for success in the areas of physics, engineering and the like. With ill-equipped labs, you might as well kiss goodbye to the dissection and in-depth study of mammals, reptiles and amphibians. Yet this is the cornerstone of biology and is supposed to partly lay the foundation for an aspiring physician or surgeon.

I once had a chat with a third-year undergraduate student of civil engineering in Nigeria about the properties of soil. Mark you that the mastery of soil mechanics is sine qua non for success in civil engineering practice. Everything you design or build will, in one way or the other, rest on soil - roads, buildings, bridges. Although the young man I spoke to had taken some courses in soil mechanics, he had no hands-on experience with using any of the soil-testing equipment out there. The reason was the absence of the testing equipment in his school. I was amazed! In this day and age, how could this young man compete in a place like USA where such equipment are commonly used by college students in the labs?

Many of us receive letters from relatives and friends that are either in the secondary schools or universities in Nigeria. If I were to grade these letters every time I get them, many of the grades would be consistent at "D" minus. They are that bad in grammar. That gives one an insight into how bad things have become. Even the emails crafted and sent by 419 scam artists who are trying to scam you and me are full of grammatical errors.

I am sure you are wondering who is to blame for the infrastructure decay and consequent degradation in the quality of education in Nigeria. The answer is simple. Much of the blame rests squarely on the shoulders of the government, both state and federal. This is because the government has refused to give education the priority that it deserves. The government has done very little to upgrade and maintain our schools, equip the labs with up- to-date testing machines, populate the libraries with good books, make the dormitories livable and conducive for studies and pay teachers their salaries promptly and regularly. In case you do not know this, then hear it from me that because teachers are not well paid and are sometimes paid late, they find other ways to make up. They operate side businesses outside the schools and divert their attention to those businesses rather than concentrate on providing good education to the future leaders of Nigeria. The resultant effect is that standard of education continues to plummet from its one-time esteemed heights in the days of Zik to the depths of abyss!

When I said that the government was to blame for infrastructural decay in our schools, some of you must have wondered if I was advocating a society where the government does everything for the people. Far from it. The elite in Nigeria who have become successful in their own rights, in various areas of endeavor, but are not doing their part to support and nurture education, are also culpable. WE, in the Diaspora, who occupy important positions here but have not made appreciable effort in giving back to our former schools in Mbaise, and in Nigeria, are also to blame. So you see, my friends, we are all guilty of wanton repudiation of what should be our responsibility. For the purpose of this speech, though, and since I am addressing Diaspora Nigerians, I will concentrate on us here in the Diaspora. "Le moment de verite!"

Take a look at how schools function in the United States. Through endowments and private donations, individuals like you and I and alumni contribute towards the upkeep of libraries, labs and construction of new buildings in public and private schools. They do not wait for the government. The lesson here is that the upkeep of schools should be a joint effort between private individuals, alumni, organizations such as MAM and the government in the case of public schools.

Whenever my commentaries air on my column, Uzokwe's Searchlight, on Nigeriaworld.com, I get floods of emails. It may interest you to know that a lot of emails also come from our brethren living in Nigeria. The common message is this, "Mr. Uzokwe, even though we appreciate the fact that you keep the discourse of Nigerian issues on the front burner, we urge you Nigerians, living in the Diaspora, to join hands and start helping us." They are right, we in the Diaspora must begin to do more back home. There is a saying that Aku lue uno, okwuo onye kpatalia. If we cannot translate our laudable successes in the Diaspora into tangible contributions towards the society we come from, how can we claim total success? Furthermore, if we cannot help the schools that gave us so much back in Nigeria, then we have lost the right to criticize whatever they are doing over there.

It is important to mention here that Mbaise Association of Maryland (MAM) is already ahead of the game. In the year 2002, MAM, through its non-profit arm, Center for Health and Education, donated $6,000 or N828,000 naira for the rehabilitation of 12 primary schools in Mbaise. At the same time, working with Morgan State University, it donated 5,000 text books to Imo State University. In 2005, MAM donated $15,000 or 2.1 million naira for the rehabilitation of 8 primary schools in three local government areas in Mbaise. This money came from donation proceeds of the 2004 fund-raiser sponsored by MAM and which took place here in Baltimore. I personally saw a letter of appreciation from the teachers and principal of Community School, Umuokirika, Ahiazu Mbaise, thanking MAM for the donation of money for uplift of the school. The list goes on.

By pulling the resources of members together as a group, MAM has been able to make tangible difference in Mbaise. If a mere 60% of Nigerians in the Diaspora periodically pull their resources together and send them home to help out schools, like MAM does, I almost guarantee you that we would collectively fight, to a standstill, the scourge that is infrastructural decay. We would together fight, to a standstill, the anomaly that is ill-equipped laboratories and libraries. We would, under one big umbrella fight to a standstill, the devastating scourge that is the graduation of academically deficient young men and women. In the end, we would have roundly succeeded in steering the ship of the Nigerian nation back to the course that our educational pioneers like the Great Zik, Alvan Ikoku, KBC Onwubiko and others originally envisaged.

As Martin Luther King Jr. once said, "The ultimate measure of a man is not where he stands in moments of comfort and convenience but where he stands at times of challenge and controversy." My friends, these are challenging times in Nigeria's educational history. Where do you stand? I'll tell you where you should stand: Next time you visit Nigeria, take a trip to that school that made you what you are today. Take a trip to that institution that laid the foundation of your essence. In the school, visit the library, visit the lab, go to the dormitories, speak with the students if they are in session, speak with the principal and teachers and assess for yourself what the school needs. When you return, join hands with organizations like Mbaise Association of Maryland and target the rehabilitation of these schools and dormitories. Target the procurement of books and equipment for the libraries and labs.

Redefining Success for Nigerians In the Diaspora -
A keynote speech on the Occasion of Inauguration of
Nigerian Association of Reading & Berks County.

The President of the Nigerian Association of Berks and Reading; the chairman; distinguished guests; ladies and gentlemen. It is with great pleasure that I stand before you, to deliver the keynote address, on the occasion of the launching of the Nigerian Association of Reading and Berks, here at the Sheraton Hotel. I thank the association for the invitation to share in your joy and felicitate with you on this epoch-making night.

It is gratifying that Nigerians, in this part of the United States, have come together, united as a people, to promote social, cultural, economic and educational development in this community. I urge you not to relent in your efforts because, in many respects, the journey you have started together, is not an easy one. First of all, whenever two or more people come together in partnership, there will be periodic disagreements. Furthermore, the task you are undertaking is huge and very daunting. But success will come your way if you strive to transcend individual differences of opinion and always keep your eyes on the goals you set for yourselves.

This keynote address was inspired by an article I wrote some years ago titled *Obligations of the citizenry in a developing Nigeria.* In the article, I posited that Nigeria needs the collective efforts of all of us, regardless of where we live, if she must develop fully. Similarly, in this keynote address, I will challenge all of us to put all hands on deck for the development of Nigeria. But before I do that, I will first take you on a jolly ride down the lane of successes that Nigerians in the Diaspora, have registered over the years.

Diaspora Nigerians are resourceful, resilient and smart. In an article published in the Houston Chronicle [May 20, 2008] titled, *"In America, Nigerians' Education Pursuit is above rest"*, Leslie Casimir concluded that amongst all ethnic groups in the United States, Nigerians have the most number of college degrees. Citing the 2006 Census Bureau's American Community Survey, she noted that a whopping 37% of

Nigerians here have bachelor's degrees, 17 percent have graduate degrees while 4 percent have PhDs. This is impressive but I am not surprised. Remember the days of the West African School Certificate Examination (WAEC) in Nigeria. The preparation for that exam laid the foundation of perseverance in academic pursuit for Nigerians. That foundation has continued to propel us to academic success wherever we go.

Delivering the key note address at Sheraton hotel Reading Pennsylvania

The success story of Nigerians in the Diaspora does not just end with academic degrees. There is hardly any area of endeavor that one would not find Nigerians in the higher echelon of responsibility, making things happen. Nigerians are widely recognized and respected in their places of work. It is not uncommon for the medical director of a reputable hospital, here, to be a Nigerian. Many reputable colleges have Nigerians as professors and department heads. The list goes on.

I have a story to share with you at this juncture. Sometime in 1996, my family moved from King of Prussia area to Harrisburg. We later attended a meeting that was organized by the Nigerian Society of South Central Pennsylvania. At the end of the meeting, I was introduced to some of the members and was pleasantly surprised by the caliber of those I met: medical doctors, college professors, agency heads, engineers, registered nurses and pharmacists.

President of the Nigerian Association, Attorney Onwudinjo third from left and wife Agatha second from left and Anthonia(my wife), first from left at the event

A few years after that encounter, during a conversation with an American lady, I mentioned that I hailed from Nigeria. She could not conceal her giddiness as she asked me, "Do you know Dr. Bakare?" Yes, I replied. With a glow in her eyes she quipped, "He is a doctors' doctor". She was referring to his medical expertise.

Those who follow the world of internet and supercomputers are familiar with the name - Philip Emeagwali. This man helped to revolutionize the way computers handle complex calculations, dramatically reducing processing speed. His work earned him the Gordon Bell prize and did I mention that he is a Nigerian living in the United States?

Even in the area of politics, Nigerians are holding their own. Many have run for public offices here in the USA, UK and France and some have won. Take the case of Ezekiel Obasohan: This past May, eighteen years after he arrived in London, he made history by defeating Evelyn Carpenter to become a Mayor in England [The Guardian, May 18, 2008]. Then there is Rotimi Adebari. Last year, he became the very first black Mayor in Dublin, Ireland and he is a Nigerian.

My friends, there are still those who question the wisdom of Nigerians running for political offices in foreign lands. My answer to them is simple: Our dreams in the Diaspora should not end with having good jobs, owning houses and driving the best cars. It should include helping to positively shape legislation that influences the destiny of our children, our children's children and Nigeria as a nation. What better way to achieve all that than through involvement in politics? Also, getting into politics in your adopted land is another way of giving back to that nation and is the height of patriotism for your adopted country.

I am equally proud to say that our children are following in the footsteps of their parents. At the close of every school quarter, Pennlive, an online newspaper, publishes the names of children in Harrisburg area schools, who are in the honors or distinguished honor list. I am always amazed at the number of Nigerian surnames on the list: Balogun, Iduoze, Jatto, Chieke, Adigwu and may I humbly add Uzokwe. Nigerian kids have blown wide open the doors of Ivy League Colleges in this country. Go to Harvard, they are there. Go to Columbia University, they are there. In Princeton, you will find them. Try Massachusetts Institute of Technology (MIT), they are there in abundance. Just a few weeks ago, we attended the graduation party of a young girl that just completed her studies at the Harvard University and headed to University of Pennsylvania to study medicine. The father is a college professor and the mother a medical doctor. Did I mention that they are both Nigerians in Harrisburg? No matter how we slice or dice it, ladies and gentlemen, these are exciting times for Nigerians in the Diaspora.

A cross section of the audience listen to the keynote speech

Now that I have taken you down this joy ride through the successes that Nigerians have attained; now that I have again reinforced in you the reason to always be proud of Nigerians in the Diaspora, I also have some cautionary note for every one of us. Our successes cannot be complete until we duplicate or share them in the country where we still have parents, brothers, sisters, aunties, uncles, nieces, nephews and friends. It makes no sense to turn our backs on the country where we drew our very first breath. Those things we do here that make us succeed; those things we do here that earn us the respect of all; those neat principles we have learnt here like keeping the environment clean, shunning bribery and corruption, lending our expertise to community development and, yes, working hard in our jobs, should also be duplicated or passed on to those in Nigeria. Simply put, we must continue to lend a helping hand to the people in the land of our birth. The wealthiest man in the world routinely offers a helping hand to Nigeria, even though he has no family ties there. Why then would those born and brought up there look the other way? Bill Gates has set a standard that we must all emulate. What you give does not have to be money, it could be your expertise or time.

When I came back from Nigeria this past January, I penned a commentary about my sojourn. In it, I pointed out, with backup pictures, how miscreants were dumping debris into open drainage gutters in Owerri, Imo State. The debris was clogging the gutters, providing breeding grounds for mosquitoes. Some months later, a reader called my attention to a new effort, by the Imo State Government, to fight the truants that clog the gutters. He felt that my commentary had something to do with the government action. Whether my article prompted the action is debatable but the issue is that I saw something wrong when I visited the country and called the attention of authorities to it. I routinely do the same thing where I live in Harrisburg. This is one way that Diaspora Nigerians, and indeed all Nigerians, can help change things in the country.

There are brilliant Nigerian civil engineers in the USA, Britain, Australia, Germany and more. They design marvelous bridges and roads where they live and provide excellent plans for rehabilitation of these structures. When they visit Nigeria, they drive on roads with potholes and bridges with structural deficiencies. If you run into them during Nigerian gatherings, they endlessly complain about the roads and bridges. My usual question to them is: what did you do about it? They always say that the authorities would not listen if they complained to them. That is a convenient excuse for doing nothing. When you see what you do not like, take pictures of it and send to the authorities if you can. As a professional, you can even suggest how it could be remedied. Simply put, make your hard-earned college degrees and expertise also relevant and useful to Nigeria not just the Diaspora.

There are many qualified Nigerians in the area of power and mechanical engineering in the Diaspora. Some have helped to design and implement complex alternative energy projects like wind, solar, geothermal and micro-hydroelectricity. Some have written complex thesis on coal energy and carbon sequestration. They do visit Nigeria and are witnesses to the perpetual electricity outages. We need them to bring their expertise to bear in helping Nigeria turn around her situation rather than just complaining. One Diaspora Nigerian, however, decided to do something about it. Dr Barth Nnaji pulled together a consortium of experts, sourced project funding and began to build a power plant in Aba. When completed, Aba will have enough power for residential neighborhoods, factories, offices and recreational facilities. Constant power means that factories will begin to produce more and employ more Nigerian youths. Sensitive hospital equipment that depends on power will start working again. Foreign businessmen and women will be attracted to Aba to establish factories and create employment. Fewer people would die from carbon monoxide inhalation because of placing generators too close to sleeping areas. All this will happen because one man, an accomplished engineer in the United States, decided to do something when all others are merely complaining.

Take the case of Dr Ifeanyi Obiakor. He was trained here in the United States in OB/GYN and internal medicine. He has a flourishing practice here. He could have pretended like he did not know that the health sector in Nigeria needed help. What did he do instead? He pulled together a consortium of medical experts, sourced funds and they are now in the process of building a $500 million hospital in Abuja. It will be a state-of -the-art hospital and will provide needed medical relief to our people. It will also provide employment for budding medical doctors in Nigeria. For people like the Nigerian president that frequent Germany for medical attention, maybe Dr Obiakor will provide the medical intervention they need right there in Abuja.

You know, I could go on and on but I believe that you got the picture. I am saying that we cannot eat our cake and still have it. If we do not help change Nigeria, who are we leaving that responsibility for? The system cannot change itself. I am also saying that my definition of true success for Nigerians in the Diaspora is lending a helping hand to the country of your birth just like you must continue to do in your adopted country.

As for the Nigerian Association of Reading and Berks, I hope you can help Nigeria by offering scholarships to kids there that have the brains but no financial means. I hope you can help Nigeria by rebuilding schools and providing computers for them. I hope you can help make Nigeria great so that when you visit in the future, you will not have bad roads to deal with nor electricity outages to complain about.

In closing, I again congratulate the Nigerian Association of Reading and Berks for this milestone. Thank you once again for having me and my wife. May God Bless Nigeria and the United States of America.

To Make Nigeria Better, be the Change
You Desire For Her - *A Keynote speech to*
Nigerians in Central Pennsylvania During the
Independence Anniversary Celebration

The President, Nigerian Association of South Central Pennsylvania, distinguished guests, ladies and gentlemen, good evening! When I was first nominated to deliver this keynote address, I was concerned that time constraints may preclude me from doing justice to it. But I later concluded that failure to rise to the occasion would be tantamount to abdication of an important social responsibility. So here I am today. I appreciate the confidence reposed in me by those whose insistence informed my standing before you today. My speech is captioned: "To Make Nigeria Better, Be the Change You Desire For Her."

Some of you are aware that I write commentaries about Nigeria on Nigeriaworld.com. The commentaries are sometimes critical of government policies and actions. But in all these writings, I never lose sight of the fact that every one of us has a role to play in making Nigeria a better nation, not just the government. My challenge to you tonight is to be the change you desire for Nigeria. Every one of us, whether in this room or outside, is endowed by the almighty with talent and intellect. Yours may be manifesting in your profession, your hobby, your daily activities or may even be dormant inside you waiting to be let loose. You can apply some of the talents towards the betterment of this 52-year-old country that is yearning for our attention.

In this room tonight, we have medical doctors of Nigerian descent, nurses, pharmacists and other health workers. There are many more all over the United States. First of all, thanks for the great work you do here of saving lives, helping to bring forth new ones and taking care of the elderly. But do you know that you can extend your great services to Nigeria? There is a humongous information gap between what the average Nigerian knows medically and what they should truly know. That information gap is causing a lot of medical havoc over there. Take diabetes for example, people who have the disease here in the United States live long lives because of knowledge about testing, eating right and exercising. But in Nigeria, people still die, lose their limbs or eyesight because of diabetic retinopathy and neuropathy. You can help change this.

If you are wondering how you can do that, let me give you a hint: You do not have to discover a new drug or find a cure. In fact, you do not have to do anything novel. Just spend a few days, during your visit

Delivering the keynote address at the independence day
celebration gala. Picture by Sam Onyeaka

to Nigeria, participating in a community health education program. There, talk to local folks about wellness, diseases, signs, symptoms, eating right and exercising. If people know how to manage what ails them, they have a better chance of survival. Or you can go on medical missions to Nigeria with your fellow professionals to treat and educate patients. Some medical missions have revealed diseases that the locals did not realize they had - breast cancers, heart diseases, liver cirrhosis, cervical cancer, asthma and the like. Helping the locals detect the diseases, especially at the early stages, could make a difference. Nigerians here sometimes solicit medical equipment and donate them to hospitals in Nigeria. You can do that too. I just read that a group of Nigerians in the Diaspora are pulling resources together to build a state-of- the-art hospital in Nigeria. All I can say is - Ain't nothin' wrong with that!

Now check this out: In July of 2010, I was in Atlanta for the reunion of alumni of University of Nigeria. I left the school three decades ago - I am obviously getting old as my kids will often remind me. Nonetheless, present at the Atlanta gathering were alumni and current and former vice chancellors. There were many presentations but the common theme was that standard of education was taking a rapid nose dive in Nigerian schools. Think about this, if Nigeria produces half-baked graduates, how can the nation advance? How can invention-based development occur? Recall that 20 or more years ago, the standard of education in Nigeria was touted as exceedingly high. But now, that academic prowess is fast dwindling to vanishing points. This is where the teachers and college professors we have in this room tonight, as well as other parts of the Diaspora, come in.

There is a clarion call for your talent and intellect in Nigeria. First of all, thank you all for the great work you do in society of imparting intellect, confidence, molding characters and shaping destinies. By spending your sabbatical time in one of the schools in Nigeria, imparting the same academic words of wisdom you do here, you can help arrest this backward slide in standard of education, one school at a time. You can share ideas, academic curriculum and research findings with students and teachers over there. You can even help facilitate visits by Nigerian teachers to this country to exchange ideas on the most effective ways to impart education. Many schools in Nigeria lack needed books, laboratory equipment and research materials. You could help in the drive to gather these items for shipment to schools in Nigeria.

Now, on to civil engineers of which I am one. Civil engineers help plan, design and build bridges, roads, box culverts, dams, buildings and other ancillaries. Again, kudos for the great work you do here. Do you realize that you too can extend your experience to Nigeria? Your contribution could be as simple as helping to organize and execute small community projects. These could include construction of culverts and roadside gutters and helping to fix potholes when you visit. Furthermore, there are always new developments in the field of civil engineering in the areas of technology, materials and the likes. You can help share or transmit the new developments to Nigeria. You may say there are Nigerians paid to do such work. Frankly, that's not a good excuse to do nothing. There is room for everyone to contribute towards the development of the country.

And how about the environment? I know that we have environmental engineers in this room tonight. You are an indispensable part of every society, ensuring clean air, clean environment and water. Air pollution alone is responsible for many respiratory and pulmonary diseases in Nigeria- asthma, COPD and even lung cancers. These diseases rob our kith and kin of long and productive lives. Do you think Nigeria needs you and your expertise? You betcha as governor Palin would say. Just visit Lagos or Bayelsa state and you will see why your contribution, no matter how small, will make a great difference. Enough said on that.

Most of you have had cause, at one time or another, while in Nigeria, to shout, "Up NEPA" or more recently, "UP PHCN". It happens when NEPA returns electricity to your home after a prolonged blackout. Because of constant blackouts, too many Nigerian homes depend on generators. But you are aware of the havoc these generators have been causing when placed too close to living quarters. The fumes or carbon monoxide have been known to wipe out entire families. We should begin to fight the electricity war from many more fronts other than just using generators or waiting for the government to build new power plants. We can harness alternative energy sources like solar and wind energy to augment what we currently have. Do you know that you can generate 2000 watts of electricity just by installing a solar panel of 2KW on the roof of your house in Nigeria?2000 watts of electricity can power several ceiling fans and light bulbs. The less the amount of electricity needed from the main grid, the less the energy burden on Nigeria's power grid. Electricity conservation should be of paramount consideration in building designs.

Buildings should be designed with ample windows for natural lighting and ventilation. This reduces the need for electric bulbs and air-conditioning that deplete electricity. This is a challenge that our architects, mechanical engineers and electrical engineers should take up. Although I have designed more than 20 buildings built in Nigeria when the green building revolution had not started or was in infancy.

These days, in line with what I am preaching tonight, I push for buildings that conserve electrical energy through functional design. I also push for low energy light bulbs and fixtures and advocate solar panels and wind turbines for lighting and running small appliances. Although geothermal energy is seen as untenable in hot climates like Nigeria, researchers have not given up. All in all, if these alternative energy measures catch on, it will help reduce excessive dependence on the central power grid and minimize erratic power supply.

By now, the business professionals in the room are wondering when Alfred will pick on them. Well, here we go. Unemployment rate is very high in Nigeria as everywhere else. Most of our graduates march directly into the unemployment line. But some in this room are business professionals that have helped companies develop business plans that propelled them to the top. You have advised individuals on business startup strategies that helped them succeed. You can do the same for young Nigerian graduates when you visit. Set up forums to educate them on how to write business plans, source funds from banks, neighbors, friends and relatives. With that knowledge, some of them may become employers themselves. You may be saying that they already have people doing this. But in a nation of more than 160 million, there are never enough mentors to guide the young and restless. My friends, are you prepared to step up to the plate and lend a helping hand?

Then there is science and technology. No nation can make appreciable strides in development without a fully developed science and technology sector. Many Nigerians have come up with inventions and discoveries that fizzled because of lack of support. A 24-year-old undergraduate in Nigeria just built a helicopter out of an old car and bike parts. Right now, everyone is praising him and talking about his feat. But mark my word, soon, the whole excitement will fizzle out because no one will sponsor him to greater heights. This happens time and time again but it does not have to be that way. If you have connections or leads in the science & technology field to support these sharp minds, please help them achieve their dreams.

And yes, you can always speak up constructively or write about something that is not working well in Nigeria. As they say in Latin – malum triumphos cum viri, boni deficiat agere - evil triumphs when good men fail to act or speak up. For 11 years, as a commentator on Nigeriaworld.com, under a column called Uzokwe's Searchlight, I have written commentaries on Nigeria's socio-economic and political situation. My writings now total two volumes of 600-pages each. These commentaries are read globally by thousands and attract hundreds of emails per week to my inbox. For those who tell me I don't go out enough, now you know what I do with my time - responding to emails – just kidding!

On a more serious note, in my commentaries, I point out what I see as wrong and then proffer solutions – I call that constructive criticism. I have written about general causes of building failures in Nigeria and proffered solutions. I have written about road failures and remedial actions. I have argued convincingly, based on structural deficiency and functional obsolescence, why a new Niger Bridge is needed in Onitsha. In fact, that article has been copied and repeated many times in Nigerian newspapers. This is a social responsibility that anyone can take up. You can do exactly the same if you love writing.

But, hold on for a second! Am I my asking you to do something that no one else is doing in Nigeria? Certainly not. There are Nigerians that engender positive changes in the country day in day out. As a result of their enterprising spirit, there have been stunning developments in so many different sectors. Now, Let's take a look at some of the positive changes occasioned by the hard work of these forward-looking Nigerians over the years:

I visited Nigeria not long ago and stopped by Tejuoso and Balogun markets in Lagos. Believe it or not folks, I was at Tejuoso market to look for onugbu - bitter leaf! Nonetheless, I was pleasantly surprised at what greeted my eyes at the markets – proliferation of cell phones, almost everyone carrying a cellphone, chatting away and making brisk businesses. Some of the folks own as many as three cell phones with three different network operators. If communication goes bad with one carrier, they will switch to the other phone. In secondary school dorms, students move about with internet-capable phones, browsing the internet and posting messages on their Facebook. I think you get the picture. These developments were unheard of as recently as in the 90s. In 1985, there was an average of one phone line per 440 Nigerians. In 1992, that number went up to one phone line per 300 inhabitants. Today, millions of Nigerians have cell phones.

But what informed this major improvement in the telecom industry? It certainly was not accidental. Simply put, in the 90s, the government realized that the monopoly enjoyed by NITEL (the sole operator at the time) was setting Nigeria back. It deregulated the sector and investors jumped at the opportunity to provide better and affordable telephone network. By mid-2002, four digital mobile operators- MTN, Econet, Nitel and Globacom, had been licensed to operate in the country. But Nigeria had very little telecom infrastructure on the ground so these investors basically had to start from scratch and install needed infrastructure. They did the heavy lifting that enabled the progress we see today.

The benefits of cell phone proliferation in Nigeria cannot be overstated. For starters, cell phone is relatively cheap in the country. The industry provides thousands of employment opportunities for Nigerians. Even the charge card phone accessories sellers are not doing too bad. Many sustain huge families with the profits they make from their trade. Some business and banking transactions are now done with cell phones, no more driving up and down. This saves transportation costs and minimizes road accidents. In medical emergencies, cell phone is a life-saver. The same is the case in security emergencies like robberies. Communication with family members and friends, even in distant lands, has improved markedly. Those of you who came here 15 or more years ago may remember how difficult it was to reach family members in Nigeria from here by phone. Now I can call up my relatives, anywhere in the village, and chat. A small step taken in the 90s, by some enterprising Nigerians, has become a giant leap for all.

One of the citizens that contributed to the success of the telecom industry in Nigeria is Chief Michael Adenuga. He is the founder of Globacom. I chose to highlight him because, just like you and I, he studied here in the United States and sometimes did menial jobs, like you and I. But back in Nigeria, in spite of the obstacles he faced, he founded Globacom and the rest is history. He is now one of the richest men in black Africa. Globacom is Nigeria's second largest national telecom operator with about 25 million subscribers. Let's be clear: Adenuga did not invent cell phone technology, but he helped revolutionize the industry in Nigeria...and so became the change he desired for Nigeria.

Now, on to information technology. In the late 80's, desk top computers began to make inroads into many African nations, including Nigeria. Recognizing the indispensability of computers and the need to make the technology part of everyday life, Nigeria formally introduced computer education into the secondary education curriculum in 1987. This increased market demand for computers and hence importation. But Nigeria's environment posed a series of challenges for the imported computers. First, the erratic power supply and fluctuating voltage tended to fry the computers. Second, the hot and humid climate resulted in frequent overheating and breakdown. Third, the imported computers lacked important local symbols like the naira sign on the keyboard. Fourth, the computers were priced out of the reach of average Nigerians.

One of the men that decided to tackle these issues was Mr. Leo Stan Ekeh, a graduate of economics from Punjab University India. In 2001, he established a computer manufacturing company called Zinox Computers. It became the first indigenous internationally certified computer system. Zinox computers are equipped with voltage stabilizers, naira symbol on the keyboard & thunder arrestor. Most of all, they are relatively affordable. Affordable computers mean that many schools, banks, businesses and individuals can own computers. It also puts the IT-technology at the fingertips of our young men and women, making them globally competitive. In 2005, Zinox received the ISO 9001 quality and management certification. It is the largest partner of Intel and Microsoft in sub Saharan Africa. The company now has more than 20 offices across West Africa. Mr. Ekeh has left his footsteps in the sands of times. Whenever the history of Nigeria's development is chronicled, I doubt that he will be left out.

Let's segue into the transportation sector. With a population of more than 160 million, there is no shortage of demand for vehicles in Nigeria. At costs of over 2 million naira, new vehicles are out of the reach of the average Nigerian. No wonder why the importation of cheaper but used vehicles is the order of the day. The problem is that most of the used vehicles, referred to as Tokunbo, easily break down due to prolonged prior use. Some pollute the environment because of defective catalytic converters. While some Nigerians were busy flooding the country with Tokunbo vehicles, one man had the dream of building a car manufacturing plant for the production of new vehicles. He wanted to build vehicles capable of withstanding.

In October 2010, Nigerian foreign dignitaries, including Nigeria's president, declared open the factory Mr. Innocent Chukwuma built for manufacture of new vehicles. His company, Innoson Motors, became the first indigenous private company that manufactures and assembles vehicles in Nigeria. They manufacture 17 & 43-seater buses, double cabin pick-up vans, sports utility vehicles & garbage compactors. Some state governments are already taking delivery of hundreds of the vehicles. They use the garbage compactors to keep the roads clean. The vehicles have a reputation for low fuel consumption, lower pollution and ability to drive well on Nigerian roads. The company provides employment for an estimated 1,600 people. So what started as a small vision by one man now has a gigantically salutary effect on a whole nation and West Africa. Some Nigerians that would never have dreamt of affording a new vehicle may now be within striking distance like teachers, small business men and women, civil servants and more. Mr. Chukwuma has become the initiator of the change he wants for Nigeria.

And then, there is Nollywood. How many people here watch Nigerian-made movies? I watch and enjoy them. Nollywood is to Nigeria what Hollywood is to the United States. For many years, Nigerians yearned for made-in-Nigeria movies showcasing local actors. In 1992, some Nigerians, on a menial budget, set out to write, produce and shoot movies locally. At first, many derided their products as inferior but they persevered. Today, Nollywood is a $200 million a year industry, providing employment for Nigerians. Nigeria's name has been elevated in many countries because of Nollywood. Go to Ghana, Trinidad, Jamaica, South Africa, Nollywood movies reign supreme. Nollywood is now the world's third largest producer of feature films. Enough said folks!

My friends, I hope you now see that I am not asking you to do something that nobody else has done. I therefore hope I have spurred you to action tonight. Thomas Edison once said - "If we did all the things we are capable of, we would literally astound ourselves". Surprise yourself by becoming or initiating the change you desire for Nigeria. For history buffs, recall that after the battle of Zela, Julius Caesar declared- veni, vidi, vici – I came, I saw and conquered. That was Julius Caesar, though.

For you and me, our own mantra should be, Veni et vidi et differentia Nigeria - I came, and saw and made a difference in Nigeria. God Bless Nigeria, God bless the United States of America.

"As MC during a Nigerian independence celebration event"

"Gathering of Nigerians during an event in Maryland USA".
Picture by Sam Onyeaka

"During a Nigerian organization event in Harrisburg.
From Left- Giwa Amu, Me, Col Sandusky and John Nwokeji"

"With my friend, Dr Mike Ukoha and my Wife
during a Nigerians event in Harrisburg"

"Speaking during the launching of my book- Surviving in Biafra- 2003"

Index

W

Z

Printed in the United States
By Bookmasters